# THE WISDOM AND WIT OF DIANE RAVITCH

C. Thomas [illegible]
January, 2020

# THE WISDOM AND WIT OF DIANE RAVITCH

DIANE RAVITCH

GARN PRESS
NEW YORK, NY

Published by Garn Press, LLC
New York, NY
*www.garnpress.com*



*Book and cover design by Ben James Taylor*

*Special thanks to Yvonne Siu-Runyan, Professor Emerita, University of Northern Colorado, and Past President, NCTE, who provided invaluable assistance in curating over 300 of Diane Ravitch's most important blog posts from the more than 19,000 Diane published between 2012 and 2017.*

First Edition, March 2019

Library of Congress Control Number: 2018963517

Publisher's Cataloging-in-Publication Data

Names: Ravitch, Diane.
Title: The Wisdom and Wit of Diane Ravitch / Diane Ravitch.
Description: First edition. | New York : Garn Press, 2019. | Includes bibliographical references.
Identifiers: LCCN 2018963517 | ISBN 978-1-942146-74-2 (pbk.) | ISBN 978-1-942146-75-9 (hardcover) | 978-1-942146-76-6 (Kindle ebook)
Subjects: LCSH: Privatization in Education--United States. | School choice--United States. | Public schools--United States. | Charter schools--United States. | Democracy and education--United States. | Educational tests and measurement. | BISAC: EDUCATION / Education Policy & Reform/General. | EDUCATION / Education Policy & Reform/Charter Schools. | EDUCATION / Standards (Incl. Common Core). | EDUCATION / Aims & Objectives. | EDUCATION / Philosophy, Theory and Social Aspects.
Classification: LCC LB1027.9 .S45 2017 (print) | LCC LB1027.9 (ebook) | DDC 371.3--dc23.
LC record available at https://lccn.loc.gov/2018963517

*I dedicate this book to the millions of men and women who teach our children, day after day, with patience, wisdom, integrity, humor, kindness, and endurance, and to the generations of teachers who have preceded them.*

# ACKNOWLEDGEMENTS

In reviewing what I have written in the past decade, I can't help but reflect on the sharp turn that I took in the period from about 2007-2010, when I came to the realization that so many of the policies I had advocated in previous years were simply wrong. Testing. Accountability. High and uniform standards for all. Making test scores the fulcrum of education. I came to see that such policies contradicted my deep belief in a liberal education, one that gives joy and insight and inspiration, one that awakens a love of learning. The policy ideas had to be jettisoned because they jeopardized genuine education.

My change of mind astonished many people. Apparently ideas are supposed to be fixed and unchanging. In explaining why I turned against my past views, I quoted John Maynard Keynes, who said, "When the facts change, I change my mind. What do you do, Sir?"

Changing my mind caused me to lose valued friends. But in time I developed close relationships with new colleagues and friends who forgave my past transgressions and welcomed me into new alliances, new debates, and a new fellowship. I thank them here: Anthony Cody, Leonie Haimson, Carol Burris, Julian Vasquez Heilig, Pasi Sahlberg, Yong Zhao, David Berliner, Gene Glass, Audrey Amrein-Beardsley, Richard Rothstein, Mercedes Schneider, Jeanne Kaplan, Jesse Hagopian, Mark Weber, Peter Greene, Andrea Gabor, Samuel Abrams, and Deborah Meier. This is by no means an exhaustive list of those from whom I learned and continue to learn.

I thank Denny Taylor and the team at Garn Press for their arduous work in bringing this collection together, in what seemed to me to be a near impossible task.

Through it all, I had the understanding, the love and support of my family: my wife, Mary, whose long experience as a teacher and principal enlightened me. My sons and my grandsons, who were always there for me through thick and thin.

I thank them all.

**Diane Ravitch**

# THERE IS NO INSTITUTION OF LEARNING THAT MATTERS MORE TO OUR FUTURE THAN THE PUBLIC SCHOOL

There is no more significant work than teaching. Teachers hold the fate of children and the nation in their hands. Anyone who disrespects or devalues the work of teachers puts their own ignorance or malice on display. It is incumbent upon us all to defend those who devote their lives to the dissemination of knowledge and the healthy development of children.

There is no institution of learning that matters more to our future than the public school. It is the one place tasked with building the citizens of our democracy. It is incumbent upon us all to prevent public funds from being diverted to private and religious entities that avoid accountability and transparency. It is our job as citizens to protect those institutions that belong to the public and to make them far better than they are today. It is our civic duty to fight for true equality of educational opportunity for all. Access to education is a basic human right.

# TABLE OF CONTENTS

# FOREWORD

# YOHURU R. WILLIAMS

*"Public schools are not chain stores that can be closed and opened at will. They are, and they should be vital community institutions, not transient agencies that come and go as test scores rise and fall." – Diane Ravitch, University of Rhode Island, 2013*

Journalism is not only the first draft of history, it is also one of the surest sparks of activism. In this regard, Diane Ravitch has been both a journalist and an activist, chronicling and speaking out against the dangers of the school privatization movement. Intrepidly, she maintained a laser-like focus on the despicable threat it poses not only to the nation's youth, but our very democracy.

A matter of conscience led Diane to boldly dissent from the thunderous voices of the proponents of the privatization movement – then masquerading as a campaign for school reform – more than a decade ago. She countered their boisterous cries of a failing system of American public education that supposedly lagged behind the rest of the world. Diane sought to challenge the narrative through her existing networks. When this bore little fruit, she took the fight public. On March 9, 2010 in the pages of *The Wall Street Journal*, in what was a shot heard across the education world, she pulled back the curtains on the charade of school reform boldly noting, "On our present course, we are disrupting communities, dumbing down our schools, giving students false reports of their progress, and creating a private sector that will undermine public education without improving it." She further explained, "Most significantly, "we are not producing a generation of students who are more knowledgeable, and better prepared for the responsibilities of citizenship. That is why I changed my mind about the current direction of school reform."

I received a copy of that article from a friend later that day and was blown away not only by the depth and clarity of the argument, but by the author. Diane had a well-established reputation as a scholar and a civil servant, even if she had once been on the other side of the political divide. As Assistant Secretary in the Office of Educational Research and Improvement in the U.S. Department of Education under George H. W. Bush, she led the federal effort to promote the creation of voluntary state and national academic standards, and she championed many of the elements of the so-called reform movement, including school choice and high stakes testing. This made her apparent defection all the more powerful. It soon became clear in her subsequent writings, speeches, and blogs that Diane would not bend to partisan politics, as she called out both Republicans and Democrats, and more than a few Billionaires, for their questionable and misguided support of initiatives like No Child Left Behind and Race to the Top. This was not about currying influence. It was about people, students, teachers and communities jeopardized by abusive and poorly conceived policies and practices.

Diane's 2013 book *Reign of Error: The Hoax of the Privatization Movement and the Danger to America's Public Schools* called out the implicit betrayal of *Brown v. Board of Education* and the false promise of educational equality. Especially for students of color, she uncovered the emergence of a separate and unequal dual system of education that privatizers promoted. Diane was quick to note the re-segregation that took place along with school closures, and she exposed the disciplinary practices and unequal investment in resources for public schools with large numbers of special education and English language learners that increased, instead of decreased, segregation and inequity.

In her writings, Diane also unflinchingly battled the narrative pushed by the disciples of privatization who brazenly sought to appropriate the legacy of the Reverend Dr. Martin Luther King. They tried to position their cause not simply as a civil rights issue but the "civil rights issue of our time." Here as elsewhere, Diane's astute training as a historian cut through the illusion. In addition to documenting the racial disparities perpetuated by school choice and the charter industry, she reminded her readers of Dr. King's support for organized labor and his emphasis on fair employment practices. As she observed in 2010, "about 98% of these schools are non-union and their teachers work 50-60 hours each week, which could not happen if they were union schools."

Diane also kept her gaze fixed on the metrics, pointing out the failings of the privatizers by their own fuzzy standards. More importantly, as she also observed in 2010, "Given the weight of studies, evaluations and federal test data, I concluded that deregulation and privately managed charter schools were not the answer to the deep-seated problems of American education. If anything, they represent tinkering around the edges of the system. They affect the lives of tiny numbers of students but do nothing to improve the system that enrolls the other 97%."

Eight years later, the situation is much the same. As Diane observed in 2018, "Today, there are more than 7,000 charter schools with about 3 million students – total enrollment in public schools is 50 million. About 90 percent of charter schools are non-union."

Over the years Diane has also used the power of her words and influence to amplify other voices through her blogs and speeches. As the cofounder of the Network for Public Education, upon whose board I proudly serve with her, she has also worked to create a powerful mobilizing organization to keep the pressure up on the privatizers and support the work of activists across the nation.

Above all she has remained committed to the idea that those with all the answers about how to fix public education – without understanding the complexities around it – are a major source of the problem. "Doubt and skepticism," she has observed, "are signs of rationality. When we are too certain of our opinions, we run the risk of ignoring any evidence that conflicts with our views. It is doubt that shows we are still thinking, still willing to reexamine hardened beliefs when confronted with new facts and new evidence." This is the wisdom of Diane Ravitch.

The great philosopher Confucius once observed there are three methods by which one may acquire such wisdom: "First, by reflection, which is noblest; second, by imitation, which is easiest; and third by experience, which is the bitterest." It may be safe to assume that the wisest among us have gained such insight through the experience of all three without losing a sense of humor. This is the wit of Diane Ravitch.

In the following pages, you will encounter some of Diane's most inspired and insightful writings full of the wit and wisdom that have made her an icon among teachers, community leaders, students, and activists concerned with preserving public education.

In revisiting these essays, we all can harness the power of her insights for the fight ahead. Those currently in the struggle, for example, may appreciate the opportunity for reflection on how far we have come and the road we have left to travel. Those new to the struggle may find a source for imitation and inspiration as well as a blueprint for engagement. It is as important and necessary now as it was a decade ago. Finally for the veterans, the book can offer new stimulation and encouragement to carry on, despite the feelings of being worn down and perhaps a bit bitter from so many years of fighting the good fight.

And has all this work been for naught? As this book goes to print in February of 2019, education reporter Dana Goldstein was moved to acknowledge in an article in *The New York Times*, that after 13 years of reporting, "So much has changed in education, as the focus shifts from calling out bad teachers and schools to listening more carefully to what educators say about their working conditions and how students are affected by them." In the wake of several high profile teacher strikes and other actions, it might be easy to forget that this has been Diane Ravitch's mantra for more than a decade.

As we await the outcome of these important labor clashes and celebrate some victories, it would be prudent to revisit the work of Diane Ravitch. We are in the process of hopefully reimagining what public education should and could be within the context of our democratic principles. We need to remain squarely focused on our most significant shared asset - our nation's youth.

As Benjamin Franklin observed, "Words may show a man's wit but actions his meaning." In the realm of the fight to preserve public education, Diane has made the same point more directly, "Without knowledge and understanding, one tends to become a passive spectator rather than an active participant in the great decisions of our time." Her own record of scholarship and activism sets a powerful example for us to get involved and stay involved until the fight is won.

**Yohuru R. Williams**
Professor of History, Dean of the College of Arts and Sciences, University of St. Thomas, Minnesota

① ideas & writing
② advocacy & activism

thought & action / brains & brawn !!

# WHY I CHANGED MY MIND ABOUT SCHOOL REFORM

## THE WALL STREET JOURNAL, MARCH 9, 2010

*"Can anyone today say with a straight face that no child has been left behind thanks to testing and accountability?" – Diane Ravitch's Blog*

I have been a historian of American education since 1975, when I received my doctorate from Columbia. I have written histories, and I've also written extensively about the need to improve students' knowledge of history, literature, geography, science, civics and foreign languages. So in 1991, when Lamar Alexander and David Kearns invited me to become assistant secretary of education in the administration of George H.W. Bush, I jumped at the chance with the hope that I might promote voluntary state and national standards in these subjects.

By the time I left government service in January 1993, I was an advocate not only for standards but for school choice. I had come to believe that standards and choice could co-exist as they do in the private sector. With my friends Chester Finn Jr. and Joseph Viteritti, I wrote and edited books and articles making the case for charter schools and accountability.

I became a founding board member of the Thomas B. Fordham Foundation and a founding member of the Koret Task Force at the Hoover Institution, both of which are fervent proponents of choice and accountability. The Koret group includes some of the nation's best-known conservative scholars of choice, including John Chubb, Terry Moe, Caroline Hoxby and Paul Peterson.

As No Child Left Behind's (NCLB) accountability regime took over the nation's schools under President George W. Bush and more and more charter schools were launched, I supported these initiatives. But over time, I became disillusioned with the strategies that once seemed so promising. I no longer believe that either approach will produce the quantum improvement in American education that we all hope for.

NCLB received overwhelming bipartisan support when it was signed into law by President Bush in 2002. The law requires that schools test all students every year in grades three through eight, and report their scores separately by race, ethnicity, low-income status, disability status and limited-English proficiency. NCLB mandated that 100% of students would reach proficiency in reading and math by 2014, as measured by tests given in each state.

Although this target was generally recognized as utopian, schools faced draconian penalties – eventually including closure or privatization – if every group in the school did not make adequate yearly progress. By 2008, 35% of the nation's public schools were labeled "failing schools," and that number seems sure to grow each year as the deadline nears.

Since the law permitted every state to define "proficiency" as it chose, many states announced impressive gains. But the states' claims of startling improvement were contradicted by the federally sponsored National Assessment of Educational Progress (NAEP). Eighth grade students improved not at all on the federal test of reading even though they had been tested annually by their states in 2003, 2004, 2005, 2006 and 2007.

Meanwhile the states responded to NCLB by dumbing down their standards so that they could claim to be making progress. Some states declared that between 80%-90% of their students were proficient, but on the federal test only a third or less were. Because the law demanded progress only in reading and math, schools were incentivized to show gains only on those subjects. Hundreds of millions of dollars were invested in test-preparation materials. Meanwhile, there was no incentive to teach the arts, science, history, literature, geography, civics, foreign languages or physical education.

In short, accountability turned into a nightmare for American schools, producing graduates who were drilled regularly on the basic skills but were often ignorant about almost everything else. Colleges continued to complain about the poor preparation of entering students, who not only had meager knowledge of the world but still required remediation in basic skills. This was not my vision of good education.

When charter schools started in the early 1990s, their supporters promised that they would unleash a new era of innovation and effectiveness. Now there are some 5,000 charter schools, which serve about 3% of the nation's students, and the Obama administration is pushing for many more.

But the promise has not been fulfilled. Most studies of charter schools acknowledge that they vary widely in quality. The only major national evaluation of charter schools was carried out by Stanford economist Margaret Raymond and funded by pro-charter foundations. Her group found that compared to regular public schools, 17% of charters got higher test scores, 46% had gains that were no different than their public counterparts, and 37% were significantly worse.

Charter evaluations frequently note that as compared to neighboring public schools, charters enroll smaller proportions of students whose English is limited and students with disabilities. The students who are hardest to educate are left to regular public schools, which makes comparisons between the two sectors unfair. The higher graduation rate posted by charters often reflects the fact that they are able to "counsel out" the lowest performing students; many charters have very high attrition rates (in some, 50%-60% of those who start fall away). Those who survive do well, but this is not a model for public education, which must educate all children.

NAEP compared charter schools and regular public schools in 2003, 2005, 2007 and 2009. Sometimes one sector or the other had a small advantage. But on the whole, there is very little performance difference between them.

Given the weight of studies, evaluations and federal test data, I concluded that deregulation and privately managed charter schools were not the answer to the deep-seated problems of American education. If anything, they represent tinkering around the edges of the system. They affect the lives of tiny numbers of students but do nothing to improve the system that enrolls the other 97%.

The current emphasis on accountability has created a punitive atmosphere in the schools. The Obama administration seems to think that schools will improve if we fire teachers and close schools. They do not recognize that schools are often the anchor of their communities, representing values, traditions and ideals that have persevered across decades. They also fail to recognize that the best predictor of low academic performance is poverty – not bad teachers.

What we need is not a marketplace, but a coherent curriculum that prepares all students. And our government should commit to providing a good school in every neighborhood in the nation, just as we strive to provide a good fire company in every community.

On our present course, we are disrupting communities, dumbing down our schools, giving students false reports of their progress, and creating a private sector that will undermine public education without improving it. Most significantly, we are not producing a generation of students who are more knowledgeable, and better prepared for the responsibilities of citizenship. That is why I changed my mind about the current direction of school reform.

# TODAY'S EDUCATION "REFORMS" WERE NOT MARTIN LUTHER KING'S DREAM

## HUFFINGTON POST, MARCH 20, 2010

There is something distinctly unsettling about seeing people invoke Martin Luther King Jr.'s name to support the current effort to privatize large swaths of American public education. It has recently become customary to claim that "education is the civil rights issue of our time." True enough, for no one can succeed in our society without an education. But the people who make this claim insist that public school students should be enrolled in schools run by for-profit corporations, hedge-fund managers, and earnest amateurs, who receive public money without any public oversight. There are now about 5,000 such schools, called charter schools, across the nation, and President Obama wants many more of them. As it happens, about 98% of these schools are non-union and their teachers work 50-60 hours each week, which could not happen if they were union schools.

Today's education "reformers" think they are advancing a civil rights agenda by creating charter schools, advocating merit pay, enshrining standardized tests of basic skills as the highest measure of achievement, closing neighborhood schools, and getting rid of unions.

Was that Martin Luther King Jr.'s dream? King fought for equality of educational opportunity, not for a "Race to the Top" for the lucky few. He fought for fundamental fairness and justice for all, not for special treatment for the few. He never promoted private management of public education. When he was assassinated, he was defending the right of workers to join a union. It is impossible to imagine him standing alongside the business executives and politically powerful who demand more standardized testing, more privatization of public schools, and more schools in which teachers have no organized voice.

# FIRST, LET'S FIRE ALL THE TEACHERS!

HUFFINGTON POST, MAY 2, 2010

Imagine that you are a teacher in a high school in a high-poverty district. Many of your students don't speak English. Some don't attend school regularly because they have to earn money or babysit with their siblings while their parents are looking for work. Some come to school unprepared because they didn't do their homework.

But you are idealistic and dedicated, you work with each of the students, you do your best to teach them reading, writing, science, math, history, whatever your subject. But despite your best efforts, many of your students can't read very well (they are struggling to learn English), and many of them don't graduate. If your school eliminated all its standards, you could easily push up the graduation rate.

About 45 minutes away is another high school in a much better neighborhood. Its statistics are far better than yours. The children are almost all born in the U.S. and their parents are almost all college graduates with good jobs. Their kids don't go to school hungry, they have their own room and their own computer, and they have stellar test scores to boot. Their graduation rate is very impressive, and most of their graduates go to college.

What is to be done about the first school? President George W. Bush signed a law called "No Child Left Behind," which required constant improvement. The Obama administration wants to rename the law but they too reject any excuses for low performance and low graduation rates.

Recently, the school committee of Central Falls, Rhode Island, voted to fire all 93 members of the staff in their low-performing high school. Central Falls is the smallest and poorest city in the state, and it has only one high school. Those fired included 74 classroom teachers, plus the school psychologist, guidance counselors, reading specialists, and administrators.

Secretary of Education Arne Duncan thought this was wonderful – he said the members of the school committee were "showing courage and doing the right thing for kids." The kids apparently didn't agree because many of them came to the committee meeting to defend their teachers.

President Obama thought it was wonderful that every educator at Central Falls High School was fired. At an appearance before the U.S. Chamber of Commerce on March 1, the President applauded the idea of closing the school and getting rid of everyone in it. At the same meeting, President Obama acknowledged Margaret Spellings, who was President George W. Bush's Education Secretary, because she "helped to lead a lot of the improvement that's been taking place and we're building on."

Well, yes, the President is right – his own education reform plans are built right on top of the shaky foundation of President Bush's No Child Left Behind program. The fundamental principle of school reform, in the Age of Bush and Obama, is measure and punish. If students don't get high enough scores, then someone must be punished! If the graduation rate hovers around 50%, then someone must be punished. This is known as "accountability."

President Obama says that Central Falls must close because only 7% of the students are proficient in math, and the graduation rate is only 48%. Sounds bad, right?

But the President has saluted a high school in Providence, Rhode Island, called "The Met" whose scores are no different from the scores at Central Falls High School. At Central Falls, 55% of the kids are classified as "proficient readers," just like

55% at The Met. In math, only 7% of students at Central Falls are proficient in math, but at The Met (which the President lauds) only 4% are proficient in math. Ah, but The Met has one big advantage over Central Falls High Schools – its graduation rate is 75.6%.

But figure this one out – how can a high school where only 4% of the students are proficient in math and only 55% are proficient readers produce a graduation rate of 75.6%? To this distant observer, it appears that the school with lower graduation standards rates higher in President Obama's eyes.

President Obama has said on several occasions that he wants to see 5,000 low-performing schools closed. So, yes, there will be plenty of teachers and principals looking for new jobs.

The question that neither President Obama nor Secretary Duncan has answered is this – where will they find 5,000 expert principals to take over the schools that are closed? Where will they find hundreds of thousands of superb teachers to fill the newly vacant positions? Or will everyone play musical chairs to give the illusion of reform?

As it happens, Central Falls High School had seen consistent improvement over the past two years. Only last year, the State Commissioner sent in a team to look at the school and commended its improvements. It noted that the school had been burdened by frequently changing programs and leadership. With more support from the district and the state, this improvement might have continued. Instead, the school was given a death warrant.

Will it be replaced by a better school? Who knows? Will excellent teachers flock to Central Falls to replace their fired colleagues? Or will it be staffed by inexperienced young college graduates who commit to stay at the school for two years? Will non-English-speaking students start speaking English because their teachers were fired? Will children come to school ready to learn because their teachers were fired?

It would be good if our nation's education leaders recognized that teachers are not solely responsible for student test scores. Other influences matter, including the students' effort, the family's encouragement, the effects of popular culture, and the influence of poverty. A blogger called "Mrs. Mimi" wrote the other day that we fire teachers because "we can't fire poverty." Since we can't fire poverty, we can't fire students, and we can't fire families, all that is left is to fire teachers.

This strategy of closing schools and firing the teachers is mean and punitive. And it is ultimately pointless. It solves no problem. It opens up a host of new problems. It satisfies the urge to purge. But it does nothing at all for the students.

# SUPPORT CONGRESSMAN OBEY'S EDUJOBS BILL

HUFFINGTON POST, JULY 1, 2010

Congressman David Obey is trying to save the jobs of tens of thousands of public school teachers who have received pink slips. As chair of the House Appropriations Committee, he proposes to shift money from President Obama's "Race to the Top" program to keep teachers employed.

Specifically, the Obey plan would keep teachers working by diverting money that is now going to be spent on charter schools and merit pay.

The Obama plan is called "reform," but it really represents the wish list of the Republican Party, which has long supported charters, vouchers, and merit pay.

The Republicans and some of their allies in the Democratic party have raised an outcry against the Obey plan, claiming that it will "gut" what they call "reform" if money is taken away from privatization and merit pay.

But there can be no school reform of any meaning if tens of thousands of teachers lose their jobs. Class sizes will soar, especially in hard-pressed urban districts, and education will suffer a serious setback for our nation's most vulnerable children.

Research and national scores have repeatedly demonstrated that charter schools in aggregate do not perform better than regular public schools. Merit pay has been tried and has failed repeatedly since the 1920s. Why should these dubious ideas, with little or no evidence to support them, take precedence over the continued employment of teachers?

The pro-privatization crowd should put their agenda on hold for a bit and support Congressman Obey's sensible plan to use every possible discretionary dollar to keep our schools fully staffed. This is the first obligation of our federal government. Thank you, Congressman David Obey for supporting the nation's hard-pressed educators!

# OBAMA'S RACE TO THE TOP WILL NOT IMPROVE EDUCATION

## HUFFINGTON POST, AUGUST 1, 2010

*"Race to the Top will someday be remembered in the history books as a Grand Detour, when ideologues gained control of federal policy and used an economic crisis to dangle money in front of the states so they would agree to implement failed policies." – Diane Ravitch's Blog*

President Obama spoke to the National Urban League this week and defended his "Race to the Top" program, which has become increasingly controversial. Mr. Obama insisted that it was the most important thing he had done in office, and that critics were merely clinging to the status quo.

Mr. Obama was unfazed by the scathing critique[1] of the Race to the Top by the nation's leading civil rights organizations, who insisted that access to federal funding should be based on need, not competition.

The program contains these key elements:

- Teachers will be evaluated in relation to their students' test scores.
- Schools that continue to get low test scores will be closed or turned into charter schools or handed over to private management.

- In low-performing schools, principals will be fired, and all or half of the staff will be fired.
- States are encouraged to create many more privately managed charter schools.

All of these elements are problematic. Evaluating teachers in relation to student test scores will have many adverse consequences. It will make the current standardized tests of basic skills more important than ever, and even more time and resources will be devoted to raising scores on these tests. The curriculum will be narrowed even more than under George W. Bush's No Child Left Behind, because of the link between wages and scores. There will be even less time available for the arts, science, history, civics, foreign language, even physical education. Teachers will teach to the test. There will be more cheating, more gaming the system.

Furthermore, charter schools on average do not get better results than regular public schools, yet Obama and Duncan are pushing them hard. Duncan acknowledges that there are many mediocre or bad charter schools, but chooses to believe that in the future, the new charters will only be high performing ones. Right.

The President should re-examine his reliance on standardized testing to identify the best teachers and schools and the worst teachers and schools. The tests are simply not adequate to their expectations.

The latest example of how test results can be doctored is the New York State testing scandal, which broke open this week. The pass rates on the state tests had soared year after year, to the point where they became ridiculous to all but the credulous. The whole house of cards came crashing down this week after the state raised the proficiency bar from the low point to which it had sunk. In 2009, 86.4% of the state's students were "proficient" in math, but the number in 2010 plummeted to 61%. In 2009, 77.4% were "proficient" in reading, but now it is only 53.2%.

The latest test scores were especially startling for New York City, where Mayor Michael Bloomberg staked his reputation on their meteoric rise. He was re-elected because of the supposedly historic increase in test scores and used them to win renewal of mayoral control. But now, the City's pass rate in reading for grades 3-8 fell from 68.8% to 42.4%, and the proficiency rate in math sunk from an incredible 81.8% to a dismal 54%.

When the mayor ran for office, he said that mayoral control would mean accountability. If things went wrong, the public would know whom to blame.

But now that the truth about score inflation is out, Mayor Bloomberg and Chancellor Klein steadfastly insist that the gains recorded on their watch did not go up in smoke and that progress was real, and they have reiterated this message through their intermediaries in the tabloids. In other words, they are using every possible rationalization and excuse to avoid accountability for the collapse of their "historic gains."

Meanwhile Secretary Duncan travels the country urging districts to adopt mayoral control, so they can emulate New York City. He carefully avoids mentioning Cleveland, which has had mayoral control for years and remains one of the lowest performing districts in the nation. Nor does he mention that Detroit had mayoral control and ended it. And it is hard to imagine that anyone would think of Chicago, which has been controlled by Mayor Richard Daley for many years, as a national model.

President Obama and Secretary Duncan need to stop and think. They are heading in the wrong direction. On their present course, they will end up demoralizing teachers, closing schools that are struggling to improve, dismantling the teaching profession, destabilizing communities, and harming public education.

# THE OBSESSION WITH TESTING IS NUTS

HUFFINGTON POST, OCTOBER 4, 2010

*"The bad ideas now infesting public education came from the corporate sector, where they failed. They are failed corporate ideas that are being imposed on public schools, where they also fail" – Diane Ravitch's Blog*

Last year I exchanged emails with a high-ranking official at the U.S. Department of Education. I complained that the accountability movement had gotten out of control, that too much time was spent preparing to take tests, learning to take tests, and taking tests, especially in low income districts. I said that the time spent on testing was reducing time for the arts, history, science, civics, geography, even physical education. Thus, kids have more tests and worse education.

His first response was "you measure what you treasure." I replied, "No, you cannot measure what you treasure." How do you measure, friendship, love, courage, honor, civility, love of learning? I suppose he was moved a little bit, because he replied, "How can we incentivize the teaching of the arts?" I should have given up then, but responded that you do some things not for economic reward, and not because they are utilitarian, but because they are right.

A couple of weeks ago, I participated in an event sponsored by *The Economist* magazine in New York City. As I waited to go on, the previous speaker talked enthusiastically about why we should look to the arts and artists as sources of inspiration, creativity, and innovation. When my panel started (billed as a "debate" between me and Eva Moskowitz, founder of Harlem Success Academy), the first question was, "How do you envision schooling five years from now?" Eva spoke of individualization and personalization. I predicted, based on current policies in the U.S., that kids will be drilled endlessly for the next test, and that the machinery will be in place to measure and test, driving out innovation, creativity, and divergent thinking. This is not wise and it is not smart.

It's a frightening scenario. I hope I am wrong. If there is not a major change in federal education policy, this is the likely outcome of where we are heading.

# THE MYTH OF CHARTER SCHOOLS

THE NEW YORK REVIEW OF BOOKS, NOVEMBER 11, 2010

Ordinarily, documentaries about education attract little attention, and seldom, if ever, reach neighborhood movie theaters. Davis Guggenheim's *Waiting for "Superman"* is different. It arrived in late September with the biggest publicity splash I have ever seen for a documentary. Not only was it the subject of major stories in *Time* and *New York* magazines, but it was featured twice on *The Oprah Winfrey Show* and was the centerpiece of several days of programming by NBC, including an interview with President Obama.

Two other films expounding the same arguments – *The Lottery* and *The Cartel* – were released in the late spring, but they received far less attention than Guggenheim's film. His reputation as the director of the Academy Award-winning *An Inconvenient Truth,* about global warming, contributed to the anticipation surrounding *Waiting for "Superman,"* but the media frenzy suggested something more. Guggenheim presents the popularized version of an account of American public education that is promoted by some of the nation's most powerful figures and institutions.

The message of these films has become alarmingly familiar: American public education is a failed enterprise. The problem is not money. Public schools already spend too much. Test scores are low because there are so many bad teachers, whose jobs are protected by powerful unions. Students drop out because the schools fail them, but they could accomplish practically anything if they were saved from bad teachers. They would get higher test scores if schools could fire more bad teachers and pay more to good ones. The only hope for the future of our society, especially for poor black and Hispanic children, is escape from public schools, especially to charter schools, which are mostly funded by the government but controlled by private organizations, many of them operating to make a profit.

*The Cartel* maintains that we must not only create more charter schools, but provide vouchers so that children can flee incompetent public schools and attend private schools. There, we are led to believe, teachers will be caring and highly skilled (unlike the lazy dullards in public schools); the schools will have high expectations and test scores will soar; and all children will succeed academically, regardless of their circumstances. *The Lottery* echoes the main story line of *Waiting for "Superman"* – it is about children who are desperate to avoid the New York City public schools and eager to win a spot in a shiny new charter school in Harlem.

For many people, these arguments require a willing suspension of disbelief. Most Americans graduated from public schools, and most went from school to college or the workplace without thinking that their school had limited their life chances. There was a time – which now seems distant – when most people assumed that students' performance in school was largely determined by their own efforts and by the circumstances and support of their family, not by their teachers. There were good teachers and mediocre teachers, even bad teachers, but in the end, most public schools offered ample opportunity for education to those willing to pursue it. The annual Gallup poll about education shows that Americans are overwhelmingly dissatisfied with the quality of the nation's schools, but 77 percent of public school parents award their own child's public school a grade of A or B, the highest level of approval since the question was first asked in 1985.

*Waiting for "Superman"* and the other films appeal to a broad apprehension that the nation is falling behind in global competition. If the economy is a shambles, if poverty persists for significant segments of the population, if American kids are not as serious about their studies as their peers in other nations, the schools must be to blame. At last we have the culprit on which we can pin our anger, our palpable sense that something is very wrong with our society, that we are on the wrong track, and that America is losing the race for global dominance. It is not globalization or deindustrialization or poverty or our coarse popular culture or predatory financial practices that bear responsibility – it's the public schools, their teachers, and their unions.

The inspiration for *Waiting for "Superman"* began, Guggenheim explains, as he drove his own children to a private school, past the neighborhood schools with low test scores. He wondered about the fate of the children whose families did not have the choice of schools available to his own children. What was the quality of their education? He was sure it must be terrible. The press release for the film says that he wondered, "How heartsick and worried did *their* parents feel as they dropped their kids off this morning?" Guggenheim is a graduate of Sidwell Friends, the elite private school in Washington, D.C., where President Obama's daughters are enrolled. The public schools that he passed by each morning must have seemed as hopeless and dreadful to him as the public schools in Washington that his own parents had shunned.

*Waiting for "Superman"* tells the story of five children who enter a lottery to win a coveted place in a charter school. Four of them seek to escape the public schools, one was asked to leave a Catholic school because her mother couldn't afford the tuition. Four of the children are black or Hispanic and live in gritty neighborhoods, while the one white child lives in a leafy suburb. We come to know each of these children and their families, we learn about their dreams for the future, we see that they are lovable, and we identify with them. By the end of the film, we are rooting for them as the day of the lottery approaches.

In each of the schools to which they have applied, the odds against them are large. Anthony, a fifth-grader in Washington, D.C., applies to the SEED charter boarding school, where there are sixty-one applicants for twenty-four places. Francisco is a first-grade student in the Bronx whose mother (a social worker with a graduate degree) is desperate to get him out of the New York City public schools and into a charter school, so she applies to Harlem Success Academy, where he is one of 792 applicants for forty places. Bianca is the kindergarten student in Harlem whose mother cannot afford Catholic school tuition, she enters the lottery at another Harlem Success Academy, as one of 767 students competing for thirty-five openings. Daisy is a fifth-grade student in East Los Angeles whose parents hope she can win a spot at KIPP LA PREP, where 135 students have applied for ten places. Emily is an eighth-grade student in Silicon Valley, where the local high school has gorgeous facilities, high graduation rates, and impressive test scores, but her family worries that she will be assigned to a slow track because of her low test scores, so they enter the lottery for Summit Preparatory Charter High School, where she is one of 455 students competing for 110 places.

The stars of the film are Geoffrey Canada, the CEO of the Harlem Children's Zone, which provides a broad variety of social services to families and children and runs two charter schools; Michelle Rhee, chancellor of the Washington, D.C., public school system, who closed schools, fired teachers and principals, and gained a national reputation for her tough policies; David Levin and Michael Feinberg, who have built a network of nearly one hundred high-performing KIPP charter schools over the past sixteen years; and Randi Weingarten, president of the American Federation of Teachers, who is cast in the role of chief villain. Other charter school leaders, like Steve Barr of the Green Dot chain in Los Angeles, do star turns, as does Bill Gates of Microsoft, whose foundation has invested many millions of dollars in expanding the number of charter schools. No successful public school teacher or principal or superintendent appears in the film

– indeed there is no mention of any successful public school, only the incessant drumbeat on the theme of public school failure.

The situation is dire, the film warns us. We must act. But what must we do? The message of the film is clear. Public schools are bad, privately managed charter schools are good. Parents clamor to get their children out of the public schools in New York City – despite the claims by Mayor Michael Bloomberg that the city's schools are better than ever – and into the charters. The mayor also plans to double the number of charters, to help more families escape from the public schools that he controls. If we could fire the bottom 5 to 10 percent of the lowest-performing teachers every year, says Hoover Institution economist Eric Hanushek in the film, our national test scores would soon approach the top of international rankings in mathematics and science.

Some fact-checking is in order, and the place to start is with the film's quiet acknowledgment that only one in five charter schools is able to get the "amazing results" that it celebrates. Nothing more is said about this astonishing statistic. It is drawn from a national study of charter schools by Stanford economist Margaret Raymond (the wife of Hanushek). Known as the CREDO study, it evaluated student progress on math tests in half the nation's five thousand charter schools, and concluded that 17 percent were superior to a matched traditional public school, 37 percent were worse than the public school, and the remaining 46 percent had academic gains no different from that of a similar public school. The proportion of charters that get amazing results is far smaller than 17 percent. Why did Davis Guggenheim pay no attention to the charter schools that are run by incompetent leaders or corporations mainly concerned with making money? Why propound to an unknowing public the myth that charter schools are the answer to our educational woes, when the filmmaker knows that there are twice as many failing charters as there are successful ones? Why not give an honest accounting?

The propagandistic nature of *Waiting for "Superman"* is revealed by Guggenheim's complete indifference to the wide variation among charter schools. There are excellent charter schools, just as there are excellent public schools. Why did he not also inquire into the charter chains that are mired in unsavory real estate deals, or take his camera to the charters where most students are getting lower scores than those in the neighborhood public schools? Why did he not report on the charter principals who have been indicted for embezzlement, or the charters that blur the line between church and state? Why did he not look into the charter schools whose leaders are paid $300,000 to $400,000 a year to oversee small numbers of schools and students?

Guggenheim seems to believe that teachers alone can overcome the effects of student poverty, even though there are countless studies that demonstrate the link between income and test scores. He shows us footage of the pilot Chuck Yeager breaking the sound barrier, to the amazement of people who said it couldn't be done. Since Yeager broke the sound barrier, we should be prepared to believe that able teachers are all it takes to overcome the disadvantages of poverty, homelessness, joblessness, poor nutrition, absent parents, etc.

The movie asserts a central thesis in today's school reform discussion – the idea that teachers are the most important factor determining student achievement. But this proposition is false. Hanushek has released studies showing that teacher quality accounts for about 7.5-10 percent of student test score gains. Several other high-quality analyses echo this finding, and while estimates vary a bit, there is a relative consensus – teachers statistically account for around 10–20 percent of achievement outcomes. Teachers are the most important factor within schools.

But the same body of research shows that non-school factors matter even more than teachers. According to University of Washington economist Dan Goldhaber, about 60 percent of achievement is explained by non-school factors, such as family income. So while teachers are the most important factor within schools, their effects pale in comparison with those of students' backgrounds, families, and other factors beyond the control of schools and teachers. Teachers can have a profound effect on students, but it would be foolish to believe that teachers alone can undo the damage caused by poverty and its associated burdens.

Guggenheim skirts the issue of poverty by showing only families that are intact and dedicated to helping their children succeed. One of the children he follows is raised by a doting grandmother, two have single mothers who are relentless in seeking better education for them, two of them live with a mother and father. Nothing is said about children whose families are not available, for whatever reason, to support them, or about children who are homeless, or about children with special needs. Nor is there any reference to the many charter schools that enroll disproportionately small numbers of children who are English-language learners or have disabilities.

The film never acknowledges that charter schools were created mainly at the instigation of Albert Shanker, the president of the American Federation of Teachers from 1974 to 1997. Shanker had the idea in 1988 that a group of public school teachers would ask their colleagues for permission to create a small school that would focus on the neediest students, those who had dropped out and those who were disengaged from school and likely to drop out. He sold the idea as a way to open schools that would collaborate with public schools and help motivate disengaged students. In 1993, Shanker turned against the charter school idea when he realized that for-profit organizations saw it as a business opportunity and were advancing an agenda of school privatization. Michelle Rhee gained her teaching experience in Baltimore as an employee of Education Alternatives, Inc., one of the first of the for-profit operations.

Today, charter schools are promoted not as ways to collaborate with public schools but as competitors that will force them to get better or go out of business. In fact, they have become the force for privatization that Shanker feared. Because of the high-stakes testing regime created by President George W. Bush's No Child Left Behind (NCLB) legislation, charter schools compete to get higher test scores than regular public schools, and thus have an incentive to avoid students who might pull down their scores.

Under NCLB, low-performing schools may be closed, while high-performing ones may get bonuses. Some charter schools "counsel out" or expel students just before state testing day. Some have high attrition rates, especially among lower-performing students.

Perhaps the greatest distortion in this film is its misrepresentation of data about student academic performance. The film claims that 70 percent of eighth-grade students cannot read at grade level. This is flatly wrong. Guggenheim here relies on numbers drawn from the federally sponsored National Assessment of Educational Progress (NAEP). I served as a member of the governing board for the national tests for seven years, and I know how misleading Guggenheim's figures are. NAEP doesn't measure performance in terms of grade-level achievement. The highest level of performance, "advanced," is equivalent to an A+, representing the highest possible academic performance. The next level, "proficient," is equivalent to an A or a very strong B. The next level is "basic," which probably translates into a C grade. The film assumes that any student below proficient is "below grade level." But it would be far more fitting to worry about students who are "below basic," who are 25 percent of the national sample, not 70 percent.

Guggenheim didn't bother to take a close look at the heroes of his documentary. Geoffrey Canada is justly celebrated for the creation of the Harlem Children's Zone, which not only runs two charter schools but surrounds children and their families with a broad array of social and medical services. Canada has a board of wealthy philanthropists and a very successful fund-raising apparatus. With assets of more than $200 million, his organization has no shortage of funds. Canada himself is currently paid $400,000 annually. For Guggenheim to praise Canada while also claiming that public schools don't need any more money is bizarre. Canada's charter schools get better results than nearby public schools serving impoverished students. If all inner-city schools had the same resources as his, they might get the same good results.

But contrary to the myth that Guggenheim propounds

about "amazing results," even Geoffrey Canada's schools have many students who are not proficient. On the 2010 state tests, 60 percent of the fourth-grade students in one of his charter schools were not proficient in reading, nor were 50 percent in the other. It should be noted – and Guggenheim didn't note it – that Canada kicked out his entire first class of middle school students when they didn't get good enough test scores to satisfy his board of trustees. This sad event was documented by Paul Tough in his laudatory account of Canada's Harlem Children's Zone, *Whatever It Takes* (2009). Contrary to Guggenheim's mythology, even the best-funded charters, with the finest services, can't completely negate the effects of poverty.

Guggenheim ignored other clues that might have gotten in the way of a good story. While blasting the teachers' unions, he points to Finland as a nation whose educational system the U.S. should emulate, not bothering to explain that it has a completely unionized teaching force. His documentary showers praise on testing and accountability, yet he does not acknowledge that Finland seldom tests its students. Any Finnish educator will say that Finland improved its public education system not by privatizing its schools or constantly testing its students, but by investing in the preparation, support, and retention of excellent teachers. It achieved its present eminence not by systematically firing 5-10 percent of its teachers, but by patiently building for the future. Finland has a national curriculum, which is not restricted to the basic skills of reading and math, but includes the arts, sciences, history, foreign languages, and other subjects that are essential to a good, rounded education. Finland also strengthened its social welfare programs for children and families. Guggenheim simply ignores the realities of the Finnish system.

In any school reform proposal, the question of "scalability" always arises. Can reforms be reproduced on a broad scale? The fact that one school produces amazing results is not in itself a demonstration that every other school can do the same. For example, Guggenheim holds up Locke High School in Los Angeles, part of the Green Dot charter chain, as a success story but does not tell the whole story. With an infusion of $15 million of mostly private funding, Green Dot produced a safer, cleaner campus, but no more than tiny improvements in its students' abysmal test scores. According to the *Los Angeles Times,* the percentage of its students proficient in English rose from 13.7 percent in 2009 to 14.9 percent in 2010, while in math the proportion of proficient students grew from 4 percent to 6.7 percent. What can be learned from this small progress? Becoming a charter is no guarantee that a school serving a tough neighborhood will produce educational miracles.

Another highly praised school that is featured in the film is the SEED charter boarding school in Washington, D.C. SEED seems to deserve all the praise that it receives from Guggenheim, CBS's *60 Minutes*, and elsewhere. It has remarkable rates of graduation and college acceptance. But SEED spends $35,000 per student, as compared to average current spending for public schools of about one third that amount. Is our society prepared to open boarding schools for tens of thousands of inner-city students and pay what it costs to copy the SEED model? Those who claim that better education for the neediest students won't require more money cannot use SEED to support their argument.

Guggenheim seems to demand that public schools start firing "bad" teachers so they can get the great results that one of every five charter schools gets. But he never explains how difficult it is to identify "bad" teachers. If one looks only at test scores, teachers in affluent suburbs get higher ones. If one uses student gains or losses as a general measure, then those who teach the neediest children – English-language learners, troubled students, autistic students – will see the smallest gains, and teachers will have an incentive to avoid districts and classes with large numbers of the neediest students.

Ultimately the job of hiring teachers, evaluating them, and deciding who should stay and who should go falls to administrators. We should be taking a close look at those who award due process rights (the accurate term for "tenure") to too many incompetent teachers. The best way to ensure that there are no bad or ineffective teachers in our public schools is to insist that we have principals and supervisors who are knowledgeable and experienced educators. Yet there is currently a vogue to recruit and train principals who have little or no education experience. The George W. Bush Institute just announced its intention to train 50,000 new principals in the next decade and to recruit non-educators for this sensitive post.

*Waiting for "Superman"* is the most important public-relations coup that the critics of public education have made so far. Their power is not to be underestimated. For years, right-wing critics demanded vouchers and got nowhere. Now, many of them are watching in amazement as their ineffectual attacks on "government schools" and their advocacy of privately managed schools with public funding have become the received wisdom among liberal elites. Despite their uneven record, charter schools have the enthusiastic endorsement of the Obama administration, the Gates Foundation, the Broad Foundation, and the Dell Foundation. In recent months, *The New York Times* has published three stories about how charter schools have become the favorite cause of hedge fund executives. According to *The New York Times,* when Andrew Cuomo wanted to tap into Wall Street money for his gubernatorial campaign, he had to meet with the executive director of Democrats for Education Reform (DFER), a pro-charter group.

Dominated by hedge fund managers who control billions of dollars, DFER has contributed heavily to political candidates for local and state offices who pledge to promote charter schools. Its efforts to unseat incumbents in three predominantly black State Senate districts in New York City came to nothing. None of its hand-picked candidates received as much as 30 percent of the vote in the primary elections, even with the full-throated endorsement of the city's tabloids. Despite the loss of these local elections and the defeat of Washington, D.C. Mayor Adrian Fenty – who had appointed the controversial schools chancellor Michelle Rhee – the combined clout of these groups, plus the enormous power of the federal government and the uncritical support of the major media, presents a serious challenge to the viability and future of public education.

It bears mentioning that nations with high-performing school systems – whether Korea, Singapore, Finland, or Japan – have succeeded not by privatizing their schools or closing those with low scores, but by strengthening the education profession. They also have less poverty than we do. Fewer than 5 percent of children in Finland live in poverty, as compared to 20 percent in the United States. Those who insist that poverty doesn't matter, that only teachers matter, prefer to ignore such contrasts.

If we are serious about improving our schools, we will take steps to improve our teacher force, as Finland and other nations have done. That would mean better screening to select the best candidates, higher salaries, better support and mentoring systems, and better working conditions. Guggenheim complains that only one in 2,500 teachers loses his or her teaching certificate, but fails to mention that 50 percent of those who enter teaching leave within five years, mostly because of poor working conditions, lack of adequate resources, and the stress of dealing with difficult children and disrespectful parents. Some who leave "fire themselves", others were fired before they got tenure. We should also insist that only highly experienced teachers become principals (the "head teacher" in the school), not retired businessmen and military personnel. Every school should have a curriculum that includes a full range of studies, not just basic skills. And if we really are intent on school improvement, we must reduce the appalling rates of child poverty that impede success in school and in life.

There is a clash of ideas occurring in education right now between those who believe that public education is not only a fundamental right but a vital public service, akin to the public provision of police, fire protection, parks, and public libraries, and those who believe that the private sector is always superior to the public sector. *Waiting for "Superman"* is a powerful weapon on behalf of those championing the "free market" and privatization. It raises important questions, but all of the answers it offers require a transfer of public funds to the private sector. The stock market crash of 2008 should suffice to remind us that the managers of the private sector do not have a monopoly on success.

Public education is one of the cornerstones of American democracy. The public schools must accept everyone who appears at their doors, no matter their race, language, economic status, or disability. Like the huddled masses who arrived from Europe in years gone by, immigrants from across the world today turn to the public schools to learn what they need to know to become part of this society. The schools should be far better than they are now, but privatizing them is no solution.

In the final moments of *Waiting for "Superman,"* the children and their parents assemble in auditoriums in New York City, Washington, D.C., Los Angeles, and Silicon Valley, waiting nervously to see if they will win the lottery. As the camera pans the room, you see tears rolling down the cheeks of children and adults alike, all their hopes focused on a listing of numbers or names. Many people react to the scene with their own tears, sad for the children who lose. I had a different reaction. First, I thought to myself that the charter operators were cynically using children as political pawns in their own campaign to promote their cause. Gail Collins in *The New York Times* had a similar reaction, and wondered why they couldn't just send the families a letter in the mail instead of subjecting them to public rejection. Second, I felt an immense sense of gratitude to the much-maligned American public education system, where no one has to win a lottery to gain admission.

# NO STUDENT LEFT UNTESTED

## THE NEW YORK REVIEW OF BOOKS - NYR DAILY, FEBRUARY 21, 2012

Last week, the New York State Education Department and the teachers' unions reached an agreement to allow the state to use student test scores to evaluate teachers. The pact was brought to a conclusion after Governor Andrew Cuomo warned the parties that if they didn't come to an agreement quickly, he would impose his own solution, though he did not explain what that would be. He further told school districts that they would lose future state aid if they didn't promptly implement the agreement after it was released to the public. The reason for this urgency was to secure $700 million promised to the state by the Obama administration's Race to the Top program, contingent on the state's creating a plan to evaluate teachers in relation to their students' test scores.

The new evaluation system pretends to be balanced, but it is not. Teachers will be ranked on a scale of 1-100. Teachers will be rated as "ineffective, developing, effective, or highly effective." Forty percent of their grade will be based on the rise or fall of student test scores, the other sixty percent will be based on other measures such as classroom observations by principals, independent evaluators, and peers, plus feedback from students and parents.

But one sentence in the agreement shows what matters most: "Teachers rated ineffective on student performance based on objective assessments must be rated ineffective overall." What this means is that a teacher who does not raise test scores will be found ineffective overall, no matter how well he or she does with the remaining sixty percent. In other words, the 40 percent allocated to student performance actually counts for 100 percent. Two years of ineffective ratings and the teacher is fired.

The New York press treated the agreement as a major breakthrough that would lead to dramatic improvement in the schools. The media assumed that teachers and principals in New York State would now be measured accurately, that the bad ones would be identified and eventually ousted, and that the result would be big gains in test scores. Only days earlier, a New York court ruled that the media will be permitted to publish the names and rankings of teachers in New York City, even if the rankings are inaccurate. Thus, the scene has been set – not only will teachers and principals be rated, but those ratings can now be released to the public online and in the press.

The consequences of these policies will not be pretty. If the way these ratings are calculated is flawed, as most testing experts acknowledge they are, then many good educators will be subject to public humiliation and will leave the profession. Once those scores are released to the media, we can expect that parents will object if their children are assigned to "bad" teachers, and principals will have a logistical nightmare trying to squeeze most children into the classes of the highest-ranked teachers. Will parents sue if their children do not get the "best" teachers?

New York's education officials are obsessed with test scores. The state wants to find and fire the teachers who aren't able to produce higher test scores year after year. But most testing experts believe that the methods for calculating teachers' assumed "value-added" qualities – that is, their abilities to produce higher test scores year after year – are inaccurate, unstable, and unreliable.[2] Teachers in affluent suburbs are likelier to get higher value-added scores than teachers of students with disabilities, students learning English, and students from extreme poverty. All too often, the rise or fall of test scores reflects the composition of the classroom and factors beyond the teachers' control, not the quality of the teacher. A teacher who is rated effective one year may well be ineffective the next year,[3] depending on which students are assigned to his or her class.

The state is making a bet that threatening to fire and publicly humiliate teachers it deems are underperforming will be sufficient to produce higher test scores. Since most teachers in New York do not teach tested subjects (reading and mathematics in grades 3-8), the state will require districts to create measures for everything that is taught – called, in state bureaucratese, "student learning objectives" – for all the others. So, in the new system, there will be assessments in every subject, including the arts and physical education. No one knows what those assessments will look like. Everything will be measured, not to help students, but to evaluate their teachers. If the district's own assessments are found to be not sufficiently rigorous by State Commissioner of Education John King – who has only three years of teaching experience, two in charter schools – he has the unilateral power to reject them.

This agreement will certainly produce an intense focus on teaching to the tests. It will also profoundly demoralize teachers, as they realize that they have lost their professional autonomy and will be measured according to precise behaviors and actions that have nothing to do with their own definition of good teaching. Evaluators will come armed with elaborate rubrics identifying precisely what teachers must do and how they must act, if they want to be successful. *The New York Times* interviewed a principal in Tennessee[4] who felt compelled to give a low rating to a good teacher, because the teacher did not "break students into groups" in the lesson he observed. The new system in New York will require school districts across the state to hire thousands of independent evaluators, as well as create much additional paperwork for principals. Already stressed school budgets will be squeezed further to meet the pact's demands for monitoring and reporting.

President Obama said in his State of the Union address that teachers should "stop teaching to the test," but his own Race to the Top program is the source of New York's hurried and wrong-headed teacher evaluation plan. According to Race to the Top, states are required to evaluate teachers based in part on their students' test scores in order to compete for federal funding. When New York won $700 million from the Obama program, it pledged to do this. What the President has now urged, "stop teaching to the test," is directly contradicted by what his own policies make necessary – teach to the test or be rated ineffective and get fired).

No high-performing nation in the world evaluates teachers by the test scores of their students, and no state or district in this nation has a successful program of this kind. The State of Tennessee and the city of Dallas have been using some type of test-score based teacher evaluation for twenty years but are not known as educational models. Across the nation, in response to the prompting of Race to the Top, states are struggling to evaluate their teachers by student test scores, but none has figured it out.

All such schemes rely on standardized tests as the ultimate measure of education. This is madness. The tests have some value in measuring basic skills and rote learning, but their overuse distorts education. No standardized test can accurately measure the quality of education. Students can be coached to guess the right answer, but learning this skill does not equate to acquiring facility in complex reasoning and analysis. It is possible to have higher test scores and worse education. The scores tell us nothing about how well students can think, how deeply they understand history or science or literature or philosophy, or how much they love to paint or dance or sing, or how well prepared they are to cast their votes carefully or to be wise jurors.

Of course, teachers should be evaluated. They should be evaluated by experienced principals and peers. No incompetent teacher should be allowed to remain in the classroom. Those who can't teach and can't improve should be fired. But the current frenzy of blaming teachers for low scores smacks of a witch-hunt, the search for a scapegoat, someone to blame for a faltering economy, for the growing levels of poverty, for widening income inequality.

For a decade, the Bush-era federal law called No Child Left Behind has required the nation's public schools to test every student in grades 3-8 in reading and mathematics. Now, the Obama administration is pressuring the states to test every grade and every subject. No student will be left untested. Every teacher will be judged by his or her students' scores. Cheating scandals will proliferate. Many teachers will be fired. Many will leave teaching, discouraged by the loss of their professional autonomy. Who will take their place? Will we ever break free of our national addiction to data? Will we ever stop to wonder if the data mean anything important? Will education survive school reform?

# FLUNKING ARNE DUNCAN

## THE NEW YORK REVIEW OF BOOKS - NYR DAILY, MARCH 7, 2012

Secretary of Education Arne Duncan loves evaluation. He insists that everyone should willingly submit to public grading of the work they do. The Race to the Top program he created for the Obama Administration requires states to evaluate all teachers based in large part on the test scores of their students. When the *Los Angeles Times* released public rankings that the newspaper devised for thousands of teachers, Duncan applauded and asked, "What's there to hide?" Given Duncan's enthusiasm for grading educators, it seems high time to evaluate his own performance as Secretary of Education.

Here are his grades:

***Does Duncan respect the limited role of the federal government in education, which all previous secretaries have recognized?***

No. Duncan has expanded the role of the federal government in unprecedented ways. He seems not to know that education is the responsibility of state and local governments, as defined by the Tenth amendment to our Constitution. States and local school districts now look to Washington to tell them how to reform their schools and must seek permission to deviate from the regulations written by the U.S. Department of Education. George W. Bush's No Child Left Behind (NCLB) created the template for this growing federal control of education, but Arne

Duncan's Race to the Top has made it possible for Washington to dictate education policy across the nation. ***Grade: F.***

***Has Duncan followed the law in his education policies?***

No. Duncan has issued waivers to states that want to be relieved from NCLB's impossible mandate of reaching 100 percent proficiency by 2014, but replaced that law's demands with those of his own devising. Duncan says his waivers allow "flexibility," but they serve simply to impose his own ideas about evaluating teachers, "transforming" low-performing schools by firing staff or closing the schools, and adopting national standards in reading and mathematics.[5] While very few people defend NCLB, which will write off almost every public school in the United States as a failure by 2014, it is still the law. Duncan has no authority to replace it with his own rules – cabinet members are not allowed to change the laws. Under our Constitution, Congress writes the laws, and the executive branch must enforce them, even as it seeks to change those that are onerous and misguided. ***Grade: F.***

***Has Duncan obeyed the clear prohibitions in law against federal involvement in creating a national curriculum?***

No. The law that governs the U.S. Department of Education clearly states that no officer of the federal government may "exercise any direction, supervision, or control" over the curriculum or program of instruction of any school or school system. Yet Duncan has insisted that states eager for race to the top funding or for NCLB waivers must adopt "college and career-ready standards," widely understood as the Common Core State Standards in mathematics and reading developed by the National Governors Association and the Council of Chief State School Officers, funded in large part by the Gates Foundation. Prodded by Duncan, 45 states have endorsed this national curriculum – despite the fact that it has never been field-tested. No one knows whether these standards are good or bad, or whether they will improve academic achievement or widen the achievement gap. A recent report by Tom Loveless from the Brookings Institution[6,7] predicted that the Common Core standards would have "little to no effect on student achievement." ***Grade: F.***

***Have the policies promulgated by Duncan been good for the children of the United States?***

No. Most parents and teachers and even President Obama (and sometimes Duncan himself) agree that "teaching to the test" makes school boring and robs classrooms of time for the imaginative instruction and activities that enliven learning. The standardized tests that are now ubiquitous are inherently boring. As President Obama said in his State of the Union address, teachers should teach with "creativity and passion," but they can't do that when tests matter so much. Spending hours preparing to take pick-the-bubble tests depresses student interest and motivation. This is not good for children. Yet Duncan's policies – which use test scores to evaluate teachers and to decide which schools to close and which teachers to pay bonuses to – intensively promote teaching to the test. This is not good for students. ***Grade: F.***

***Do Duncan's Policies Encourage Teachers and Inspire Good Teaching?***

No. Duncan's policies demean the teaching profession by treating student test scores as a proxy for teacher quality. A test that a student takes on one day of the year cannot possibly measure the quality of a teacher. Officially, the administration suggests that test scores are supposed to be only one of multiple measures of teacher quality, but invariably the scores outweigh every other component of any evaluation program,[8] as they did in New York City's recent release of the teacher ratings. Nor do most teachers want to compete with one another for merit pay.

Duncan cheered when the superintendent of the Central Falls, Rhode Island, school district threatened to fire every teacher in the town's only high school. The Education Secretary memorably said that Hurricane Katrina – which wiped out public schools and broke the teachers' union in New Orleans – was the best thing that ever happened to the school system in that city. Teachers are demoralized by such statements. They want to collaborate around the needs of the children they teach, but federal policy commands them instead to compete with one another for dollars and higher test scores if they want to stay employed. The *MetLife Survey of the American Teacher*, released March 6, 2012,[9,10] reports a sharp decline in teacher morale since 2009 – the percentage of teachers who are "very satisfied" with their job dropped from 59 percent to 44 percent, and the percentage who said they were likely to leave the profession grew from 17 percent to 29 percent. This happened on Duncan's watch. ***Grade: F.***

***Have Duncan's Policies Strengthened Public Education?***

No. Duncan has required states to create more privately-managed charter schools to be eligible for Race to the Top funding, putting pressure on state governments to privatize public education. In response, state legislatures are authorizing many more such schools, whose budgets are drawn from the funds of local public schools. A small proportion of these new charter schools will get high scores, and some will get those scores by skimming the top students in poor communities and by excluding children with disabilities and children who are English language learners. Such practices are harmful to public schools, which will continue to educate the overwhelming majority of students – with *fewer resources* than before. In some states, such as Michigan and Ohio, large numbers of charters are run for profit, which creates additional incentives for them to avoid *low-performing* and thus expensive-to-educate students. Although charters vary widely in quality, they do not produce better results on average than regular public schools. Conservative governors such as Mitch Daniels in Indiana and Bobby Jindal in Louisiana have taken Duncan's advocacy of choice to the next level and endorsed vouchers, which further undermine public education. Despite these well-documented issues, Duncan continues to urge the expansion of the charter sector and has ignored the depredations of the for-profit charter sector. ***Grade: F.***

***Has Duncan defended public education and public school educators against attacks on them?***

No. Although he is a Democrat, he has been absent when public education and public school educators were under siege. When Wisconsin Governor Scott Walker decided to eliminate collective bargaining rights for teachers and other public sector workers, Duncan was silent. When Indiana Governor Mitch Daniels pushed through a voucher bill that provides public funding for students to attend private and religious schools, Duncan was silent. When Louisiana Governor Bobby Jindal endorsed sweeping voucher and charter legislation, Duncan was silent – indeed, he described Governor Jindal's choice for state commissioner to promote his extremely conservative education agenda as "a visionary leader". When other governors proposed legislation to remove due process rights from teachers, to slash education spending, and to expand the privatization of public schools, Duncan was silent. ***Grade: F.***

***Will Duncan's policies improve public education?***

No. Under pressure to teach to tests – which assess only English and math skills – many districts are reducing the time available for teaching the arts, history, civics, foreign languages, physical education, and other non-tested subjects. Other districts are spending scarce dollars to create new tests for the arts, physical education, and those other subjects so they can evaluate all their teachers, not just those who teach reading and mathematics. Reducing the time available for the arts, history, and other subjects will not improve education. Putting more time and money into testing reduces the time and money available for instruction. None of this promotes good education. None of this supports love of learning or good character or any other ideals for education. Such a mechanistic, anti-intellectual approach would not be tolerated for President Obama's children, who attend an excellent private school. It should not be tolerated for the nation's children, 90 percent of whom attend public schools. ***Grade: F.***

***Overall, Secretary Duncan rates an F.***

We will someday view this era as one in which the nation turned its back on its public schools, its children, and its educators. We will wonder why so many journalists and policymakers rejected the nation's obligation to support public education as a social responsibility, and accepted the unrealistic, unsustainable promises of entrepreneurs and billionaires. And we will, with sorrow and regret, think of this as an era when an obsession with testing and data obliterated any concept or definition of good education. Some perhaps may recall this as a time when the nation forgot that education has a greater purpose than preparing our children to compete in the global economy.

Secretary of Education Duncan should have fought vigorously against all these pernicious developments. He should have opposed the misuse of test scores. He should have opposed the galloping privatization of public education. He should have demanded the proper funding of public education, instead of tolerating deep budget cuts as "the new normal." He should have spoken out against states that passed along the cost of higher education to students, putting it out of reach for many. But he has not. He should have upheld, in word and deed, the dignity of the teaching profession. Unfortunately he has not.

Even more unfortunately, it is hard to find any leader of either party who stands forthrightly today as a champion of students, teachers, public schools, and good education. This is a tragedy of our times.

***Report Card: Arne Duncan***

| | |
|---|---|
| Fidelity to the Constitution | F |
| Doing what's right for children | F |
| Doing what's right for public education | F |
| Respecting the limits of federalism | F |
| Doing what's right for teachers | F |
| Doing what's right for education | F |

# SCHOOLS WE CAN ENVY

## THE NEW YORK REVIEW OF BOOKS, MARCH 8, 2012

In recent years, elected officials and policymakers such as former president George W. Bush, former schools chancellor Joel Klein in New York City, former schools chancellor Michelle Rhee in Washington, D.C., and Secretary of Education Arne Duncan have agreed that there should be "no excuses" for schools with low test scores. The "no excuses" reformers maintain that all children can attain academic proficiency without regard to poverty, disability, or other conditions, and that someone must be held accountable if they do not. That someone is invariably their teachers.

Nothing is said about holding accountable the district leadership or the elected officials who determine such crucial issues as funding, class size, and resource allocation. The reformers say that our economy is in jeopardy, not because of growing poverty or income inequality or the outsourcing of manufacturing jobs, but because of bad teachers. These bad teachers must be found out and thrown out. Any laws, regulations, or contracts that protect these pedagogical malefactors must be eliminated so that they can be quickly removed without regard to experience, seniority, or due process.

The belief that schools alone can overcome the effects of poverty may be traced back many decades, but its most recent manifestation was a short book published in 2000 by the conservative Heritage Foundation in Washington, D.C., titled *No Excuses*. In this book, Samuel Casey Carter identified twenty-one high-poverty schools with high test scores. Over the past decade, influential figures in public life have decreed that school reform is the key to fixing poverty. Bill Gates told the National Urban League, "Let's end the myth that we have to solve poverty before we improve education. I say it's more the other way around: improving education is the best way to solve poverty." Gates never explains why a rich and powerful society like our own cannot address both poverty and school improvement at the same time.

For a while, the Gates Foundation thought that small high schools were the answer, but Gates now believes that teacher evaluation is the primary ingredient of school reform. The Gates Foundation has awarded hundreds of millions of dollars to school districts to develop new teacher evaluation systems. In 2009, the nation's chief reformer, Secretary of Education Arne Duncan, launched a $4.35 billion competitive program called Race to the Top, which required states to evaluate teachers by student test scores and to remove the limits on privately managed charter schools.

The main mechanism of school reform today is to identify teachers who can raise their students' test scores every year. If the scores go up, reformers assume, then the students will enroll in college and poverty will eventually disappear. This will happen, the reformers believe, if there is a "great teacher" in every classroom and if more schools are handed over to private managers, even for-profit corporations.

The reformers don't care that standardized tests are prone to measurement error, sampling error, and other statistical errors. They don't seem to care that experts like Robert L. Linn at the University of Colorado, Linda Darling-Hammond at Stanford, and Helen F. Ladd at Duke, as well as a commission of the National Research Council, have warned about misuse of standardized tests to hold individual teachers accountable with rewards or sanctions. Nor do they see the absurdity of gauging the quality of a teacher by the results of a multiple-choice test given to students on one day of the year.

Testing can provide useful information showing students

and teachers what is and is not being learned, and scores can be used to diagnose learning problems. But bad things happen when tests become too consequential for students, teachers, and schools, such as narrowing the curriculum only to what is tested or cheating, or lowering standards to inflate scores. In response to the federal and state pressure to raise test scores, school districts across the nation have been reducing the time available for the arts, physical education, history, civics, and other non-tested subjects. This will not improve education and is certain to damage its quality.

No nation in the world has eliminated poverty by firing teachers or by handing its public schools over to private managers, nor does research support either strategy. But these inconvenient facts do not reduce the reformers' zeal. The new breed of school reformers consists mainly of Wall Street hedge fund managers, foundation officials, corporate executives, entrepreneurs, and policymakers, but few experienced educators. The reformers' detachment from the realities of schooling and their indifference to research allow them to ignore the important influence of families and poverty. The schools can achieve miracles, the reformers assert, by relying on competition, deregulation, and management by data – strategies similar to the ones that helped produce the economic crash of 2008. In view of the reformers' penchant for these strategies, educators tend to call them "corporate reformers," to distinguish them from those who understand the complexities of school improvement.

The corporate reformers' well-funded public relations campaign has succeeded in persuading elected officials that American public education needs shock therapy. One is tempted to forget that the United States is the largest and one of the most successful economies in the world, and that some part of this success must be attributed to the institutions that educated 90 percent of the people in this nation.

Faced with the relentless campaign against teachers and public education, educators have sought a different narrative, one free of the stigmatization by test scores and punishment favored by the corporate reformers. They have found it in Finland. Even the corporate reformers admire Finland, apparently not recognizing that Finland disproves every part of their agenda.

It is not unusual for Americans to hold up another nation as a model for school reform. In the mid-nineteenth century, American education leaders hailed the Prussian system for its professionalism and structure. In the 1960s, Americans flocked to England to marvel at its progressive schools. In the 1980s, envious Americans attributed the Japanese economic success to its school system. Now the most favored nation is Finland, and for four good reasons.

First, Finland has one of the highest-performing school systems in the world, as measured by the Programme for International Student Assessment (PISA), which assesses reading, mathematical literacy, and scientific literacy of fifteen-year-old students in all thirty-four nations of the Organisation for Economic Co-operation and Development (OECD), including the United States. Unlike our domestic tests, there are no consequences attached to the tests administered by the PISA. No individual or school learns its score. No one is rewarded or punished because of these tests. No one can prepare for them, nor is there any incentive to cheat.

Second, from an American perspective, Finland is an alternative universe. It rejects all of the "reforms" currently popular in the United States, such as testing, charter schools, vouchers, merit pay, competition, and evaluating teachers in relation to the test scores of their students.

Third, among the OECD nations, Finnish schools have the least variation in quality, meaning that they come closest to achieving equality of educational opportunity – an American ideal.

Fourth, Finland borrowed many of its most valued ideas from the United States, such as equality of educational opportunity, individualized instruction, portfolio assessment, and cooperative learning. Most of its borrowing derives from the work of the philosopher John Dewey.

In *Finnish Lessons: What Can the World Learn from Educational Change in Finland?* Pasi Sahlberg explains how his nation's schools became successful. A government official, researcher, and former mathematics and science teacher, Sahlberg attributes the improvement of Finnish schools to bold decisions made in the 1960s and 1970s. Finland's story is important, he writes, because "it gives hope to those who are losing their faith in public education."

Detractors say that Finland performs well academically because it is ethnically homogeneous, but Sahlberg responds that "the same holds true for Japan, Shanghai or Korea," which are admired by corporate reformers for their emphasis on testing. To detractors who say that Finland, with its population of 5.5 million people, is too small to serve as a model, Sahlberg responds that "about 30 states of the United States have a population close to or less than Finland."

Sahlberg speaks directly to the sense of crisis about educational achievement in the United States and many other nations. U.S. policymakers have turned to market-based solutions such as "tougher competition, more data, abolishing teacher unions, opening more charter schools, or employing corporate-world management models." By contrast, Finland has spent the past forty years developing a different education system, one that is focused on improving the teaching force, limiting student testing to a necessary minimum, placing responsibility and trust before accountability, and handing over school- and district-level leadership to education professionals.

To an American observer, the most remarkable fact about Finnish education is that students do not take any standardized tests until the end of high school. They do take tests, but the tests are drawn up by their own teachers, not by a multinational testing corporation. The Finnish nine-year comprehensive school is a "standardized testing-free zone," where children are encouraged "to know, to create, and to sustain natural curiosity."

I met Pasi Sahlberg in December 2010. I was one of a dozen educators invited to the home of the Finnish consul in New York

City to learn about the Finnish education system on the day after the release of the latest international test results. Once again, Finland was in the top tier of nations, as it has been for the past decade. Sahlberg assured the guests that Finnish educators don't care about standardized test scores and welcomed the international results only because they protected the schools against conservative demands for testing and accountability.

Finnish teachers, Sahlberg said, are well educated, well prepared, and highly respected. They are paid about the same as teachers in the United States in comparison to other college graduates, but Finnish teachers with fifteen years' experience in the classroom are paid more than their American counterparts. I asked Sahlberg how it was possible to hold teachers or schools accountable when there were no standardized tests. He replied that Finnish educators speak not of accountability, but of responsibility. He said, "Our teachers are very responsible; they are professionals." When asked what happens to incompetent teachers, Sahlberg insisted that they would never be appointed – once qualified teachers are appointed, it is very difficult to remove them. When asked how Finnish teachers would react if they were told they would be judged by their students' test scores, he replied, "They would walk out and they wouldn't return until the authorities stopped this crazy idea."

Sahlberg invited me to Finland to tour several schools, which I eventually did in September 2011. With Sahlberg as my guide, I visited bright, cheerful schools where students engaged in music, dramatics, play, and academic studies, with fifteen-minute recesses between classes. I spoke at length with teachers and principals in spacious, comfortable lounges. Free from the testing obsession that now consumes so much of the day in American schools, the staff has time to plan and discuss the students and the program.

Before I left Finland, Sahlberg gave me a book called *The Best School in the World: Seven Finnish Examples from the 21st Century*, about the architecture of Finnish schools. The book is based on an exhibition presented at the Venice Biennale of Architecture in 2010. When we visited one of the featured schools, I thought, how delightful to discover a nation that cares passionately about the physical environment in which children learn and adults work.

To be sure, Finland is an unusual nation. Its schools are carefully designed to address the academic, social, emotional, and physical needs of children, beginning at an early age. Free preschool programs are not compulsory, but they enroll 98 percent of children. Compulsory education begins at the age of seven. Finnish educators take care not to hold students back or label them as "failing," since such actions would cause student failure, lessen student motivation, and increase social inequality. After nine years of comprehensive schooling, during which there is no tracking by ability, Finnish students choose whether to enroll in an academic or a vocational high school. About 42 percent choose the latter. The graduation rate is 93 percent, compared to about 80 percent in the U.S.

Finland's highly developed teacher preparation program is the centerpiece of its school reform strategy. Only eight universities are permitted to prepare teachers, and admission to these elite teacher education programs is highly competitive – only one of every ten applicants is accepted. There are no alternative ways to earn a teaching license. Those who are accepted have already taken required high school courses in physics, chemistry, philosophy, music, and at least two foreign languages. Future teachers have a strong academic education for three years, and then enter a two-year master's degree program. Subject matter teachers earn their master's degree from the university's academic departments, not – in contrast to the U.S. – the department of teacher education, or in special schools for teacher education. Every candidate prepares to teach all kinds of students, including students with disabilities and other special needs. Every teacher must complete an undergraduate degree and a master's degree in education.

Because entry into teaching is difficult and the training is rigorous, teaching is a respected and prestigious profession in

Finland. So selective and demanding is the process that virtually every teacher is well prepared. Sahlberg writes that teachers enter the profession with a sense of moral mission and the only reasons they might leave would be "if they were to lose their professional autonomy" or if "a merit-based compensation policy (tied to test scores) were imposed." Meanwhile, the United States is now doing to its teachers what Finnish teachers would find professionally reprehensible – judging their worth by the test scores of their students.

Finland's national curriculum in the arts and sciences describes what is to be learned but is not prescriptive about the details of what to teach or how to teach it. The national curriculum requires the teaching of a mother tongue (Finnish or Swedish), mathematics, foreign languages, history, biology, environmental science, religion, ethics, geography, chemistry, physics, music, visual arts, crafts, physical education, health, and other studies.

Teachers have wide latitude at each school in deciding what to teach, how to teach, and how to gauge their pupils' progress. Finnish educators agree that "every child has the right to get personalized support provided early on by trained professionals as part of normal schooling." Sahlberg estimates that some 50 percent of students receive attention from specialists in the early years of schooling. Teachers and principals frequently collaborate to discuss the needs of the students and the school. As a result of these policies, Sahlberg writes:

> Most visitors to Finland discover elegant school buildings filled with calm children and highly educated teachers. They also recognize the large amount of autonomy that schools enjoy, with little interference by the central education administration in schools' everyday lives, systematic methods for addressing problems in the lives of students, and targeted professional help for those in need.

The children of Finland enjoy certain important advantages

over our own children. The nation has a strong social welfare safety net, for which it pays with high taxes. More than 20 percent of our children live in poverty, while fewer than 4 percent of Finnish children do. Many children in the United States do not have access to regular medical care, but all Finnish children receive comprehensive health services and a free lunch every day. Higher education is tuition-free.

Sahlberg recognizes that Finland stands outside what he refers to as the "Global Education Reform Movement," to which he appends the apt acronym "GERM". GERM, he notes, is a virus that has infected not only the United States, but the United Kingdom, Australia, and many other nations. President George W. Bush's No Child Left Behind law and President Barack Obama's Race to the Top program are examples of the global education reform movement. Both promote:

- Standardized testing as the most reliable measure of success for students, teachers, and schools.
- Privatization in the form of schools being transferred to private management.
- Standardization of curriculum.
- Test-based accountability such as merit pay for high scores, closing schools with low scores, and firing educators for low scores.

In contrast, the central aim of Finnish education is the development of each child as a thinking, active, creative person, not the attainment of higher test scores. The primary strategy of Finnish education is cooperation, not competition. I consider the Teach for America organization – the subject of Wendy Kopp's *A Chance to Make History* – in comparison to the Finnish model in the next essay.

# HOW, AND HOW NOT, TO IMPROVE THE SCHOOLS

THE NEW YORK REVIEW OF BOOKS, MARCH 22, 2012

In his 2012 State of the Union address, President Barack Obama proposed that teachers should "stop teaching to the test" and that the nation should "reward the best ones" and "replace teachers who just aren't helping kids learn." This all sounds sensible, but it is in fact a contradictory message. The president's signature education program, called Race to the Top, encourages states to award bonuses to teachers whose students get higher test scores – they are, presumably "the best ones" – and to fire teachers if their students get lower test scores – presumably the teachers "who just aren't helping kids". If teachers want to stay employed, they must "teach to the test." The president recommends that teachers stop doing what his own policies make necessary and prudent.

Like George W. Bush's No Child Left Behind, Barack Obama's Race to the Top program is part of what Pasi Sahlberg calls "the Global Education Reform Movement," or GERM. GERM demands teaching to the test. GERM assumes that students must be constantly tested, and that the results of these tests are the most important measures and outcomes of education. The scores can be used not only to grade the quality of every school, but to punish or reward students, teachers, principals, and schools. Those at the top of the education system, the elected officials and leaders who make the rules, create the budgets, and allocate resources, are never accountable for the consequences of their decisions. GERM assumes that people who work in schools need carrots and sticks to persuade (or compel) them to do their best.

In Finland, the subject of the first part of this essay, teachers work collaboratively with other members of the school staff; they are not "held accountable" by standardized test scores because there are none. Teachers devise their own tests to inform them about their students' progress and needs. They do their best because it is their professional responsibility. Like other professionals, as Pasi Sahlberg shows in his book *Finnish Lessons,* Finnish teachers are driven by a sense of intrinsic motivation, not by the hope of a bonus or the fear of being fired. Intrinsic motivation is also what they seek to instill in their students. In the absence of standardized testing by which to compare their students and their schools, teachers must develop, appeal to, and rely on their students' interest in learning.

The GERM model seeks to emulate the free market by treating parents as consumers and students as products, with teachers as compliant workers who are expected to obey orders and follow scripts. Advocates of GERM are often hostile to teachers' unions, which are considered obstacles to the managerial ethos necessary to control the daily life of a school. Unions also make it hard, if not impossible, to carry out cost savings, such as removing the highest-paid teachers and replacing them with low-wage, entry-level teachers.

Finland's success confounds the GERM theorists, because almost every teacher and principal in Finland belongs to the same union. The union works closely with the Ministry of Education to improve the quality of education, and it negotiates for better salaries, benefits, and working conditions for educators.

The American school reform movement – the odd coalition of corporate-friendly Democrats, right-wing Republicans, Tea Party governors, Wall Street executives, and major foundations – proudly advocates the tenets of GERM. More testing, more privately managed schools, more deregulation, more firing of teachers, more school closings, they believe, and eventually every student will go to college and poverty will be eliminated. There is little evidence to support this approach.

The Duke University economist Helen F. Ladd recently delivered a major address titled "Education and Poverty: Confronting the Evidence," in which she demonstrated that poverty drags down academic performance, not only in the U.S., but in other nations as well. To argue, as so many of the corporate reformers blithely do, that poverty is used as "an excuse" for bad teachers is either naive or ignorant. Or it may be a way of avoiding the politically difficult subjects of poverty and income inequality, both of which are rising and threaten the well-being of our society.

The corporate reformers believe that entrepreneurship will unleash a new era of innovation and creativity, but it seems mostly to have unleashed canny entrepreneurs who seek higher test scores by any means possible – such as excluding students with disabilities or students learning English as a second language – or who seek maximum profit. One facet of the business plan for reform is reducing the cost of instruction. Many governors tackle this head-on by slashing the budget and laying off teachers. Others, claiming to act in the name of "reform," replace teachers with online instruction. Another way to reduce costs is to rely on inexperienced teachers, who are at the bottom of the salary scale and are likely to leave teaching for more remunerative, less demanding jobs before they are eligible for a pension.

Experienced teachers are fleeing American public education in response to the testing demands of No Child Left Behind, which reduce professional autonomy. According to federal data, the "modal years" of teacher experience in our public schools in 1987–1988 was fifteen, meaning that there were more teachers with fifteen years of experience than any other group. By 2007-2008, the largest number of teachers were in their first year of teaching. In response to the ongoing drumbeat of public opprobrium inspired by corporate-style school reform, we are losing the experienced teachers that students and new teachers need.

Unlike Finland, where entry into teaching is limited and

competitive, the United States has low standards for new teachers. In Finland the profession is highly esteemed; in the United States it is not. Some states require master's degrees, some do not. The difference is not compensation, but the high degree of professionalism that Finland expects of its teachers. In the United States, some states and districts require teachers to have a degree in the subject they teach or to pass a test to demonstrate their mastery of their subject, some do not.

Schools of education are held in low esteem within the university system. Online universities now award the largest numbers of master's degrees in education. The teaching profession in the United States is a revolving door. It's easy to enter, and many teachers leave – up to 40 to 50 percent – in their first five years as teachers. The turnover is highest in low-scoring urban districts. We do not support new teachers with appropriate training and mentoring, and we have a problem retaining teachers. No other profession in the United States has such a high rate of turnover.

For those who take seriously the need to improve the teaching profession, this would seem to be the right time to raise entry standards and to improve teacher education. If we were to learn from Finland's example, we would select well-educated candidates for entry into teaching, require academic excellence and a master's degree, and make certification as an education professional meaningful. But corporate reformers have shown no interest in raising standards for the teaching profession. They believe that entry-level requirements such as certification, master's degrees, and other credentials are unrelated to "performance," that is, student test scores. They also scorn seniority, experience, tenure, and other perquisites of the profession. Instead, they believe that a steady infusion of smart but barely trained novices will change the face of teaching. In no other field but education would such judgments be tolerated, because they reinforce the low status of education as a profession, one where no prolonged preparation is thought necessary.

The corporate reformers' favorite remedy for the ills of the profession is the Teach for America (TFA) program. By now, everyone in the education field knows the story of how the Princeton student Wendy Kopp developed the idea for TFA as her senior thesis in 1989, then raised millions of dollars from corporations and turned her idea into a wildly successful brand. TFA enlists new graduates from the nation's best colleges and universities, who commit themselves to teach in distressed urban and rural schools for two years. In the past decade, Kopp has raised hundreds of millions of dollars for TFA.

Just in the past eighteen months, TFA received $50 million from the U.S. Department of Education, $49.5 million from the ultra-conservative Walton Family Foundation, and $100 million from a consortium of other foundations, as well as additional millions from corporations and other major donors. Each year, TFA selects several thousand idealistic young people, gives them five weeks of training, and sends them out to teach. The school districts pay members of TFA a starting teacher's salary and typically pay TFA $5,000 for each new teacher.

TFA, like the Peace Corps, is an admirable idea. The young people who join TFA are typically among our brightest students from top-tier universities. On some campuses, more students apply to TFA than to any other prospective employer. Like others who become teachers, they want to make a difference in the lives of children, particularly those who are poor.

And yet TFA has aroused the anger of veteran educators because of the organization's arrogance. TFA claims that its young recruits are better than other teachers, presumably because they are carefully selected and therefore smarter than the average teacher. It also claims that its corps members produce remarkable results even in the two or three years that most are likely to teach. But researchers such as Linda Darling-Hammond at Stanford, Barbara Torre Veltri at Northern Arizona University, Philip Kovacs at the University of Alabama, and Julian Vasquez Heilig at the University of Texas have challenged TFA 's claims. They maintain that the students of TFA's young recruits have not achieved the remarkable test score gains that the organization boasts about. Critics ask why inexperienced young graduates are permitted to teach the nation's most vulnerable children. Veteran educators resent the suggestion that new college graduates have arrived to save their schools. They know that novices with a few weeks' training, no matter how smart and idealistic, can't be expected to produce dramatic results in two or three years as a teacher.

In *A Chance to Make History,* Kopp ignores the critics and concentrates instead on telling stories about successful classrooms and schools led by TFA alumni and teachers. The message of the book is that TFA has discovered the secrets to producing astonishing changes in schools, and needs to keep growing to bring these changes to entire districts.

The book is written in the first person and consists of anecdotes intended to demonstrate that TFA has discovered how to provide an excellent education for every child in America, regardless of poverty or other handicaps. Kopp confidently asserts that there is "hard evidence that we can ensure all of our children in urban and rural communities have the opportunity to attain an excellent education." Back when she started, she writes, "many assumed that fixing education would require fixing poverty first." She is now convinced, however, that TFA teachers, "even in their first and second years of teaching, are proving it is possible for economically disadvantaged children to compete academically with their higher-income peers." She points to the KIPP network of charter schools, the YES Prep charter schools in Houston, and the Mastery charter schools in Philadelphia as remarkable success stories, where disadvantaged children achieve high test scores. Kopp acknowledges that her husband, Richard Barth, is the chief executive officer of KIPP, which also received $50 million from the U.S. Department of Education in 2010. These examples make her confident that "we don't need to wait to fix poverty in order to ensure that all children receive an excellent education."

But what is bringing about these miraculous results? Kopp has one word that she uses on almost every page of the book, "transformational." She applauds transformational teachers, transformational leadership, and transformational schools. Transformational teachers change the trajectory of children's lives. They tell every child that they are going to go to college, and that, according to Kopp, seems to cause major changes. So does tracking data and extra time. KIPP schools have:

> ... total central control over the indicators used to track progress ... such as college matriculation and completion of eighth grade, student attrition, and teacher retention. Other non-negotiables include more time and the requirement that every adult who works at KIPP chooses to be there.

Some of those schools offer the extra health services that our society apparently can't afford to provide to all children, and some provide extra tutoring and help for families. In the schools she calls transformational, poverty does not get in the way of high test scores.

But can these individual charter schools or charter networks generate the same success in entire urban districts? After all, it took eighteen years for the handsomely funded KIPP charter network to grow to ninety-nine schools enrolling 26,000 students, a tiny number compared to a nation with millions of impoverished, low-performing students. Kopp points to New York City, Washington, D.C., and New Orleans as districts with significant numbers of TFA recruits that have made "historic progress and improvement."

However, her evidence is shaky. She says that New York City is a model where "the needle is moving against the achievement gap in ways that are meaningful for students." She refers to the city's gains on federal tests, but does not acknowledge that the gains were no larger than those of other urban districts. She refers to the city's improvement on New York State tests, but curiously fails to mention that those dramatic gains evaporated following a widely publicized investigation in July 2010. After the state acknowledged that its tests had become easier over time, the city's test scores dropped back almost to where they had been in 2002, and the achievement gaps among racial and ethnic groups reverted as well.

Is Washington, D.C., a promising model? Kopp believes that the TFA alumni who have managed the district's schools since 2007 have made remarkable improvements by imposing new demands for data, measurement, and accountability on every school, as well as a new teacher evaluation system. But a few months after Kopp's book appeared, *USA Today* revealed evidence of a major cheating scandal. The newspaper disclosed that test scores at certain schools showed a remarkably high rate of erasures from wrong to right.

The investigation centered on a school that Chancellor Michelle Rhee had celebrated, where scores rose sharply in a short period of time. Kopp could not have known about the cheating allegations, but she surely knew that the district's steady improvement in reading and mathematics scores on the federally sponsored tests called the National Assessment of Educational Progress had begun in 2003, long before the arrival in 2007 of Rhee, a TFA alumna, as chancellor of schools for the district. Unfortunately, despite its improved test scores, the District of Columbia continues to have the largest achievement gap between white and black students in the nation – fully double that of most other big cities tested by the federal government.

As for New Orleans, it is the poster child of the corporate reformers because the public school system and the teachers' union were wiped out by Hurricane Katrina. Now about 70 percent of the students in the district attend charter schools, staffed by TFA and other young teachers. Reformers have portrayed New Orleans as an educational miracle, and the media have faithfully parroted this characterization as proof that nonunion charter schools are successful. But few paid attention when the state of Louisiana recently released grades for every school in the state and 79 percent of the charter schools formed by the state received a grade of D or F.

TFA is a worthy idea. It is wonderful to encourage young

people to commit themselves to public service for two years. The program would be far more admirable if the organization showed some modesty, humility, and realism in its claims for its inexperienced teachers. Many foundations, corporations, and even the U.S. Department of Education, treat TFA as a systemic solution to the critical needs of the teaching profession. But it is foolhardy to expect that a profession of more than three million teachers will be transformed by the annual addition of a few thousand college graduates who agree to stay for only two years.

TFA is no substitute for the deep changes needed in the recruitment, support, and retention of career educators. Our nation's schools need professional teachers who have had the kind of intensive preparation and practice that nations like Finland insist upon. The Peace Corps sends out young people to do whatever is required in impoverished communities, not to serve as full-fledged Foreign Service officers for two years. Nor is it realistic to claim that these young people, because they are smart, can fix American schools and end the inequities in American society by teaching for a few years. If only it were that easy!

The current reform movement in education has embraced TFA and privately managed charter schools as remedies for the nation's schools. But this combination is unlikely to succeed because one alienates career educators and the other destabilizes our public education system. It is hard to imagine improving the schools without the support and trust of the people who work in them every day.

Under pressure from the Obama administration's Race to the Top program, many state legislatures have recently passed laws to evaluate the effectiveness of teachers in relation to the test scores of their students. This is very questionable, not least because most teachers do not teach subjects that are tested – only reading and mathematics in grades 3 to 8 are regularly tested, but not history, science, civics, the arts, foreign languages, or other subjects. Many economists are excited about measuring teachers by "results" in this way, but test publishers warn that the tests measure student performance, not teacher quality.

Although many legislatures want student scores to count for as much as 50 percent of a teacher's evaluation, these measures turn out to be inaccurate, unreliable, and unstable. Students are not randomly assigned, and the scores say more about the composition of a class than about the quality of the teacher. A teacher may look highly effective one year but ineffective the next, depending on which students end up in his or her classroom. Research has demonstrated that those who teach students with disabilities, students who are just learning English, and other students with high needs are less likely to get big test score gains and more likely to be rated as "bad" teachers. By imposing such indiscriminate standards, some excellent teachers will be fired, and others of less distinction will get bonuses. No profession worthy of being considered a profession would allow legislatures to determine how to assess the quality of its practitioners. They are not competent to do so. Part of the definition of a profession is that it is self-regulating, not subservient to external mandates. More self-regulation and professionalism is needed in teaching, not less.

The problems of American education are not unsolvable, but the remedies must be rooted in reality. Schools are crucial institutions in our society and teachers can make a huge difference in changing children's lives, but schools and teachers alone cannot cure the ills of an unequal and stratified society. Every testing program – whether the SAT, the ACT, or state and national tests – demonstrates that low scores are strongly correlated to poverty. On the SAT, for example, students from the most affluent families have the highest scores, and children from the poorest families have the lowest scores. Children need better schools, and they also need health clinics, high-quality early childhood education, arts programs, after-school activities, safe neighborhoods, and basic economic security. To the extent that we reduce poverty, we will improve student achievement.

So what does Finland teach us? We need to raise the standards for entry into the teaching profession, and future teachers should have intensive professional and academic preparation.

If we were to improve the teaching profession, then perhaps more of the talented young people who now apply to TFA would choose to enter teaching as a career, not as a stepping stone to graduate school or another more remunerative line of work. If teaching were to become admired and prestigious, our schools would certainly benefit. But no matter how admired the teaching profession becomes, our society must do much more to reduce poverty and to improve the lives of children and families.

# IN DEFENSE OF FACING REALITY

## HUFFINGTON POST, MARCH 18, 2012

*The most reactionary and anti-union of the major foundations – the billionaire Walton Family Foundation – has awarded $20 million to Teach for America to send bright, ill-prepared new college graduates into the nation's classrooms. – Diane Ravitch's Blog*

I recently wrote two review articles for *The New York Review of Books* about the teaching profession. The first was a review of Pasi Sahlberg's *Finnish Lessons*,[11] about the exceptional school system of Finland, which owes much to the high professionalism of its teachers.

The second of the two articles was a review of Wendy Kopp's *A Chance to Make History*,[12] and it focused on her organization, Teach for America.

I expressed my admiration for the young people who agree to teach for two years, with only five weeks of training. But I worried that TFA was now seen – and promoting itself – as the answer to the serious problems of American education. Even by naming her book *A Chance to Make History*, Wendy Kopp reinforced the idea that TFA was the very mechanism that American society could rely upon to lift up the children of poverty and close the achievement gaps between different racial and ethnic groups.

Wendy Kopp responded to my review of her book with a blog called *In Defense of Optimism*.[13] She wrote that:

> ... over the last twenty years we in the United States have discovered that we don't have to wait to fix poverty to dramatically improve educational outcomes for underprivileged students. In fact, there's strong evidence that one of the most effective ways to break the cycle of poverty is to expand the mission of public schools in low-income communities and put enormous energy into providing children with the extra time and support they need to reach their potential.

Now I certainly agree with Kopp that schools are enormously important, and that it's vital to have talented educators working in them. We both want to see the day when every child has access to an excellent education. She believes that the teachers and the leaders produced by TFA have figured this out. I disagree. I think that the lesson of Finland and other high-performing nations is that we must improve the teaching profession, so that career educators receive the respect and working conditions they need to succeed, and we must also reduce poverty.

If it were true that we now know how to break the cycle of poverty, poverty would be declining. But poverty is growing in the United States – child poverty is more than 20 percent and rising. Among the world's advanced nations, we are number one in child poverty. It's facile to blame schools and teachers, but more realistic to recognize that poverty is a reflection of economic conditions. Schools cannot create jobs, provide homes for the homeless, or change the economy.

Kopp is right that TFA has become a training ground for leaders. Some of its alumni have moved into high-level positions, like Michelle Rhee, former chancellor of the public schools of the District of Columbia, who now works closely with the nation's most conservative governors to strip teachers of due process rights and to promote charter schools, vouchers, and for-profit education corporations. Another TFA alum, John White, Commissioner of Education in Louisiana, advances the same hard-right agenda for Governor Bobby Jindal.

In my reviews, I contrasted the five-year preparation of teachers in Finland with the American hodge-podge approach to the recruitment and training of teachers. In the U.S. states offer many ways to become a teacher, and our non-system has produced low standards for entry and a revolving door, with 40-50 percent leaving in their first five years of teaching. Finnish teachers are highly respected and seldom leave their profession.

Kopp dismisses Finland as a model because less than 4 percent of its children are poor. But that's part of the story of their success and should not be waved aside as unimportant. Teacher professionalism is also part of Finnish success. In this country, our public school teachers are constantly criticized and disrespected, and few are recognized for their dedication and hard work despite budget cuts, growing class sizes, and a hostile media. So long as the attacks on teachers continue, so long as the politicians continue defunding the schools, and so long as our society continues to tolerate high levels of child poverty and intense racial segregation, we will continue to have low-performing students and "failing" schools.

We will have to learn to hold two ideas in our heads at the same time. We must both reduce poverty and improve our schools. We cannot fix our schools without strengthening the teaching profession and addressing the social conditions that shape their outcomes.

# DO OUR PUBLIC SCHOOLS THREATEN NATIONAL SECURITY?

THE NEW YORK REVIEW OF BOOKS, JUNE 7, 2012

In his Pulitzer Prize winning book, *Anti-Intellectualism in American Life*, Richard Hofstadter characterized writing on education in the United States as:

> ... a literature of acid criticism and bitter complaint.... The educational jeremiad is as much a feature of our literature as the jeremiad in the Puritan sermons.

Anyone longing for the "good old days," he noted, would have difficulty finding a time when critics were not lamenting the quality of the public schools. From the 1820s to our own time, reformers have complained about low standards, ignorant teachers, and incompetent school boards.

Most recently, in 1983, an august presidential commission somberly warned that we were (in the title of its statement) "A Nation at Risk" because of the low standards of our public schools. The Reagan-era report said:

> Our once unchallenged preeminence in commerce, industry, science, and technological innovation is being overtaken by competitors throughout the world.

Our national slippage was caused, said the commission, by "a rising tide of mediocrity that threatens our very future as a Nation and a people." This mediocre educational performance was nothing less than "an act of unthinking, unilateral educational disarmament."

Imagine the peril, the threat of national disaster: "our very future as a Nation and a people" hung in the balance unless we moved swiftly to improve our public schools. What were we to do? The commission proposed a list of changes, starting with raising graduation requirements for all students and making sure they studied a full curriculum of English, math, science, history, computer science, as well as foreign languages (for the college-bound), the arts, and vocational education.

It also proposed more student time in school, higher standards for entry into teaching, higher salaries for teachers, and an evaluation system for teachers that included peer review. Nothing was said about the current fad of evaluating teachers by their students' test scores. The federal government distributed half a million copies of the report, and many states created task forces and commissions to determine how to implement the recommendations. Many states did raise graduation requirements, but critics were unappeased, and complaints about our educational failures continued unabated.

Somehow, despite the widely broadcast perception that educational achievement was declining, the United States continued to grow and thrive as an economic, military, and technological power. As President Barack Obama put it in his 2011 State of the Union address:[14]

> Remember – for all the hits we've taken these last few years, for all the naysayers predicting our decline, America still has the largest, most prosperous economy in the world. No workers – no workers are more productive than ours. No country has more successful companies, or grants more patents to inventors and entrepreneurs. We're the home to the world's best colleges and universities, where more students come to study than any place on Earth.

How is it possible that this nation became so successful if its public schools, which enroll 90 percent of its children, have been consistently failing for the past generation or more?

Now comes the latest jeremiad, this one from a task force sponsored by the Council on Foreign Relations and led by Joel I. Klein, former chancellor of the New York City public schools – now employed by Rupert Murdoch's News Corporation to sell technology to schools and to advise Murdoch on his corporation's hacking scandals – and Condoleezza Rice, former Secretary of State during the administration of President George W. Bush. This report has the cumbersome title *U.S. Education Reform and National Security*[15] and a familiar message – our nation's public schools are so dreadful that they are a threat to our national security. Once again, statistics are marshaled to prove that our schools are failing, our economy is at risk, our national security is compromised, and everything we prize is about to disappear because of our low-performing public schools. Make no mistake, the task force warns: "Educational failure puts the United States' future economic prosperity, global position, and physical safety at risk."

Despite its alarmist rhetoric, the report is not a worthy successor to the long line of jeremiads that it joins. Unlike *A Nation at Risk*, which was widely quoted as a call to action, this report is a plodding exercise in groupthink among mostly like-minded task force members. Its leaden prose contains not a single sparkling phrase for the editorial writers. The only flashes of original thinking appear in the dissents to the report.

What marks this report as different from its predecessors, however, is its profound indifference to the role of public education in a democratic society, and its certainty that private organizations will succeed where the public schools have failed. Previous hand-wringing reports sought to improve public schooling; this one suggests that public schools themselves are the problem, and the sooner they are handed over to private operators, the sooner we will see widespread innovation and improved academic achievement.

The report is a mishmash of misleading statistics and incoherent arguments, intended to exaggerate the failure of public education. Richard Haass, the president of the Council on Foreign Relations, introduces the report with this claim: "It will come as no surprise to most readers that America's primary and secondary schools are widely seen as failing." Many scholars of education would disagree with this conclusion; they would probably respond that the United States has many excellent public schools and that the lowest-performing schools are overwhelmingly concentrated in districts with high levels of poverty and racial isolation. Haass then writes, "High school graduation rates, while improving, are still far too low, and there are steep gaps in achievement between middle class and poor students." He does not seem aware that, according to the latest federal data, high school graduation rates are at their highest point in history for students of all races and income levels. Certainly they should be higher, but the actual data do not suggest a crisis.

Of course, there are achievement gaps between middle-class and poor students, but this is true in every nation where there are large income gaps. While the task force points out the problems of concentrated poverty in segregated schools, exacerbated by unequal school funding, it offers no recommendations to reduce poverty, racial segregation, income gaps, or funding inequities. It dwells on the mediocre standing of American schools on international tests, but does not acknowledge that American schools with a low level of poverty rank first in the world on international tests of literacy.

The task force has many complaints. American students don't study foreign languages. American employers can't find enough skilled workers. Too many young people do not qualify for military service because of criminal records, lack of physical fitness, or inadequate educational skills. Not enough scientists and engineers are trained "to staff the military, intelligence agencies, and other government-run national security offices, as well as the aerospace and defense industries." Thus, the public schools are failing to prepare the soldiers, intelligence agents, diplomats, and engineers for the defense industry that the report assumes are needed. This failure is the primary rationale for viewing the schools as a national security risk.

To right these conditions, the task force has three recommendations.

First, the states should speedily implement the Common Core State Standards in English and mathematics and add to them national standards in science, technology, foreign languages, and possibly civics.

Second, states and districts "should stop locking disadvantaged students into failing schools without any options." The task force proposes an expansion of competition and choice, for example with vouchers – meaning that states and districts should allow students to attend private and religious schools with public funding. The task force also favors charter schools – privately managed schools that directly receive public funding. If all these private schools get an equal share of public dollars, the task force opines, this will "fuel the innovation necessary to transform results."

Third, the United States should have "a national security readiness audit" to determine whether students are learning the necessary skills "to safeguard America's future security and prosperity," and "to hold schools and policymakers accountable for results."

None of these recommendations has any clear and decisive evidence to support it.

The Common Core State Standards in reading and mathematics were developed over the past few years by groups representing the National Governors Association, the Council of Chief State School Officers, and Achieve, and funded largely by the Bill and Melinda Gates Foundation. The Obama administration encouraged adoption of these standards through its Race to the Top program. To be eligible for a share of the billions of dollars in competitive federal grants, states were expected to express willingness to adopt the standards, and forty-five states have done so.

They may be excellent standards, or they may not be. They

may help improve achievement, or they may not. But no one knows, because the Common Core standards have never been implemented or tried out anywhere. If they are sufficiently rigorous, they might increase the achievement gap between high-performing students and low-performing students and might leave students who struggle with English even further behind than they are now.

Tom Loveless, an analyst at the Brookings Institution, recently predicted that the standards will have no impact on student achievement,[16] but perhaps he is wrong. Until they are implemented somewhere, their value cannot simply be assumed. It must be demonstrated. Thus, the task force goes out on a limb by claiming that these untried standards are the very linchpin of defending our nation's borders and securing our future prosperity.

Certainly the task force is right to insist upon the importance of foreign-language study, but it is wrong to blame the nation's public schools for a shortage of specialists in Chinese, Dari, Korean, Russian, and Turkish. Although some American high schools teach Chinese, these languages are usually taught by universities or specialized language programs. It is peculiar to criticize public elementary and secondary schools for the lack of trained linguists in Afghanistan and other international hotspots.

Students who sign up to study a language this year have no way of knowing in which region or nation we will need linguists five or ten years from now. How are students or schools to know where the next military action or political crisis will emerge? Furthermore, the effort to expand foreign language instruction in K-12 schools requires not just standards, but a very large new supply of teachers of foreign languages to staff the nation's 100,000 or so public schools. This won't happen without substantial new funding for scholarships to train tens of thousands of new teachers.

Similarly, there is mixed evidence, to be generous, to support the task force's recommendation to increase competition and choice. Although it cites a few studies that show higher test scores for some charter schools, most studies of charters show no difference in test scores between charter students and students in public schools. Vouchers have generally produced results no different from regular public schools. Milwaukee has had vouchers for twenty-one years, intended to allow disadvantaged students to escape from failing public schools, but on average the students in voucher schools achieve the same test scores as those in regular public schools. And Milwaukee, which has a very competitive environment of charters and vouchers, is, according to federal assessments, one of the nation's lowest-performing urban school districts.

The task force's claim that charter schools will be beacons of innovation rests on hope, not on any evidence presented in the report. The most "innovative" of the charters are the for-profit academies that teach online – a fast-growing sector that recruits students to take their courses by computer at home. These virtual academies have been the subject of negative stories in *The New York Times* and *The Washington Post*, criticized both for their focus on profits and for their poor academic results. The Task Force's enthusiasm for charter schools is not surprising. As chancellor of New York City's public school system, Klein enthusiastically supported charter schools and opened one hundred of them, regardless of community opposition. Another member of the task force was Richard Barth, the chief executive officer of the KIPP charter school chain.

The task force asserts that charters will lead the way to innovative methods of education. But the charters with the highest test scores are typically known not for innovation, but for "no excuses" discipline policies, where students may be fined or suspended or expelled if they fail to follow the rules of the school with unquestioning obedience, such as not making eye contact with the teacher or slouching or bringing candy to school or being too noisy in gym or the lunchroom.

Some of the high-performing charter schools have high attrition rates, and some have achieved high scores by excluding or limiting students who are apt to get low test scores, such as students who are English-language learners. There is no evidence that charters are more likely to teach foreign languages and advanced courses in science than public schools. The schools with the most extensive range of courses in foreign languages, advanced science, and advanced mathematics are large comprehensive high schools, which have been in disfavor for the past decade, after the Gates Foundation decided that large high schools were a bad idea and invested $2 billion in breaking them up into small schools. This program was abandoned in 2008.

The task force's proposal for "a national security readiness audit" is bizarre. It is not clear what it means, who would conduct it, or who would pay for it. Will schools be held accountable if they do not produce enough fit candidates for the military, the intelligence agencies, the defense industry, and the foreign service? Some high school graduates do join the military, but no high school prepares its students for the diplomatic corps or the defense industry or the Central Intelligence Agency. Who will be held accountable if colleges and universities don't produce an adequate supply of teachers of Turkish, Russian, Chinese, Korean, and Dari to the high schools? Should every high school offer these languages? Should universities be held accountable if there are not enough physics teachers? What will happen to schools that fail their national security readiness audit? Will they be closed?

Three big issues are unaddressed by the Klein-Rice report. One is the damage that No Child Left Behind and Race to the Top, which rely on standardized testing to measure the worth of teachers and schools, have caused to public education. The second is its misleading economic analysis. And the third is its failure to offer any recommendation to improve the teaching profession.

Instead of criticizing the ruinous effects of the Bush-era No Child Left Behind policy (NCLB), the task force praises it. This is not surprising, since Margaret Spellings, the architect of NCLB and former secretary of education, was a member of the task force. The task force chides public schools for losing sight of civics, world cultures, and other studies, but never pauses to recognize that NCLB has compelled schools everywhere to focus solely on reading and mathematics, the only subjects that count in deciding whether a school is labeled a success or a failure. NCLB has turned schooling into a joyless experience for most American children, especially in grades three through eight, who must spend weeks of each year preparing to take standardized tests.

In pursuing its policy of Race to the Top, the Obama administration has promoted the teach-to-the-test demands of NCLB. Most of America's teachers will now be evaluated by their students' scores on those annual multiple-choice tests. Students will, in effect, be empowered to fire their teachers by withholding effort, or will bear responsibility if their lack of effort, their home circumstances, or their ill health on testing day should cause their teacher to lose her job. NCLB and Race to the Top have imposed on American education a dreary and punitive testing regime that would gladden the hearts of a Gradgrind but demoralizes the great majority of teachers, who would prefer the autonomy to challenge their students to think critically and creatively. This dull testing regime crushes the ingenuity, wit, playfulness, and imagination that our students and our society most urgently need to spur new inventions and new thinking in the future.

In its economic analysis, the task force is surely right that we need more and better education, though it does not propose – in this era of widespread cuts in budgets for education – that we must be willing to pay more to get it. Instead it offers a chart showing that the median annual earnings of high school dropouts and high school graduates have fallen since 1980. The same chart shows that the earnings of college graduates are higher than those with less education but have been stagnant since 1985. It is not clear why this is so. The task force report occasionally refers to income inequality and poverty, which surely depress academic outcomes, but never considers their causes or proposes ways to reduce them.

Surely the economy will need more highly educated workers and everyone should have the chance to go to college, but the task force does not adequately acknowledge the costs of higher education or suggest how they will be paid. Nor does it discuss projections by the federal Bureau of Labor Statistics (BLS) that the majority of new jobs for the next several years will require on-the-job training, not a bachelor's degree. According to the BLS, the economy will need 175,000 computer engineers, 582,000 nurses, 461,000 home health aides, 400,000 customer service agents, 394,000 fast food workers, 375,000 retail sales clerks, 255,000 construction workers, and so on.

While the report laments the inadequacy of current efforts to recruit and prepare teachers, it offers no recommendation about how to attract better-qualified men and women into teaching and how to prepare them for the rigors of the classroom. The only program that it finds worthy of endorsement is Teach for America, whose recruits receive only five weeks of training and agree to teach for only two years. This is not surprising, because Wendy Kopp, the founder and chief executive officer of Teach for America, was a member of the task force.

Without the added comments at the end of the report, signed by seven of its thirty members, the task force report might be perceived as an essentially urgent appeal for more testing of students, more top-down control, and more privatization of the public schools. That is, more of what the federal government and many state governments have been doing for at least the past decade. But two of the dissents demolish its basic premises.

In her dissent, Linda Darling-Hammond of Stanford University takes apart the claim that competition and privatization will produce great improvement. She points out that the highest-performing nations in the world (Finland, Singapore, and South Korea):

> ... have invested in strong public education systems that serve virtually all students, while nations that have aggressively pursued privatization, such as Chile, have a huge and growing divide between rich and poor that has led to dangerous levels of social unrest.

Charter schools, she notes, are more likely to underperform in comparison to district-run public schools when they enroll similar students, and they are more likely to enroll a smaller proportion of students with disabilities and English-language learners. Darling-Hammond, who advised President Obama during his 2008 campaign, takes issue with the report's praise of New Orleans, where nearly 80 percent of students are enrolled in charter schools. Charters in New Orleans, she observes, have not only been criticized for excluding students with disabilities, but New Orleans "remains the lowest-ranked district in the low-performing state of Louisiana."

Whatever credibility remains to the report is finally shredded by task force member Stephen M. Walt of Harvard University. Walt faintly praises the task force for its "effort to draw attention to the issue of public education," but then delivers a withering critique of its claims and findings. He does not see any convincing evidence that the public education system is "a very grave national security threat" to the United States. Walt writes that "the United States spends more on national security than the next twenty nations combined, has an array of powerful allies around the world, and remains the world leader in science and technology." Walt is unimpressed by the task force's indictment of public education. Not only do American schools rank among the top 10 percent of the world's 193 nations, he writes, but:

> ... none of the states whose children outperform U.S. students is a potential rival. Barring major foreign policy blunders unrelated to K–12 education, no country is likely to match U.S. military power or overall technological supremacy for decades. There are good reasons to improve K-12 education, but an imminent threat to our national security is not among them.

Walt's critique leaves the task force report looking naked, if not ridiculous. If the international tests are indicators of our national security weakness, should we worry that we might be invaded by Finland or South Korea or Japan or Singapore or Canada or New Zealand or Australia? Obviously not. The nations with higher test scores than ours are not a threat to our national security. They are our friends and allies. If education were truly the key to our national security, perhaps we should allocate sufficient funding to equalize resources in poor neighborhoods and make higher education far more affordable to more Americans than it is today.

If there is no national security crisis, as the task force has vainly tried to establish, what can we learn from its deliberations?

Commissions that gather notable figures tend not to be venturesome or innovative, and this one is no different. When a carefully culled list of corporate leaders, former government officials, academics, and prominent figures who have a vested interest in the topic join to reach a consensus, they tend to reflect the status quo. If future historians want to see a definition of the status quo in American education in 2012, they may revisit this report by a task force of the Council on Foreign Relations. It offers no new directions, no new ideas, just a stale endorsement of the federal, state, and corporate policies of the past decade that have proven so counterproductive to the genuine improvement of American education.

# THE PARTNERSHIP FOR 19TH CENTURY SKILLS

## DIANE RAVITCH BLOG POST, JULY 11, 2012

Yesterday the National Research Council released a report supporting the need to develop what it calls "deeper learning," drawing on cognitive skills, interpersonal skills, and interpersonal skills. All of this sounds swell, excellent, worthy of doing and endorsing. I'm for it. Yes, yes, yes.

But I could not help but be reminded of something I wrote a few years ago. It was in response to a great hullabaloo about 21st century skills. The hullabaloo grew so insistent and so loud that I did my contrarian thing and decided that what we are really missing in our society is what I thought of as 19th century skills.

I don't know how different they are from 21st century skills, but they are worth talking about, and I would say, defending.

Every time I dial a business on the telephone and get one of those endless loops, I find myself missing an earlier era when you could call and actually talk to a human being. When I get extra frustrated with the loop, I start shouting, "Human being, human being." But that's not the magic word, so they send me back to the beginning of the loop.

But why stop in middle of the 20th century.

Why not a Partnership for 19th century skills? Here is what I wrote for the Core Knowledge blog in 2009:

**The Partnership for 19th Century Skills**

I for one have heard quite enough about the 21st century

skills that are sweeping the nation. Now, for the first time, children will be taught to think critically (never heard a word about that in the 20th century, did you?), to work in groups (I remember getting a grade on that very skill when I was in third grade a century ago), to solve problems (a brand new idea in education), and so on. Let me suggest that it is time to be done with this unnecessary conflict about 21st century skills. Let us agree that we need all those forenamed skills, plus lots others, in addition to a deep understanding of history, literature, the arts, geography, civics, the sciences, and foreign languages.

But allow me also to propose a new entity that will advance a different set of skills and understandings that are just as important as what are now called 21st century skills. I propose a Partnership for 19th Century Skills. This partnership will advocate for such skills, values, and understandings as:

- The love of learning
- The pursuit of knowledge
- The ability to think for oneself (individualism)
- The ability to work alone (initiative)
- The ability to stand alone against the crowd (courage)
- The ability to work persistently at a difficult task until it is finished (industriousness) (self-discipline)
- The ability to think through the consequences of one's actions on others (respect for others)
- The ability to consider the consequences of one's actions on one's well-being (self-respect)
- The recognition of higher ends than self-interest (honor)
- The ability to comport oneself appropriately in all situations (dignity)
- The recognition that civilized society requires certain kinds of behavior by individuals and groups (good manners) (civility)
- The ability to believe in principles larger than one's own self-interest (idealism)

- The willingness to ask questions when puzzled (curiosity)
- The readiness to dream about other worlds, other ways of doing things (imagination)
- The ability to believe that one can improve one's life and the lives of others (optimism)
- The ability to speak well and write grammatically, using standard English (communication)

I invite readers to submit other 19th century skills that we should cultivate assiduously among the rising generation, on the belief that doing so will lead to happier lives and a better world.

Diane Ravitch
PS: Feel free to add your own.

# TWO VISIONS FOR CHICAGO'S SCHOOLS

THE NEW YORK REVIEW OF BOOKS - NYR DAILY, SEPTEMBER 12, 2012

According to most news reports, the teachers in Chicago are striking because they are lazy and greedy. Or they are striking because of a personality clash between Mayor Rahm Emanuel and union president Karen Lewis. Or because this is the last gasp of a dying union movement. Or because Emanuel wants a longer school day and the teachers oppose it.

None of this is true. All reports agree that the two sides are close to agreement on compensation issues – it is not money that drove them apart. Last spring the union and the school board agreed to a longer school day, so that is not the issue either. The strike is a clash of two very different visions about what is needed to transform the schools of Chicago – and the nation.

Chicago schools have been a petri dish for school reform for nearly two decades. Beginning in 1995, they came under tight mayor control, and Mayor Richard Daley appointed his budget director, Paul Vallas, to run the schools; Vallas set out to raise test scores, open magnet schools and charter schools, and balance the budget. When Vallas left to run for governor (unsuccessfully), Daley selected another non-educator, Arne Duncan, who was Vallas's deputy and a strong advocate of charter schools. Vallas had imposed reform after reform, and Duncan added even more. Duncan called his program Renaissance 2010, with the goal of closing low-performing schools and opening one hundred new schools. Since 2009, Duncan has been President Obama's Education Secretary, where he launched the $5 billion Race to the Top program, which relies heavily on student test scores to evaluate teacher quality, to award merit pay, and to close or reward schools.[17] It also encourages the proliferation of privately managed charter schools.

This is the vision that Washington now supports, and that the Chicago school board, appointed by current mayor and former Obama chief of staff Rahm Emanuel, endorses – more school closings, more privately managed schools, more testing, merit pay, longer school hours. But in Chicago itself, where these reforms started, most researchers agree that the results have been mixed at best. There has been no renaissance. After nearly twenty years of reform, the schools of Chicago remain among the lowest performing in the nation.

The Chicago Teachers Union has a different vision. It wants smaller classes, more social workers, air-conditioning in the sweltering buildings where summer school is conducted, and a full curriculum, with teachers of arts and foreign languages in every school. Some schools in Chicago have more than forty students in a class, even in kindergarten. There are 160 schools without libraries; more than 40 percent have no teachers of the arts.

What do the teachers want? The main sticking point is the seemingly arcane issue of teacher evaluations. The mayor wants student test scores to count heavily in determining whether a teacher is good (and gets a bonus) or bad (and is fired). The union points to research showing that test-based evaluation is inaccurate and unfair. Chicago is a city of intensely segregated public schools and high levels of youth violence. Teachers know that test scores are influenced not only by their instruction but by what happens outside the classroom.

The strike has national significance because it concerns policies endorsed by the current administration, and it also raises issues found all over the country. Not only in Chicago but in other cities, teachers insist that their students need smaller classes and a balanced curriculum. Reformers want more privately-managed charter schools, even though they typically get the same results as public schools. Charter schools are a favorite of the right because almost 90 percent of them are non-union. Teachers want job protection so that they will not be fired for capricious reasons, and have academic freedom to teach controversial issues and books. Reformers want to strip teachers of any job protections.

The strike is a headache for President Obama, because he is trapped between two allies that he needs for the November election. He needs the support of organized labor, especially the four million teachers, many of whom enthusiastically campaigned for him in 2008. But how can he abandon Rahm Emanuel? Even more problematic for the president, the teachers are rebelling against the core principles of the Obama administration's Race to the Top program. That program – which provides grants to states, including Illinois,[18] which demonstrate they are pursuing its reforms – relies heavily on standardized testing to enable states to evaluate teachers, to award merit pay, and to identify schools as "failing" and set them up for mass firings and closure.

Ultimately, the strike may be resolved around seemingly technical issues having to do with pay scales – whether teachers continue to earn more for degrees and experience – and regulations governing layoffs and rehiring. But what are likely to remain are the biggest issues:

- Will carrots and sticks for teachers produce better education for students?
- Should Chicago continue privatizing public education?
- Are standardized tests appropriate measures of teacher quality and school quality?
- Do school closings lead to better schools?
- Can school reform overcome concentrated racial segregation and poverty?
- Can our society afford to give children in urban districts a far higher quality of education than is now

available?

Predictably, the striking teachers are taking a beating in the national media,[19] which admires Rahm Emanuel's tough position, but teachers elsewhere are rallying around the Chicago strikers. Many see them as standing up for teachers and their right to bargain collectively, a right that was settled – or so it seemed – during the Depression with the passage of the Wagner Act of 1935, which protected the right of workers to join unions. Education researchers, who have been concerned about the overuse and misuse of standardized testing, may fear to see issues settled politically instead of by reference to evidence. If the mayor wins, it will be perceived as a victory for a continued assault on teachers and their unions and an endorsement of school closings and privatized charters. If the teachers win, which is a long shot, the children of Chicago might get smaller classes and a better curriculum. The best outcome would be an amicable settlement, one that assures not more testing but better education.

# HOLDING EDUCATION HOSTAGE

## THE NEW YORK REVIEW OF BOOKS - NYR DAILY, FEBRUARY 1, 2013

For weeks, New York City Mayor Michael Bloomberg and the United Federation of Teachers have been battling over the issue of teacher evaluation. Governor Andrew Cuomo set a deadline for them to reach an agreement, but they failed to do so, potentially costing the city schools hundreds of millions of dollars. The state education commissioner, John King, jumped into the fray by threatening to withhold over a billion dollars in state and federal aid if there was no settlement between the parties. Now, Governor Cuomo says that he may intervene and take charge of the stalemated negotiations.

What's going on here? Why can't the mayor and the union reach an agreement? Why does Commissioner King intend to punish the city's children if the grown-ups don't agree?

The imbroglio began with the Obama administration's Race to the Top program. Immediately after Barack Obama's inauguration in January 2009, with the economy in free fall, Congress passed the huge economic stimulus package, which included $100 billion to aid schools, $95 billion to be disbursed to states to avoid massive layoffs of teachers and the remaining $5 billion to be given to the U.S. Department of Education to promote education reforms.

The new Secretary of Education Arne Duncan huddled with

his advisors and decided to create the so-called Race to the Top, a competition among states for the new funds. Instead of asking states to come up with their own best ideas for education reform, Duncan laid out a laundry list of policies that states must put in place to be eligible to win millions of dollars.[20] Among them was a requirement that state governments base teacher evaluations to a significant degree on the test scores of their students. The assumption was that good teachers produce higher test scores every year, while ineffective teachers do not.

In a time of fiscal stringency, New York, like almost every other state,[21] wanted a share of the federal windfall. New York promptly repealed a law that explicitly prohibited using test courses to assess teacher performance. New York applied for Race to the Top funds and was a finalist. In order to win, the state needed the cooperation of the teachers union. Michael Mulgrew, head of the union, joined city and state officials in applying for the funding. In return, the union received a promise that test scores would count for no more than 20 percent of any teacher's evaluation. The state won $700 million, and was expected to do what Secretary Duncan wanted – evaluate teachers by test scores, open more charter schools, adopt "college-and-career ready" standards, and undertake a variety of other measures intended to produce rewards for successful schools and punishment for schools with low scores.

Implementation of these measures has been slow. Governor Cuomo jumped into the act by demanding that test scores count for 40 percent of teachers' evaluations, not 20 percent. The federal government did not set a specific percentage, the most conservative states have made it as high as 50 percent.

The New York State Regents hired a new state commissioner, John King, who has only a few years of experience as a teacher or administrator, gained in the charter sector. King is an accountability hawk who has pressed hard to get a top-down, test-based system in place quickly. He pressed so hard and moved so quickly, brooking no dissent, that more than a third of the principals in the state signed a petition opposing the state's new

– and itself untested – evaluation system.

Despite their qualms, most school districts reached agreements with their local unions, but New York City did not. Mayor Bloomberg believes that teachers can be measured by the rise or fall of their students' test scores. He believes it so ardently that last year he released the names and rankings of 18,000 teachers to the media. The information was released in response to a Freedom of Information lawsuit filed by the *New York Post*. Although the city had promised the union that it would fight such a request, it did not, and the teachers' names were made public.

The list contained many inaccuracies. The city admitted that the margin of error in the rankings was so large that the numbers were essentially meaningless. Bill Gates published an opinion piece in *The New York Times* opposing the public release of teachers' names and rankings. Governor Cuomo agreed. Only Mayor Bloomberg remains adamant[22] that "the public has a right to know," even if the rankings are inaccurate and needlessly humiliating.

This is the background for today's bad blood between the mayor and the union. But there is more to it than a personal vendetta. The recent negotiations collapsed because the union wanted the agreement to have a one-year sunset clause, at which time the process would be reviewed and fine-tuned. Most districts in the state have done this. Mayor Bloomberg objected to the sunset, fearing that it would make the agreement moot. He has a point. The process might take three to five years to show results, for good or ill.

Many researchers and testing experts have cautioned that evaluating teachers by the test scores of their students – called value-added assessment – is fraught with problems. Linda Darling-Hammond, a prominent scholar at Stanford University and one of the nation's leading authorities on issues of teacher quality, has written that the measures say more about which students are in the classroom than about the competence of the teacher.

The National Academy of Education and the American

Educational Research Association issued a joint statement saying the same thing.[23] Those who teach students with disabilities, English-language learners, and low-performing students are likely to get smaller gains in test scores than those who teach students from affluent homes in well-funded schools. Using test scores to rate teachers will penalize those who teach the students in greatest need. Over time, teachers will avoid the students who jeopardize their jobs and their reputations. This will be harmful to the students who need talented and experienced teachers most urgently.

Across the nation, as districts put into effect the "reform" that Secretary Duncan wants, the consequences have been counterproductive. Houston fired its teacher of the year. Other districts are discovering that their best teachers are getting low ratings. A teacher in Florida was recently photographed in front of her elementary school, whose billboard honored her as teacher of the month, as she held up a placard saying she had just been rated "ineffective."

So what we have here is an effort by politicians to devise a metric to rate professionals. The measure makes no sense. No other nation – unless it is following our own bad example – is rating teachers in so crude a fashion. Even researchers at the company that designed New York's evaluation system warned that it was too soon to use it to make high-stakes decisions about teachers.

It is simply wrong to devise a measure of teacher quality based on standardized tests. The tests are not yardsticks. They are not scientific instruments. They are social constructions, and quite apart from how contingent their results are on the social and economic background of the students being tested, they are also subject to human error, sampling error, random error, and other errors. It is true that the cleanliness of restaurants can be given a letter grade (another of Bloomberg's test-oriented innovations in New York City), and agribusiness can be measured by crop yields, and corporations can be measured by their profits. But to apply a letter grade or a numerical ranking to a professional is to radically misunderstand the complex set of qualities that make someone good at what they do. It is an effort by economists and statisticians to quantify activities that are at heart matters of judgment, not productivity. Professionals must be judged by other professionals, by their peers. Nowhere is this more true than among educators, whose success at teaching character, wisdom, and judgment cannot be measured by standardized tests.

# KEEP YOUR 'DISRUPTION' OUT OF OUR SCHOOLS

HUFFINGTON POST, AUGUST 21, 2013

*"Privatization via charters and vouchers has intensified racial segregation and is reversing the Brown Decision of 1954. The disreputable concept of "separate but equal" is returning under the guise of "school choice." – Diane Ravitch's Blog*

Judith Shulevitz recently wrote a brilliant essay[24] on "disruption" as a business strategy.

As we know, mega-corporations believe they must continually reinvent themselves in order to have the latest, best thing and beat their competitors, who are about to overtake them in the market.

They believe in disruption as a fundamental rule of the marketplace.

By some sloppy logic or sleight-of-hand, the financial types and corporate leaders who think they should reform the nation's schools have concluded that the schools should also be subject to "creative disruption" or just plain "disruption."

And so we have the unaccredited Broad Superintendents Academy, underwritten by billionaire Eli Broad, sending out superintendents who are determined to "disrupt" schools by closing them and handing them over to private management.

Unfortunately, Secretary Arne Duncan agrees that disruption is wonderful, so he applauds the idea of closing schools, opening new schools, inviting the for-profit sector to compete for scarce funds, and any other scheme that might disrupt schools as we know them.

He does this believing that U.S. education is a failed enterprise and needs a mighty shaking-up.

First, he is wrong to believe that U.S. public education is failing. That is untrue. I document that he is wrong in my book, *Reign of Error: The Hoax of the Privatization Movement and The Danger to America's Public Schools*, using graphs from the U.S. Department of Education website.

Second, "disruption" is a disaster for children, families, schools, and communities.

Think of little children. They need continuity and stability, not disruption. They need adults who are a reliable presence in their lives. But, following the logic of the corporate reformers, their teachers must be fired, their school must be closed, everything must be "turned around" and brand new or the kids won't learn. No matter how many parents and children appear at school board meetings, no matter how much they plead for the life of their neighborhood school, the hammer falls and it is closed. This is absurd.

Think of adolescents. When they misbehave, we say they are "disruptive." Now we are supposed to believe that their disruptive behavior represents higher order thinking.

But no one can learn when one student in a class of thirty is disruptive.

Disruptive policies harm families because after the closing of the neighborhood school, they are expected to shop for a school. They are told they have "choice," but the one choice denied them is their neighborhood school. Maybe one of their children is accepted at the School of High Aspirations, but the other didn't get accepted and is enrolled instead in the School for Future Leaders, which happens to be on the other side of town. That is not good for families.

Disruption is not good for communities. In most communities, the public school is the anchor of community life. It is where parents meet, talk about common problems, work together, and learn the fundamental processes of democratic action.

Disruption destroys local democracy. It atomizes families and communities, destroying their ability to plan and act together on behalf of their community.

By closing their neighborhood school, disruption severs people from the roots of their community. It fragments community.

It kneecaps democracy.

City after city is now suffering a "disruptive" assault on public education. Mayor Rahm Emanuel closed dozens of schools in Chicago, Mayor Michael Bloomberg closed dozens of schools in New York City, public education in Detroit is dying, and Philadelphia public schools are on life support, squeezed by harsh budget cuts and corporate faith in disruption and privatization.

But the disruptive strategy won't be confined to urban districts. As the tests for the new national Common Core standards are introduced in state after state, test scores will collapse as predicted because they are so "hard." Parents will be outraged. Disruption and havoc will produce what corporate reformers are hoping for – a loss of faith in public education, a conviction that it is broken beyond repair, and a willingness to try anything, even to allow for-profit vendors to take over the responsibilities of the public sector. That is already happening in many states, where hundreds of millions of dollars are siphoned away from public schools and handed over to disruptive commercial enterprises. It doesn't produce better education, but it produces profits.

Maybe that is the point of disruption.

# CHARLES BLOW IS WRONG ABOUT THE COMMON CORE

HUFFINGTON POST, AUGUST 22, 2013

*"Billions spent on testing instead of teaching. ... The latest international test results show no gains in reading. None. This failure belongs to Reformers." – Diane Ravitch's Blog*

Charles Blow is one of the columnists in *The New York Times* that I usually count on to challenge the conventional wisdom and to speak up for the powerless.

Sadly, in this column,[25] he parrots the conventional wisdom and voices the opinions of the elites.

Imagine, he calls the Broad Foundation a "reform" organization. The Broad Foundation is the source of policies that are privatizing public schools and destroying communities. Some of the worst, most arrogant leaders in U.S. education have been "trained" by the unaccredited Broad Academy. The foundation's guide[26] on how to close schools is a bible for the corporate reform movement.

As for the international test scores, Blow should not have relied on *Time* magazine's Amanda Ripley. He should have looked at the Rothstein-Carnoy study,[27] which demonstrates that the PISA results were misleading, or the recent article in the UK *Times Educational Supplement*,[28] where test experts maintained that the scores on PISA are "meaningless," or considered the more recent TIMSS test,[29] where American students did very well. Or read the chapter in my book *Reign of Error: The Hoax of the Priva-*

*tization Movement and the Danger to America's Public Schools*, which explains the myths and facts about international testing.

Why in the world would he enthuse about the Common Core tests? As we saw recently in New York, the new tests widened the gaps between affluent and poor, between black and white, between English language learners and native speakers, between children with disabilities and those without. Common Core has no evidence to support its claims. The Common Core tests are deepening the stratification of society and falsely labeled two-thirds of the state's children as failures. "Harder" tests do not make kids smarter. It will take smaller classes, experienced teachers, and a greater investment in the neediest children to do that.

# THE BIGGEST FALLACY OF THE COMMON CORE STANDARDS

HUFFINGTON POST, AUGUST 24, 2013

*"Accountability begins at the top." – Diane Ravitch's Blog*

Boosters of the Common Core national standards have acclaimed them as the most revolutionary advance in the history of American education.

As a historian of American education, I do not agree.

Forty-five states have adopted the Common Core national standards, and they are being implemented this year.

Why did 45 states agree to do this? Because the Obama administration had $4.35 billion of Race to the Top federal funds, and states had to adopt "college-and-career ready standards" if they wanted to be eligible to compete for those funds. Some states, like Massachusetts, dropped their own well-tested and successful standards and replaced them with the Common Core, in order to win millions in new federal funds.

Is this a good development or not?

If you listen to the promoters of the Common Core standards, you will hear them say that the Common Core is absolutely necessary to prepare students for careers and college.

They say, if we don't have the Common Core, students won't be college-ready or career-ready.

Major corporations have published full-page advertisements in *The New York Times* and paid for television commercials, warning that our economy will be in serious trouble unless every school and every district and every state adopts the Common Core standards.

A report from the Council on Foreign Relations last year (chaired by Joel Klein and Condoleezza Rice)[30] warned that our national security was at risk unless we adopt the Common Core standards.

The Common Core standards, its boosters insist, are all that stand between us and economic and military catastrophe.

All of this is simply nonsense.

How does anyone know that the Common Core standards will prepare everyone for college and careers since they are now being adopted for the very first time?

How can anyone predict that they will do what their boosters claim?

There is no evidence for any of these claims.

There is no evidence that the Common Core standards will enhance equity. Indeed, the Common Core tests in New York caused a collapse in test scores, causing test scores across the state to plummet. Only 31 percent "passed" the Common Core tests. The failure rates were dramatic among the neediest students. Only 3.2 percent of English language learners were able to pass the new tests, along with only 5 percent of students with disabilities, and 17 percent of black students. Faced with tests that are so far beyond their reach, many of these students may give up instead of trying harder.

There is no evidence that those who study these standards will be prepared for careers, because there is nothing in them that bears any relationship to careers.

There is no evidence that the Common Core standards will enhance our national security.

How do we know that it will cause many more students to study math and science? With the collapse in test scores that Common Core brings, maybe students will doubt their ability and opt for less demanding courses.

Why so many promises and ungrounded predictions? It is

a mystery.

Even more mysterious is why the nation's major corporations and chambers of commerce now swear by standards that they have very likely never read.

Don't get me wrong. I am all for high standards. I am opposed to standards that are beyond reach. They discourage, they do not encourage.

But the odd thing about these standards is that they seem to be written in stone. Who is in charge of revising them? No one knows.

When I testified by Skype to the Michigan legislative committee debating the Common Core a couple of weeks ago, I told them to listen to their teachers and be prepared to revise the standards to make them better. Someone asked if states were "allowed" to change the standards. I asked, why not? Michigan is a sovereign state. If they rewrite the standards to fit the needs of their students, who can stop them? The federal government says it doesn't "own" the standards. And that is true. The federal government is forbidden by law from interfering with curriculum and instruction.

States should do what works best for them. I also urged Michigan legislators to delay any Common Core testing until they were confident that teachers had the professional development and resources to teach them and students had had adequate time to learn what would be tested.

Do we need national standards to compare the performance of children in Mississippi to children in New York and Iowa? We already have the National Assessment of Educational Progress (NAEP), which has been making these comparisons for 20 years.

Maybe I am missing something. Can anyone explain how the nation can adopt national standards without any evidence whatever that they will improve achievement, enrich education, and actually help to prepare young people – not for the jobs of the future, which are unknown and unknowable – but for the challenges of citizenship and life? The biggest fallacy of the Common Core standards is that they have been sold to the nation without any evidence that they will accomplish what their boosters claim.

Across the nation, our schools are suffering from budget cuts.

Because of budget cuts, there are larger class sizes and fewer guidance counselors, social workers, teachers' assistants, and librarians.

Because of budget cuts, many schools have less time and resources for the arts, physical education, foreign languages, and other subjects crucial for a real education.

As more money is allocated to testing and accountability, less money is available for the essential programs and services that all schools should provide.

Our priorities are confused.

# WHAT CAN MARTIN LUTHER KING, JR. TEACH US ABOUT OUR EDUCATION SYSTEM?

HUFFINGTON POST, AUGUST 30, 2013

I received a note from an outstanding superintendent in a fine suburban district in New York, someone I greatly admire. He is experienced and wise. He has the support of parents, staff, and community. He runs one of the state's best school districts.

He wrote of the excitement and joy of the beginning of the school year. He talked about the commemoration of Dr. King's legacy. But he ended on a sad note. He said he experienced the sadness and humiliation of telling teachers and students about their test scores and ratings, about how many students had failed the absurd Common Core tests, which meant their teachers too had "failed."

Suddenly, it struck me that the best way to remember Martin Luther King was not to think of him as a statue or an icon, but to take to heart his example. He did not bow his head in the face of injustice. He did not comply. He said no. He said it in a spirit of love and non-violence. But he resisted.

He said no. He resisted. He said, we will not acquiesce to what we know is wrong. We will not acquiesce. We will not comply. We will not obey unjust laws.

How does that apply to the situation of public education today? Public schools are drowning in nonsensical mandates.

They are whipsawed by failed ideas coming from D.C. and state capitals that are following D.C.'s demands. They are subject to regulations and programs that no one understands. These mandates are ruining schooling, not making it better. The incessant testing is not making kids smarter, it is making kids bored and turned off by school. Schools are trapped in bureaucratic mazes that make no sense.

What would Martin Luther King, Jr., do? Would he passively submit?

No. He would resist. He would organize and join with others. He would build coalitions of parents, students, teachers, administrators, school board members, and members of the community who support their public schools. He would demand true education for all children. He would demand equality of educational opportunity, not a Race to some mythical Top or ever higher scores on bubble tests. He would not be silent as our public schools are worn down and torn down by mindless mandates. He would recognize that the victims of this political and bureaucratic malfeasance are our children. He would build a political movement so united and clear in its purpose that it would be heard in every state Capitol and even in Washington, D.C.

And that is how we should commemorate his life.

# WHAT IS A 'FAILING' SCHOOL?

## HUFFINGTON POST, SEPTEMBER 3, 2013

Two years ago, Kevin Kosar, a former graduate student of mine, conducted an Internet search for the term "failing school." What he discovered was fascinating.[31] Until the 1990s, the term was virtually unknown. About the mid-1990s, the term began appearing with greater frequency. With the passage of No Child Left Behind, the use of the expression exploded and became a commonplace.

Kosar did not speculate on the reasons. But I venture to say that the rise of the accountability movement created the idea of "failing schools."

"Accountability" was taken to mean that if students have low test scores, someone must be blamed. Since Bush's NCLB, it became conventional to blame the school. With President Obama's Race to the Top, blame shifted to teachers. The solution to "failing schools," according to Secretary of Education Arne Duncan, is to fire the staff and close the school.

New York Governor Andrew Cuomo recently took this idea to an extreme[32] by saying that he wanted a "death penalty" for "failing schools." He believes that when schools have persistently low test scores, they should lose democratic control.

They should be taken over by the state, given to private charter corporations, or put under mayoral control. In fact, none of these ideas has been successful.

Low-performing school districts in New Jersey have been under state control for more than 20 years without turning them into high-performing districts. Mayoral control in Cleveland and Chicago has been a flop. And private charters typically do no better than public schools, except when they exclude low-scoring students.

Undoubtedly there are some schools where the leadership is rotten and corrupt. In such cases, the responsibility lies with the district superintendent to review the staff and programs, and make significant changes as needed.

But these days, any school with low test scores is called a "failing school," without any inquiry into the circumstances of the school.

Instead of closing the school or privatizing it, the responsible officials should act to improve the school, they should ask:

- What proportion of the students are new immigrants and need help learning English?
- What proportion entered the school far behind their grade level?
- What proportion have disabilities and need more time to learn?
- What resources are available to the school?

An in-depth analysis is likely to reveal that most "failing schools" are not failing schools, but are schools that enroll high proportions of students who need extra help, extra tutoring, smaller classes, social workers, guidance counselors, psychologists, and a variety of other interventions.

Firing the staff does not turn around a low-performing school. Nor does handing it over to a charter chain. Nor does mayoral control. Most of the time, what we call a "failing school" is a school that lacks the personnel and resources to meet the needs of its students.

Closing schools does not make them better. Nor does closing schools help students. It's way past time to stop blaming the people who work in troubled schools and start helping them by providing the tools they need and the support their students need.

# WHY NEW YORK'S SUPER WEALTHY OPPOSE THE UNIVERSAL PRE-K PLAN

HUFFINGTON POST, SEPTEMBER 6, 2013

*"The basic idea of trickle-down economics is that enriching those with the most will encourage them to invest in productive industries, create jobs, and thus help those at the bottom, as Money trickles down from the top. The late Senator Daniel Patrick Moynihan described this as feeding the horses to feed the sparrows." – Diane Ravitch's Blog*

*Bloomberg News* reports[33] that the city's corporate leaders and super-wealthy are offended by mayoral candidate Bill de Blasio's plan to raise taxes on those earning over $500,000 a year to fund universal pre-K and after school programs for middle school kids.

The head of the business leaders' group was astonished by de Blasio's indifference to the needs of corporate executives. "It shows lack of sensitivity to the city's biggest revenue providers and job creators," said Kathryn Wylde, president of the Partnership for New York City, a network of 200 chief executive officers, including Co-Chairman Laurence Fink of BlackRock Inc. (BLK), the world's biggest money manager.

Some predicted an exodus of rich people from the city.

These are the same people who raise $80 million in a single night at a benefit for the Robin Hood Foundation dinner to support charter schools in New York City. Of course, those gifts are tax-deductible, not taxes. What has de Blasio proposed? According to *Bloomberg News*:

> De Blasio's plan would raise the marginal tax rate on incomes above $500,000 to 4.4 percent from almost 3.9 percent.
>
> For the 27,300 city taxpayers earning $500,000 to $1 million, the average increase would be $973 a year, according to the Independent Budget Office, a municipal agency.
>
> For those making $1 million to $5 million, the average extra bite would rise to $7,793, the budget office said.
>
> At incomes of $5 million to $10 million, it would climb to $33,518, and for those earning more than $10 million, it would mean paying $182,893 more.

Here is the reaction of one hedge fund manager, E.E. "Buzzy" Geduld, who runs the hedge fund Cougar Capital LLC in the city and is a trustee of Manhattan's Dalton School, where annual tuition tops $40,000. He said that de Blasio's plan "is the most absurd thing I've ever heard" and "not a smart thing to do."

Think of the billions that Bloomberg squandered on technology projects that fizzled (like the $600 million Citytime project), the failed merit pay plan ($53 million wasted), the failed plan to pay students to get higher test scores, etc.

The business executives said nothing because no one suggested that they would be taxed to pay for it.

De Blasio is proposing research-based programs. Those who care about education and kids should be cheering and should gladly pay an extra $973 (or more if their income is higher) to do what is right for kids. Oh, and one more thing. The *Bloomberg News* article says:

> The city's richest 1 percent took home 39 percent of all earnings in 2012, up from 12 percent in 1980, accord-

ing to the Fiscal Policy Institute, a nonprofit research group in New York.

Don't cry for me, Argentina.

# WHAT THE NEW YORK TIMES LEFT OUT

## HUFFINGTON POST, SEPTEMBER 12, 2013

Yesterday, *The New York Times* published an article[34] about my forthcoming book *Reign of Error* that turned out to be a profile of me. The reporter, Motoko Rich, did a good job of describing me, my dog Mitzi, and the basic facts of my unusual philosophical and political journey over the past few decades.

The headline was wrong, however, and I know that reporters don't write headlines. Whoever wrote it is out of touch. The headline said, "Loud Voice Fighting Tide of New Trend in Education." I would have preferred an adjective other than "loud," like "strong" or "persistent." My megaphone is actually rather small, consisting of nothing more than my pen (actually, my computer). I don't know how "loud" my computer is. I also found objectionable the suggestion that I was fighting a "new trend." In fact, I am fighting the status quo. When a policy is shared by the U.S. Department of Education, the U.S. Congress, most governors and state legislatures, ALEC (the American Legislative Exchange Council), Jeb Bush, the U.S. Chamber of Commerce, and the president of the United States, how can it be called "new"?

I wish the article had said that the book refutes every claim of the privatization movement, that it provides ample documentation to show that American education is not failing or declining, that it demonstrates that test scores for American students are at an all-time high, that high-school graduation rates are at an all-time high, that dropout rates are at a historic low, and that privatization of public education is bad for our democracy.

It turns out I was not the only one who harbored these concerns. Read *The Daily Howler*[35] on this topic.

# I KNOW WHO I AM AND I LOVE WHAT I DO

HUFFINGTON POST, SEPTEMBER 30, 2013

A blogger who is a Los Angeles parent asked the question,[36] "Who is Diane Ravitch?" – and explored the answer.

I know who I am.

I am one of eight children, born in Houston and a graduate of the Houston public schools.

I was lucky enough to be admitted to Wellesley College, where my friends included incredibly talented women.

I married a wonderful man two weeks after college, moved to New York City, and began having children. I had three sons, one of whom died of leukemia at the age of two.

I earned a Ph.D. in the history of American education from Columbia University in 1975. My mentor was the great historian Lawrence A. Cremin.

My first book was a history of the New York public school system, published in 1974. It was also my doctoral dissertation.

I was divorced in 1986. My ex-husband and I are good friends.

From 1991-93, I was Assistant Secretary of Education in the first Bush administration. Then I worked as a senior fellow at the Brookings Institution for two years.

I missed New York City and moved back to Brooklyn and became an adjunct at New York University. I published more books.

In 1997, the Clinton administration appointed me to serve on the National Assessment Governing Board, which oversees federal testing. Secretary Richard Riley reappointed me in 2001, and I served on that board for seven years, learning a lot about testing.

I was a fellow at three different conservative think tanks in the 1990s and the early years of this century – the Manhattan Institute, the Thomas B. Fordham Institute, and the Koret Task Force at the Hoover Institution.

In 2010, I published a book explaining that the ideas I had thought were good in theory turned out not to work, and that they were actually damaging education. I became a critic of testing, accountability, choice, and competition. My book explained why and how I lost faith in these ideas. It is *The Death and Life of the Great American School System: How Testing and Choice Are Undermining American Education.*

I have lived with my best friend for the past 25 years.

I still live in Brooklyn. I have written ten or eleven books and edited many more.

I have four grandsons.

My latest book *Reign of Error* is the #1 book in education and the #1 book on public policy as of this moment on Amazon.

This week I visited Denver, Seattle, Sacramento, and Berkeley. Tonight I speak in Palo Alto, then twice in Los Angeles. I have no staff, no secretary, no assistant. I am not funded by anyone.

I am 75 years old.

I love what I am doing.

I love children, and I admire those who dedicate their lives to educating children and improving the lives of children, families, and communities.

I want all children to have a wonderful education, not just the basics and testing.

I will work for a better education for all as long as I have strength and breath.

# SOME ADVICE FOR MY CRITICS

## HUFFINGTON POST, OCTOBER 6, 2013

I have been more than thrilled by the response to my new book *Reign of Error*. Today it is #10 on *The New York Times* best seller list, next week it will be #15. My guess is that as more educators and parents read it, they will recommend it to others. I hope they will form study groups to discuss the issues it raises. My hope was to provide indisputable facts about where we are, and research-based evidence about what we need to do to improve our schools and our society-not one first, then the other, but both.

As you might expect, the book is controversial because it disputes the popular narrative that our schools are failing and broken, that we must do all sorts of things that have never been done before, must test more often, more than any other nation in the world, must fire teachers and principals, lay off guidance counselors, social workers and librarians, eliminate the arts to make more time for testing, and close schools. And if we do all these things, someday, all schools will be great!

Humbug, I say. A hoax, I say.

Speaking plainly, however, is dangerous, if you are a woman. When men speak plainly and mince no words, they are direct and forceful. When women speak plainly and mince no words, they are abrasive, harsh, and just plain – well – rude. The same people who object to my tone waste no time denouncing me in abusive language. I will not deign to notice them. Nor will they intimidate me by their swagger.

So, to pay tribute to those who want me to be quiet and deferential, here is a video for them.[37] Enjoy.

# MERCEDES SCHNEIDER EXPLAINS: WHO PAID FOR THE COMMON CORE STANDARDS

HUFFINGTON POST, OCTOBER 10, 2013

Mercedes Schneider has undertaken an immense task. She decided to spend her free time – when she is not teaching – trying to figure out how much the Gates Foundation paid various organizations to write, develop, implement, promote, and advocate for the Common Core state standards (CCSS).

This is a herculean job because the foundation has been so free-handed with its money. To its credit, the Gates Foundation has a website that enables researchers to identify their grants over time. At a certain point, as you go through the list of who got how much money to "promote" the CCSS, you start to wonder "who DIDN'T get Gates money?"

This is her first post,[38] where she shows that the Gates Foundation underwrote the organizations writing the Common Core standards – the National Governors Association, Student Achievement Partners (David Coleman), the Council of Chief State School Officers, and Achieve. She sums up what she found: "In total, the four organizations primarily responsible for CCSS – NGA, CCSSO, Achieve, and Student Achievement Partners – have taken $147.9 million from Bill Gates."

This first post also includes a list of think tanks and major education organizations that received funding from Gates to promote the CCSS.

Her second post[39] lists organizations that influence state and local decisions, to encourage them to promote CCSS.

The third post[40] lists the state education departments and local school districts that have received grants from the Gates Foundation to implement CCSS.

The fourth post[41] lists 16 universities that received Gates' funding to promote CCSS.

The fifth post[42] lists the foundations and institutes that have received Gates' funding to promote CCSS.

In her sixth and final post in the series,[43] Schneider lists the businesses and nonprofits that have received Gates' funding to promote CCSS. Schneider writes:

> My desire is that the information I have presented in this series (and elsewhere on my blog) might be used as ammunition in the hands of those oppressed by the likes of Gates and his reform purchasing power. Contact your legislators. Attend those school board meetings equipped with information about the driving forces behind CCSS and other detrimental so-called reforms. Speak out, and when you are ignored, speak again.

The larger question is posed in the first post:

> Bill Gates likes Common Core. So, he is purchasing it. In doing so, Gates demonstrates (sadly so) that when one has enough money, one can purchase fundamentally democratic institutions.
>
> I do not have billions to counter Gates. What I do have is this blog and the ability to expose the purchase.
>
> I might be without cash, but I am not without power.
>
> Can Bill Gates buy a foundational democratic insti-

tution? Will America allow it? The fate of CCSS will provide crucial answers to those looming questions.

The bottom line is that the U.S. Department of Education badly wants national standards, but it is prohibited by law from influencing curriculum and instruction in the nation's schools. So, a deal is struck. Gates pays to create the CCSS, Arne Duncan uses the power of the federal purse to push states and districts to adopt them, and then uses his bully pulpit to warn that the future of the nation is in peril unless these very standards are swiftly implemented.

The problem is that all this happened so swiftly, and with so little public understanding, that the public is in the dark. A recent Gallup poll showed that most people never heard of the CCSS and had no idea what they were. Instead of taking a decade to build consensus, the Gates Foundation and the Department of Education plunged ahead.

Instead of developing a democratic process in which teachers, teacher educators, scholars, specialists in the education of children with disabilities, specialists in the education of English learners, and specialists in early childhood education were consulted at every step in the process, instead of trying out the standards to see how they work in real classrooms with real children, the Gates Foundation and the Department of Education took a shortcut.

Now, they are paying a price for taking the shortcut. In the absence of knowledge, evidence, experience, and a genuine consensus, ignorance is feeding the flames of distrust and suspicion.

Conspiracy theories abound. People make wild claims about the standards, saying they will "dumb down" the children, or saying whatever they want because so few people – aside from the ones who are on Gates' expansive payroll – have read the standards and have any idea how we suddenly came to have national standards that every district and every school must adopt.

Some states have dropped out of the assessment consortia that Arne Duncan created to test the CCSS with a grant of $350 million of federal dollars. Some districts and some states may drop the CCSS if the opposition continues to build.

Twenty years from now, will CCSS exist? It is hard to tell at this point. If history is any guide, teachers will adapt the standards to conform to what they already know. They will be changed, they will be revised on the ground. If the CCSS assessments continue to fail large majorities of students, as they did in Kentucky and New York, parents will turn angry at the assessments, not their schools or their teachers.

It is a mess, and it gets messier every day.

In a country as diverse as this one, in a country with fifty state systems and a high degree of decentralized authority, there are no shortcuts to the democratic process. When historians look back, that is very likely the conclusion they will draw.

# DEAR REFORMERS: I DIDN'T MEAN TO HURT YOUR FEELINGS

## HUFFINGTON POST, OCTOBER 15, 2013

*"The game goes on. ... Contagious. Nauseating. But profitable." – Diane Ravitch's Blog*

In his review of my book *Reign of Error* in Schools Matter,[44] historian and teacher John Thompson contemplates the urgent issue of whether I hurt reformers' feelings.

To be precise, the question posed by his review is, "Should Diane Ravitch Be More Careful to Not Hurt Reformers' Feelings?"

This is an interesting question that I have pondered these past few weeks, indeed, for the past few years.

It is true. I heard from a mutual friend (well, not so much a friend anymore) that Bill Gates was very hurt by my comments about his effort to remake American education.

He frankly could not understand how anyone could question his good intentions.

Actually I have never questioned his intentions, but I certainly question his judgment and his certainty that he can "fix" education by creating metrics to judge teachers.

He recently said that it would take a decade to find out whether "this stuff" works. In the meanwhile, teachers and principals are losing their jobs, schools are being closed, communities are being shattered – because Bill Gates got a new idea that he wanted to try out using human subjects.

I have also heard from other sources that reformers say I am "mean" or "harsh" when I say that some "reformers" have a profit motive or that their grand plans actually hurt poor minority children instead of helping them.

They are baffled that I do not admire their efforts to create charters and vouchers to allow poor kids to "escape" public schools.

I confess that I was not thinking about their feelings.

I was thinking about the consequences of their actions.

I was thinking about purposeful efforts to dismantle public education.

I was thinking about the constant repetition of the blatant lie that American public education is a failure.

One of the things that a historian tries to do is to correct the record. When people say things again and again, even though these things are not true, it is the job of the historian to tell the truth. If others disagree, they should put their facts on the table too.

Historians understand that debate and dissent are part of the work of understanding history.

There is not one truth, but on the other hand, you can't just make up facts and narratives, hire a fancy PR firm, and rewrite history to suit yourself.

Are there profiteers in the business of school reform? Yes, indeed, and I document their profitable activities amply in the book.

Meanwhile, dear reformers, please know that I didn't mean to hurt your feelings.

I just wanted to let you know that your efforts to create a dual system of publicly funded schools turns back the clock to the shameful era before the Brown decision.

And I wanted you to know that your reliance on standardized testing is a grand mistake.

I urge every one of you to take the tests that you think are the measure of all students and publish your scores.

If you won't take the test, if you fear the results, don't be so vigorous in using them to label children and evaluate teachers.

And please know that your speculative plans are not "hurting the feelings" of teachers and principals, they are ruining their careers, ruining their reputations, doing real and tangible damage to the lives of real people.

Their feelings are not hurt by your theoretical reforms. Their lives are.

# OUR KIDS TODAY: THE GREATEST GENERATION?

HUFFINGTON POST, OCTOBER 16, 2013

The members of the Providence Student Union are the most creative and best informed critics of high-stakes testing in the nation. They can run rings around the public officials in Rhode Island when they explain the damage done by high-stakes testing. They know that a large percentage of students will be denied a high school diploma because they could not pass a standardized test called NECAP.

I had the good fortune to meet some of the leaders of the PSU when I recently spoke at the University of Rhode Island in Kingston. The students drove from Providence, some 45 minutes away. When I spoke, I was introduced by Claudierre McKay, who had distinguished himself as a participant in the student Town Hall on Education Nation. When young McKay introduced me, he presaged everything I was about to say. The students are the consumers of the mandates, why not listen to them?

What I love about the PSU, aside from its determination and style, is that it has mastered the art of political theater. PSU held a zombie march in front of the Rhode Island Department of Education last year to express its contempt for the NECAP as a requirement for graduation.

When officials didn't listen, the PSU found 60 accomplished professionals to take the test, composed of released items from the actual NECAP exam. Sixty percent of the professionals, distinguished in law, government, architecture, and journalism, failed the high school graduation test.

Most if not all of the members of PSU will easily pass the NECAP – they are very smart young people. They are demonstrating on behalf of their peers – those who are bound to fail because of circumstances beyond their control because they are new immigrants, because they have a disability that interferes with test-taking, or whose desperate poverty is disabling. PSU understands that a large percentage of students will not earn a high school diploma and their lives will be blighted. With a high school diploma, they have a chance to learn a trade, to be successful in a line of work that doesn't require algebra. Without one, their lives are ruined.

Does this bother the bureaucrats? Not at all.

But it bothers the students of the PSU.

Recently, they staged a talent show[45] in front of the Rhode Island Department of Education. The point – students have many talents, and test-taking is only one of them, probably not the most important. These young people will save American education from the dead, cold hands of the robots who now are in charge of the nation's schools. They have heart, they have creativity, they have wit, they are innovative, they are alive with spirit. They have the qualities that made America great.

They know this great secret – we are not Singapore, we are not Korea, we are not China. We are America. We should cultivate the wit and wisdom of Ben Franklin, the ingenuity of Thomas Alva Edison, the spirit of the Wright brothers. Were they good test-takers? Who knows? Who cares? I bet the guys at Enron and Madoff had great test scores.

Thanks, Providence Student Union, for reminding us of the greatness of your generation. We will do whatever we can to keep the machine from crushing your heart and spirit.

# THE SHAME OF OUR NATION

## HUFFINGTON POST, OCTOBER 19, 2013

Remember all the times that "reformers" like Arne Duncan, Bill Gates, Wendy Kopp, and Joel Klein have said that the answer to poverty is to "fix" schools first? Remember their claims that school reform – more testing, more charters, more inexperienced teachers, larger classes, more technology – would vanquish poverty? For the past decade, our society has followed their advice, pouring billions into the pockets of the testing industry, consultants, and technology companies, as well as the over-hyped charter industry, Teach for America, and the multi-billion-dollar search for a surefire metric to evaluate teachers.

But what if they are wrong? What if all those billions were wasted on their pet projects, ambitions, and hunches, while child poverty kept growing?

The latest study, reported by Lyndsey Layton of *The Washington Post*[46] reports a staggering increase in child poverty across the nation. The majority of public school students in the South and the West now qualify for free or reduced price lunch. By federal standards, that means they are poor.

The United States has a greater proportion of children living in poverty than any other advanced nation in the world. We are #1 in child poverty. This is shameful.

The late Senator Daniel Patrick Moynihan once remarked on the phenomenon of "feeding the horses to feed the sparrows." In this case, the horses are the educational industrial complex. They are gobbling up federal, state, and local funding while children and families go hungry, lacking the medical care, economic security, and essential services they need. Instead of helping their families to become self-sufficient, we are fattening the testing industry. Instead of ensuring that their schools have the guidance counselors, social workers, psychologists, and librarians the children need, our states are stripping their schools to the bare walls. Instead of supplying the arts and physical education that children need to nourish body and soul, we let them eat tests. Instead of giving the reduced class size where they get the attention they need, they sit in packed classrooms.

Every dollar that fattens the educational industrial complex – not only the testing industry and the inexperienced, ill-trained Teach for America, but the corporations now collecting hundreds of millions of dollars to tell schools what to do – is a dollar diverted from what should be done now to address directly the pressing needs of our nation's most vulnerable children, whose numbers continue to escalate, demonstrating the utter futility and self-serving nature of what is currently and deceptively called "reform."

Once these futile programs have collapsed, once they have been exposed as hollow (though lucrative) gestures, we will look back with sorrow at the lives wasted, the billions squandered, and the incalculable damage to our children and our society.

Someday we will say, as we should be saying now, that we cannot tolerate the loss of so many young lives. We cannot continue to blame teachers, principals, and schools for our society's collective abandonment of so many children. We cannot allow, and should no longer permit, the income inequality that protects the billionaires and corporate executives while neglecting the growth of a massive underclass. The age of the Robber Barons has returned. Good for them, but bad, very bad, for America.

# INTERNATIONAL TEST SCORES PREDICT NOTHING

HUFFINGTON POST, OCTOBER 24, 2013

Uh-oh! Another study has appeared warning that we are falling behind other nations on international standardized tests.

The National Assessment Governing Board released the results of a study comparing the performance of U.S. states to nations that participated in the 2011 TIMSS.

Students in most U.S. states were above the international average but the nations known for their test-taking culture dominated the results. That is, the top performing nations were Singapore, Korea, Chinese Taipei, and Japan.

The usual hand-wringers were wringing their hands about how awful we were, how terribly we compare to those at the top.

The reporters from *The New York Times*[47] and *The Washington Post*[48] tried to reach me but I was at an all-day event in Vermont-New Hampshire and did not see their messages.

If I had responded, I would have said this – international test scores do not predict the economic future. Once a nation is above a basic threshold of literacy, the numbers reflect how good that nation is at test-taking. They are meaningless as economic predictors.

In 1964, when the first international test was offered in two grades to 12 nations, we came in last and next to last in the two grades but went on to have a stronger economy in the next half century than the other 11 nations that were tested.

In 1983, a federal report called "A Nation at Risk" warned that our international test scores were a symbol of a "rising tide of mediocrity" and that we were losing our major industries to Japan and Germany because of our terrible schools. As it happened, we lost our automobile industry to Japan not because of our schools or test scores but because of our short-sighted auto executives, who did not anticipate the demand for fuel-efficient cars.

Meanwhile, despite those test scores, our country continued to grow its economy, to be the most militarily powerful and technologically innovative nation in the world, and Japan went into a prolonged period of economic stagnation.

In the latest round of international test scores, Japan outscored us. So what? Singapore, Korea, and the other Asian tigers have cultures that put incredible pressure on young people to get high test scores. *The Washington Post* had a sensible comment by someone who studies labor markets: [42]

> But Hal Salzman, a professor of public policy at Rutgers University, said hand-wringing over international tests is misguided.
>
> "What's really peculiar about the whole test-score hysteria is that they use it as a proxy for the U.S. 'competitiveness and innovation' as though we don't have actual measurements," said Salzman, an expert in science and engineering labor markets and the globalization of innovation. "The country continues to lead on innovation, economic performance and all the results that these things are supposed to indicate."
>
> There are more than enough strong math and science students in U.S. classrooms to fill future jobs in this country, he said.
>
> "It doesn't mean we don't want to improve education," Salzman said. "But the fear that's driving it is unfounded. The problem we have is not at the top or at the middle. It's at the bottom. That's what gets lost

in averages and rankings."

Professor Salzman is right. The international test scores are poor economic barometers. What matters most in the decades ahead is the extent to which we cultivate creativity, ingenuity, curiosity, innovation, and thinking differently. These qualities have been the genius of American culture. These traits are not measured by standardized tests.

The students who learn to select the correct box on a multiple-choice question are not the inventors and innovators of the future. They are the clerks of the future.

# HOW DOES THE NEW MAYOR GO ABOUT REBUILDING A SCHOOL SYSTEM THAT HAS GONE THROUGH A DOZEN YEARS OF BEING THE TARGET OF A WRECKING BALL?

HUFFINGTON POST, NOVEMBER 6, 2013

*"Parents get it. They see their children stressed out by constant testing. Their children bear the burden of knowing that their performance may cause their teacher to be fired. That's a heavy burden. Parents understand that tests don't teach children. Teachers teach children. Without teachers, there is no instruction." – Diane Ravitch's Blog*

The election of Bill de Blasio as mayor of New York City represents a major national setback for the agenda shared not only by Mayor Bloomberg, but by George W. Bush, Michelle Rhee, Arne Duncan, Jeb Bush, Scott Walker, Bobby Jindal, ALEC (the American Legislative Exchange Council), the Koch brothers and many others. What they had in common was that they had the gall to call themselves "reformers" as they determined to replace public education with a choice system that gave preference to privatized management over democratic governance.

Make no mistake. In New York City, the drive to privatize public education has ground to a halt with de Blasio's election.

Bill de Blasio now has the opportunity to provide national leadership to the growing movement to rebuild and strengthen public education as a fundamental institution in our democratic society. He can make clear that the past decade of relying on testing and punishment has failed and that wise policy can restore the public schools as agencies of social progress.

De Blasio understands the failure of the Bloomberg education policies. Not only were his own children students in New York City's public schools (one is now in high school, the other in college), but he was a member of a local school board. He knows better than most how authoritarian the mayor was, and how indifferent he was to the concerns of parents and communities. De Blasio understands that decisions about the fate of schools should not be made arbitrarily and capriciously by one man, but only after the most earnest deliberation with those most directly affected – students, parents, educators, and the local community.

De Blasio must restore trust in public education in New York City, which Bloomberg eroded. The public school system enrolls 1.1 million students, and New Yorkers made clear in this election that they want a mayor who intends to make it work better for all children, not demean and destroy it. For a dozen years, we have had a mayor whose main message was that charter schools – the schools outside his control – were far, far superior to the schools for which he was directly responsible. He looked down on the public schools that enrolled 94 percent of all students, and by word and deed, sought to undermine public confidence in them.

Bloomberg did his best to destroy neighborhood schools and turn all schools into schools of choice. De Blasio must reverse that policy. He should restore neighborhood schools and the sense of community that builds strong schools and strong communities. Where Bloomberg sought to eliminate the school system and make every school into an autonomous unit, responsible for nothing more than test score data, de Blasio must rebuild the school system so that every school has competent oversight and supervision.

How does a new mayor go about rebuilding a school system that has gone through a dozen years of being the target of a wrecking ball?

First, he must restore the contiguous community school districts, each of which has a superintendent to oversee the condition and progress of the schools. In a de Blasio administration, there should be neighborhood elementary schools, neighborhood middle schools, and neighborhood high schools. There should be a district office where parents can go and get an answer if they have problems, rather than trying to penetrate the secluded, indifferent, and distant bureaucracy that Bloomberg created.

Second, the restoration of neighborhood schools would eliminate the byzantine "choice" process that Bloomberg initiated, whereby parents of children applying to middle school and high school visited schools, listed a dozen choices, and hoped for the best. Choosing a middle school should not be as difficult and complicated as applying to college. Every parent should be able to count on admission to a neighborhood school. At the same time, de Blasio should retain the specialized high schools that students want to attend, even if they must leave their neighborhood. In a city as big as New York City, there is room for both neighborhood schools and a limited number of schools that students choose, like the Bronx High School of Science, Stuyvesant High School, and Brooklyn Tech (where de Blasio's son Dante is a student).

Third, de Blasio should assemble a team of expert educators – recruited from the ranks of the city's most respected retired educators – who will take on a double assignment. First, they should review the quality of every principal in the system because many who were appointed by Bloomberg had minimal experience as educators. Second, his council of expert evaluators should create a regular inspection process to visit every struggling school and devise an action plan to provide the help it needs for the children it serves.

Fourth, de Blasio should follow through on his campaign promise to set higher expectations for the city's charter sector. The policy of co-location does not work. Instead, it has created a system of separate and unequal schools housed in the same building. Charter schools that are munificently funded and that pay their executives munificent salaries, far more than the chancellor of the entire city school system, should pay rent for using public space, as the law requires. Charter schools should be expected to enroll the same population as neighborhood schools, with the same proportions of students who are English learners and the same proportions of students with disabilities – accepting students with all kinds of disabilities, not just those with the least challenging ones, as they now do. Charters should be expected to collaborate, not compete, with the city's public schools.

Fifth, and far from last, the new mayor should de-emphasize testing and accountability. We have learned again and again that students with the greatest needs get the lowest test scores. The mayor should eliminate Bloomberg's flawed accountability system, whose sole purpose seems to be to set up schools for closure and privatization. Most testing should be done by teachers, who know what they have taught and can use test results to learn quickly what students need and how to give them support. It would be a breath of fresh air if the mayor announced a three-year moratorium on Common Core testing while the city is restoring integrity to a badly damaged school system.

The most immediate goal of Mayor Bill de Blasio is to select a chancellor who agrees with his vision of rebuilding the New York City public school system. This should be an experienced educator who shares the mayor's view that the needs of children really do come first and that data are far less important than the restoration of respect for learning, respect for educators, and the realization that a new day has dawned for public education in New York City.

# NAEP NONSENSE: DON'T BELIEVE THE HYPE

## HUFFINGTON POST, NOVEMBER 10, 2013

*"I can accept that people disagree. What I find hard to understand is an unwillingness to face plain and incontrovertible facts." – Diane Ravitch's Blog*

The latest NAEP reports on reading and math[49] have been heralded as evidence for the success of the "reforms" that involve test prep, testing, punishing teachers if scores don't go up, rewarding them if they do, closing schools, and other versions of the carrot and stick method of school reform.

Here is my one-word comment: Balderdash!

There are just as many states using the same misguided strategies who made few or no gains as there were reformy states making big gains.

If test-and-punish strategies work, why don't they work everywhere?

D.C., Tennessee, and Indiana raised test scores, but the gains in other reformy states were small or negligible.

Below the national average were hard-driving reformy states including Colorado, Delaware, Louisiana, Rhode Island, Ohio, Connecticut, and North Carolina.

That highly reformy state Wisconsin made no gains at all.

Michigan, New Jersey, and Massachusetts actually lost ground.

It is impossible to conclude, as some leaders have, that D.C., Tennessee, and Indiana have the right formula because so many states with exactly the same formula made no progress at all. Some of the states that were unlucky enough to win Race to the Top mandates made little or no gains or lost ground.

As a former member of the NAEP board, let me say that I find this statistical horse race utterly stupid. Are students in D.C. getting a better education than those in Massachusetts? Highly unlikely.

Are the students in the states with the biggest gains getting better education or more test prep?

Let me say it as bluntly as I know how. These state comparisons are stupid and say nothing about the quality of education available in different states. Anyone who takes them seriously is either a sports writer covering education or someone who thinks that education can be reduced to the scores on standardized tests.

Will families rush to enroll their children in the schools of D.C. or Tennessee because of these scores? Don't be ridiculous.

# THE DAY PRESIDENT KENNEDY DIED

HUFFINGTON POST, NOVEMBER 22, 2013

I remember the day President Kennedy died. I was 25 years old. I was living on East 86th Street in Manhattan. I was walking home to my apartment. A shopkeeper ran out on the street and shouted, "They killed the President." More people started coming out of shops, looking stunned, weeping and in shock. I ran home. My husband was at work, my one-year-old was napping. I told the babysitter to go home. I turned on the television and remained glued to it, crying as the facts emerged from the early confusion.

I met John Kennedy twice. When I was in college in Massachusetts, he was Senator. He came to meet with the political science majors in 1958, and we spent an hour or so talking about the issues facing the nation. He was charming, handsome, funny, well-informed. We had no idea that the Senator would be President in two years.

In 1960, I graduated from college and was married a few weeks later. That summer, I volunteered to work in the Kennedy campaign. I worked at the headquarters at 277 Park Avenue, an old and beautiful building that has since been torn down and replaced by a skyscraper. I still have cards inviting wealthy matrons to a tea party at the home of Mrs. Elinor Gimbel, signed by Rose Kennedy, the candidate's mother. During the fall, he came to thank the volunteers individually. I was struck by how freckled he was. Funny what you remember.

I was part of the generation that was moved by his eloquence, his humor, his charm, his intellect. He encouraged us to dream of a new world.

I felt shattered by his assassination. It was one of the darkest days the nation had known. Five years later came the terrible deaths, the murders of Martin Luther King, Jr., then Robert F. Kennedy. It seemed we would never dare to dream again.

# WHY DO WE TREAT SCHOOLS LIKE SPORTS TEAMS?

HUFFINGTON POST, NOVEMBER 22, 2013

I have been wondering lately why we are so obsessed with giving every student, every teacher, and every school a ranking, rating, and/or grade.

It seems to me that we are thinking about children, teachers, and schools the same way we think about sports teams. In every league, there are winners and losers.

But if we think about education as a culture that is very different from that of a competitive sports league, then the picture and the questions change.

What if we thought of schools as if they were akin to families?

Then we would work to develop school cultures that are collaborative and supportive. We would make sure that those with the greatest needs got the resources they need. We would stop thinking of winners and losers (and "racing to the top") and think instead about the full development of each human's potential.

It is a paradigm shift, to be sure. But the present paradigm of ranking, rating, and grading ends up demoralizing children, teachers, and schools.

We must think and act differently. If we do, we will not only have better schools, but a better society, where people help one another instead of finding a way to beat out their competitors.

Save the competition for the sports field, save it for the arenas where it is appropriate.

Think of each child as a precious human being, one of a kind. Think of teachers as professionals, who should be well prepared, supported, and given the autonomy to decide what works best in their classrooms. And treasure each community's school as an invaluable and irreplaceable institution, one that is central to the community and essential to our democracy.

# WHAT YOU NEED TO KNOW ABOUT THE INTERNATIONAL TEST SCORES

HUFFINGTON POST, DECEMBER 3, 2013

The news reports say that the test scores of American students on the latest PISA test are "stagnant," "lagging," "flat," etc.

The U.S. Department of Education would have us believe – yet again – that we are in an unprecedented crisis and that we must double down on the test-and-punish strategies of the past dozen years.

The myth persists that once our nation led the world on international tests, but we have fallen from that exalted position in recent years.

Wrong, wrong, wrong.

Here is the background history that you need to know to interpret the PISA score release, as well as Secretary Duncan's calculated effort to whip up national hysteria about our standing in the international league tables.

The U.S. has *never* been first in the world, nor even near the top, on international tests.

Over the past half century, our students have typically scored at or near the median, or even in the bottom quartile.

International testing began in the mid-1960s with a test of mathematics. The First International Mathematics Study tested

13-year-olds and high-school seniors in 12 nations. American 13-year-olds scores significantly lower than students in nine other countries and ahead of students in only one. On a test given only to students currently enrolled in a math class, the U.S. students scored last, behind those in the 11 other nations. On a test given to seniors not currently enrolled in a math class, the U.S. students again scored last.

The First International Science Study was given in the late 1960s and early 1970s to 10-year-olds, 14-year-olds, and seniors. The 10-year-olds did well scoring behind only the Japanese, the 14-year-olds were about average. Among students in the senior year of high schools, Americans scored last of eleven school systems.

In the Second International Mathematics Study (1981-82), students in 15 systems were tested. The students were 13-year-olds and seniors. The younger group of U.S. students placed at or near the median on most tests. The American seniors placed at or near the bottom on almost every test. The "average Japanese students achieved higher than the top 5 percent of the U.S. students in college preparatory mathematics" and "the algebra achievement of our most able students (the top 1 percent) was lower than that of the top 1 percent of any other country." The quote is from Curtis C. McKnight and others, *The Underachieving Curriculum: Assessing U.S. Mathematics from an International Perspective* (pp. 17, 26-27). I summarized the international assessments from the mid-1960s to the early 1990s in a book called *National Standards in American Education: A Citizen's Guide* (Brookings, 1995).

The point worth noting here is that U.S. students have never been top performers on the international tests. We are doing about the same now on PISA as we have done for the past half century.

Does it matter?

In my recent book, *Reign of Error*, I quote extensively from a brilliant article by Keith Baker, called "Are International Tests Worth Anything?" which was published by Phi Delta Kappan in

October 2007. Baker, who worked for many years as a researcher at the U.S. Department of Education, had the ingenious idea to investigate what happened to the 12 nations that took the First International Mathematics test in 1964. He looked at the per capita gross domestic product of those nations and found that "the higher a nation's test score 40 years ago, the worse its economic performance on this measure of national wealth – the opposite of what the Chicken Littles raising the alarm over the poor test scores of U.S. children claimed would happen." He found no relationship between a nation's economic productivity and its test scores. Nor did the test scores bear any relationship to quality of life or democratic institutions. And when it came to creativity, the U.S. "clobbered the world," with more patents per million people than any other nation.

Baker wrote that a certain level of educational achievement may be "a platform for launching national success, but once that platform is reached, other factors become more important than further gains in test scores. Indeed, once the platform is reached, it may be bad policy to pursue further gains in test scores because focusing on the scores diverts attention, effort, and resources away from other factors that are more important determinants of national success." What has mattered most for the economic, cultural, and technological success of the U.S. he says, is a certain "spirit," which he defines as "ambition, inquisitiveness, independence, and perhaps most important, the absence of a fixation on testing and test scores."

Baker's conclusion was that "standings in the league tables of international tests are worthless."

I agree with Baker. The more we focus on tests, the more we kill creativity, ingenuity, and the ability to think differently. Students who think differently get lower scores. The more we focus on tests, the more we reward conformity and compliance, getting the right answer.

Thirty years ago, a federal report called "A Nation at Risk"[50] warned that we were in desperate trouble because of the poor academic performance of our students. The report was written by a distinguished commission appointed by the Secretary of Education. The commission pointed to those dreadful international test scores and complained that "on 19 academic tests American students were never first or second and, in comparison with other industrialized nations, were last seven times." With such terrible outcomes, the commission said, "the educational foundations of our society are presently being eroded by a rising tide of mediocrity that threatens our very future as a Nation and a people." Yet we are still here, apparently the world's most dominant economy. Go figure.

Despite having been proved wrong for the past half century, the Bad News Industry is in full cry, armed with the PISA scores, expressing alarm, fright, fear, and warnings of imminent economic decline and collapse.

Never do they explain how it was possible for the U.S. to score so poorly on international tests again and again over the past half century and yet still emerge as the world's leading economy, with the world's most vibrant culture, and a highly productive workforce. From my vantage point as a historian, here is my takeaway from the PISA scores:

> **Lesson 1:** If they mean anything at all, the PISA scores show the failure of the past dozen years of public policy in the United States. The billions invested in testing, test prep, and accountability have not raised test scores or our nation's relative standing on the league tables. No Child Left Behind and Race to the Top are manifest failures at accomplishing their singular goal of higher test scores.
>
> **Lesson 2:** The PISA scores burst the bubble of the alleged "Florida miracle" touted by Jeb Bush. Florida was one of three states – Massachusetts, Connecticut, and Florida – that participated in the PISA testing.[51] Massachusetts did very well, typically scoring above the OECD average and the U.S. average, as you might expect of the nation's highest performing state

on NAEP. Connecticut also did well. But Florida did not do well at all. It turns out that the highly touted "Florida model" of testing, accountability, and choice was not competitive, if you are inclined to take the scores seriously. In math, Florida performed below the OECD average and below the U.S. average. In science, Florida performed below the OECD average and at the U.S. average. In reading, Massachusetts and Connecticut performed above both the OECD and U.S. average, but Florida performed at average for both.

**Lesson 3:** Improving the quality of life for the nearly one-quarter of students who live in poverty would improve their academic performance.

**Lesson 4:** We measure only what can be measured. We measure whether students can pick the right answer to a test question. But what we cannot measure matters more. The scores tell us nothing about students' imagination, their drive, their ability to ask good questions, their insight, their inventiveness, their creativity. If we continue the policies of the Bush and Obama administration in education, we will not only *not* get higher scores – the Asian nations are so much better at this than we are – but we will crush the very qualities that have given our nation its edge as a cultivator of new talent and new ideas for many years.

Let others have the higher test scores. I prefer to bet on the creative, can-do spirit of the American people, on its character, persistence, ambition, hard work, and big dreams, none of which are ever measured or can be measured by standardized tests like PISA.

# GROWING UP JEWISH IN TEXAS: CHRISTMAS

HUFFINGTON POST, DECEMBER 25, 2013

I was born and raised in Houston, Texas.

I am third of eight children.

My parents were both Jewish, as am I.

Yet every year we celebrated Christmas.

Is this puzzling? It wasn't at all puzzling to me and my siblings.

Every Christmas, the family bought a Christmas tree, and we all joined in decorating it with lights, ornaments, and tinsel.

Every Christmas morning, we woke up like a noisy tribe about 5 a.m. and rushed to discover that we all had presents under the tree.

Why did our Jewish family celebrate Christmas?

To begin with, my parents had been born into observant Jewish families. My father was born in Savannah, Georgia, where he was the youngest of nine children and the only boy. He was spoiled rotten, left high school without graduating, and tried (but failed) to make it in vaudeville as a hoofer and comedian. My mother was born in Bessarabia and came to America at the end of World War I as a nine-year-old girl with her mother and little sister. They traveled on a ship (the "Savoie") loaded with returning American soldiers, then made their way to Houston to meet my grandfather, who was a tailor and had come to America before the war broke out.

What my parents wanted most was to be seen as "real Americans." My mother was especially zealous about wanting to speak perfect English (she arrived speaking only Yiddish). She was very proud that she earned a high school diploma from the Houston public schools. In her eyes, real Americans celebrated Christmas. So, of course, we had a tree, and we believed that Santa Claus brought the presents. There was no religious content to our tree and our gifting.

We went to public school, where we learned all the Christmas songs. We went to assemblies and sang "Silent Night," "Joy to the World," "O Little Town of Bethlehem," and all the other traditional songs. I knew I was Jewish, and I usually hummed certain words instead of saying them, but nonetheless I loved the songs and I love them still. I was never offended by singing Christmas songs at public school. It was what we did.

Of course, my siblings and I went to Sunday School at the synagogue, and my brothers were bar mitzvah. I was "confirmed," which was a ceremony that occurred at the end of tenth grade, when we read from the prayer book as a group.

I should add that we started every day in public school with a short reading from the Bible, over the loudspeaker, followed by a prayer and the recitation of the Pledge of Allegiance.

I was okay with the Bible reading, the prayers, the Christmas songs. I was also okay with our family putting up a Christmas tree while belonging to a synagogue and practicing our Jewish rituals and holy days.

I committed one major faux pas as a result of my upbringing in two religious traditions. On one occasion, when I was about 12, the rabbi at my reform temple invited me to join him on the altar and say a prayer. I said "The Lord's Prayer," the one that begins, "Our father, who art in heaven, hallowed be thy name" prayer, and there was some awkwardness afterwards. I had no idea that I was saying a Christian prayer, drawn from the Gospel of Matthew, in the synagogue! I had heard it hundreds of times in school. I think I was forgiven my error. After that, the rabbi was careful to propose a specific prayer from the prayer book for children who were invited to speak from the altar.

Many things have changed, and I understand that. But when I go with my partner to midnight Mass on Christmas Eve at the Oratory of St. Boniface in Brooklyn, I am glad I know the words to the songs. I learned them in public school in Houston. I look around and am not surprised to see a fairly large number of other Jews from the neighborhood, also joining in singing the songs with the choir. It is Christmas. It is a time to celebrate peace and joy and goodwill towards all. We can all share those hopes.

# COMMON CORE STANDARDS: PAST, PRESENT, FUTURE

## SPEECH TO THE MODERN LANGUAGE ASSOCIATION (MLA), JANUARY 11, 2014

*"Now students and policymakers alike see higher education as career training, a way to get a better job. Lost is the idea of learning for learning's sake. That is an intellectual luxury we can no longer afford or even remember." – Diane Ravitch's Blog*

As an organization of teachers and scholars devoted to the study of language and literature, MLA should be deeply involved in the debate about the Common Core standards.

The Common Core standards were developed in 2009 and released in 2010. Within a matter of months, they had been endorsed by 45 states and the District of Columbia. At present, publishers are aligning their materials with the Common Core, technology companies are creating software and curriculum aligned with the Common Core, and two federally-funded consortia have created online tests of the Common Core.

What are the Common Core standards? Who produced them? Why are they controversial? How did their adoption happen so quickly?

As scholars of the humanities, you are well aware that every historical event is subject to interpretation. There are different ways to answer the questions I just posed. Originally, this session was designed to be a discussion between me and David Coleman, who is generally acknowledged as the architect of the Common

Core standards. Some months ago, we both agreed on the date and format. But Mr. Coleman, now president of the College Board, discovered that he had a conflicting meeting and could not be here.

So, unfortunately, you will hear only my narrative, not his, which would be quite different. I have no doubt that you will have no difficulty getting access to his version of the narrative, which is the same as Secretary Arne Duncan's.

He would tell you that the standards were created by the states, that they were widely and quickly embraced because so many educators wanted common standards for teaching language, literature, and mathematics. But he would not be able to explain why so many educators and parents are now opposed to the standards and are reacting angrily to the testing that accompanies them.

I will try to do that.

I will begin by setting the context for the development of the standards.

They arrive at a time when American public education and its teachers are under attack. Never have public schools been as subject to upheaval, assault, and chaos as they are today. Unlike modern corporations, which extol creative disruption, schools need stability, not constant turnover and change. Yet for the past dozen years, ill-advised federal and state policies have rained down on students, teachers, principals, and schools.

George W. Bush's No Child Left Behind and Barack Obama's Race to the Top have combined to impose a punitive regime of standardized testing on the schools. NCLB was passed by Congress in 2001 and signed into law in 2002. NCLB law required schools to test every child in grades 3-8 every year, by 2014 said the law, every child must be "proficient" or schools would face escalating sanctions. The ultimate sanction for failure to raise test scores was firing the staff and closing the school.

Because the stakes were so high, NCLB encouraged teachers to teach to the test. In many schools, the curriculum was narrowed, the only subjects that mattered were reading and mathematics. What was not tested – the arts, history, civics, literature, geography, science, physical education – didn't count. Some states, like New York, gamed the system by dropping the passing mark each year, giving the impression that its students were making phenomenal progress when they were not. Some districts, like Atlanta, El Paso, and the District of Columbia, were caught up in cheating scandals. In response to this relentless pressure, test scores rose, but not as much as they had before the adoption of NCLB.

Then along came the Obama administration, with its signature program called Race to the Top. In response to the economic crisis of 2008, Congress gave the U.S. Department of Education $5 billion to promote "reform." Secretary Duncan launched a competition for states called "Race to the Top." If states wanted any part of that money, they had to agree to certain conditions:

- They had to agree to evaluate teachers to a significant degree by the rise or fall of their students' test scores.
- They had to agree to increase the number of privately managed charter schools.
- They had to agree to adopt "college and career ready standards" which were understood to be the not-yet-finished Common Core standards.
- They had to agree to "turnaround" low-performing schools by such tactics as firing the principal and part or all of the school staff.
- They had to agree to collect unprecedented amounts of personally identifiable information about every student and store it in a data warehouse.

It became an article of faith in Washington and in state capitols, with the help of propagandistic films like *Waiting for "Superman,"* that if students had low scores, it must be the fault of bad teachers. Poverty, we heard again and again from people like Bill Gates, Joel Klein, and Michelle Rhee, was just an excuse for bad teachers, who should be fired without delay or due process.

These two federal programs, which both rely heavily on standardized testing, have produced:

- A massive demoralization of educators
- An unprecedented exodus of experienced educators who were replaced in many districts by young, inexperienced, low-wage teachers.
- The closure of many public schools, especially in poor and minority districts.
- The opening of thousands of privately managed charter schools.
- An increase in low-quality for-profit charter schools and low-quality online charter schools.
- A widespread attack on teachers' due process rights and collective bargaining rights.
- The near-collapse of public education in urban districts like Detroit and Philadelphia as public schools are replaced by privately managed charter schools.

A burgeoning educational-industrial complex of testing corporations, charter chains, and technology companies that view public education as an emerging market. Hedge funds, entrepreneurs, and real estate investment corporations invest enthusiastically in this emerging market, encouraged by federal tax credits, lavish fees, and the prospect of huge profits from taxpayer dollars. Celebrities, tennis stars, basketball stars, and football stars are opening their own name-brand schools with public dollars, even though they know nothing about education.

No other nation in the world has inflicted so many changes or imposed so many mandates on its teachers and public schools as we have in the past dozen years. No other nation tests every student every year as we do. Our students are the most over-tested in the world. No other nation – at least no high-performing nation – judges the quality of teachers by the test scores of their students. Most researchers agree that this methodology is fundamentally flawed, that it is inaccurate, unreliable, and unstable, that the highest ratings will go to teachers with the most affluent students and the lowest ratings will go to teachers of English learners, teachers of students with disabilities, and teachers in high-poverty schools. Nonetheless, the U.S. Department of Education wants every state and every district to do it. Because of these federal programs, our schools have become obsessed with standardized testing, and have turned over to the testing corporations the responsibility for rating, ranking, and labeling our students, our teachers, and our schools.

The Pearson Corporation has become the ultimate arbiter of the fate of students, teachers, and schools.

This is the policy context in which the Common Core standards were developed. Five years ago, when they were written, major corporations, major foundations, and the key policymakers at the Department of Education agreed that public education was a disaster and that the only salvation for it was a combination of school choice – including privately managed charters and vouchers – national standards, and a weakening or elimination of such protections as collective bargaining, tenure, and seniority. At the same time, the political and philanthropic leaders maintained a passionate faith in the value of standardized tests and the data that they produced as measures of quality and as ultimate, definitive judgments on people and on schools. The agenda of both Republicans and Democrats converged around the traditional Republican agenda of standards, choice, and accountability. In my view, this convergence has nothing to do with improving education or creating equality of opportunity, but everything to do with cutting costs, standardizing education, shifting the delivery of education from high-cost teachers to low-cost technology, reducing the number of teachers, and eliminating unions and pensions.

The Common Core standards were written in 2009 under the aegis of several D.C.-based organizations – the National Governors Association, the Council of Chief State School Officers, and Achieve. The development process was led behind closed doors by a small organization called Student Achievement Partners, headed by David Coleman. The writing group of 27 contained few educators, but a significant number of representatives of the testing industry. From the outset, the Common Core standards were marked by the absence of public participation, transparency, or educator participation. In a democracy, transparency is crucial, because transparency and openness builds trust. Those crucial ingredients were lacking.

The U.S. Department of Education is legally prohibited from exercising any influence or control over curriculum or instruction in the schools, so it could not contribute any funding to the expensive task of creating national standards. The Gates Foundation stepped in and assumed that responsibility. It gave millions to the National Governors Association, to the Council of Chief School Officers, to Achieve, and to Student Achievement Partners. Once the standards were written, Gates gave millions more to almost every think tank and education advocacy group in Washington to evaluate the standards, even to some that had no experience evaluating standards, and to promote and help to implement the standards. Even the two major teachers' unions accepted millions of dollars to help advance the Common Core standards. Altogether, the Gates Foundation has expended nearly $200 million to pay for the development, evaluation, implementation, and promotion of the Common Core standards. And the money tap is still open, with millions more awarded this past fall to promote the Common Core standards.

Some states like Kentucky adopted the Common Core standards sight unseen. Some, like Texas, refused to adopt them sight unseen. Some, like Massachusetts, adopted them even though their own standards were demonstrably better and had been proven over time.

The advocates of the standards saw them as a way to raise test scores by making sure that students everywhere in every grade were taught using the same standards. They believed that common standards would automatically guarantee equity. Some spoke of the Common Core as a civil rights issue. They emphasized that the Common Core standards would be far more rigorous than most state standards and they predicted that students would improve their academic performance in response to raising the bar.

Integral to the Common Core was the expectation that they would be tested on computers using online standardized exams. As Secretary Duncan's chief of staff wrote at the time, the Common Core was intended to create a national market for book publishers, technology companies, testing corporations, and other vendors.

What the advocates ignored is that test scores are heavily influenced by socioeconomic status. Standardized tests are normed on a bell curve. The upper half of the curve has an abundance of those who grew up in favorable circumstances, with educated parents, books in the home, regular medical care, and well-resourced schools. Those who dominate the bottom half of the bell curve are the kids who lack those advantages, whose parents lack basic economic security, whose schools are overcrowded and under-resourced. To expect tougher standards and a renewed emphasis on standardized testing to reduce poverty and inequality is to expect what never was and never will be.

Who supported the standards? Secretary Duncan has been their loudest cheerleader. Governor Jeb Bush of Florida and former DC Chancellor Michelle Rhee urged their rapid adoption. Joel Klein and Condoleezza Rice chaired a commission for the Council on Foreign Relations, which concluded that the Common Core standards were needed to protect national security. Major corporations purchased full-page ads in *The New York Times* and other newspapers to promote the Common Core. ExxonMobil is especially vociferous in advocating for Common Core, taking out advertisements on television and other news media saying that the standards are needed to prepare our workforce for global competition. The U.S. Chamber of Commerce endorsed the standards, saying they were necessary to prepare workers for the global marketplace. The Business Roundtable stated that its #1 priority is the full adoption and implementation of the Common Core standards. All of this excitement was generated despite the fact that no one knows whether the Common Core will fulfill any of these promises. It will take 12 years before we know what its effects are.

The Common Core standards have both allies and opponents on the right. Tea-party groups at the grassroots level oppose the standards, claiming that they will lead to a federal takeover of education. The standards also have allies and opponents on the left.

I was aware of Common Core from the outset. In 2009, I urged its leaders to plan on field testing them to find out how the standards worked in real classrooms with real teachers and real students. Only then would we know whether they improve college-readiness and equity. In 2010, I was invited to meet at the White House with senior administration officials, and I advised them to field test the standards to make sure that they didn't widen the achievement gaps between haves and have-nots.

After all, raising the bar might make more students fail, and failure would be greatest amongst those who cannot clear the existing bar.

Last spring, when it became clear that there would be no field testing, I decided I could not support the standards. I objected to the lack of any democratic participation in their development, I objected to the absence of any process for revising them, and I was fearful that they were setting unreachable targets for most students. I also was concerned that they would deepen the sense of crisis about American education that has been used to attack the very principle of public education. In my latest book *Reign of Error,* using data on the U.S. Department of Education website, I demonstrated that the current sense of crisis about our nation's public schools was exaggerated, that test scores were the highest they had ever been in our history for whites, African Americans, Latinos, and Asians, that graduation rates for all groups were the highest in our history, and that the dropout rate was the lowest ever in our history.

My fears were confirmed by the Common Core tests. Wherever they have been implemented, they have caused a dramatic collapse of test scores. In state after state, the passing rates dropped by about 30%. This was not happenstance. This was failure by design. Let me explain.

The Obama administration awarded $350 million to two groups to create tests for the Common Core standards. The testing consortia jointly decided to use a very high passing mark, which is known as a "cut score." The Common Core testing consortia decided that the passing mark on their tests would be aligned with the proficient level on the federal tests called NAEP. This is a level typically reached by about 35-40% of students. Massachusetts is the only state in which as many as 50% ever reached the NAEP proficient level. The testing consortia set the bar so high that most students were sure to fail, and they did.

In New York State, which gave the Common Core tests last spring, only 30% of students across the state passed the tests. Only 3% of English language learners passed. Only 5% of students with disabilities passed. Fewer than 20% of African American and Hispanic students passed. By the time the results were reported in August the students did not have the same teachers, and the teachers saw the scores but did not get any item analysis. They could not use the test results for diagnostic purposes, to help students. Their only value was to rank students.

When New York State education officials held public hearings, parents showed up en masse to complain about the Common Core testing. Secretary Duncan dismissed them as "white suburban moms" who were disappointed to learn that their child was not as brilliant as they thought, and that their public school was not as good as they thought. But he was wrong. The parents were outraged not because they thought their children were brilliant but because they did not believe that their children were failures. What, exactly, is the point of crushing the hearts and minds of young children by setting a standard so high that 70% are certain to fail?

The financial cost of implementing Common Core has barely been mentioned in the national debates. All Common

Core testing will be done online. This is a bonanza for the tech industry and other vendors. Every school district must buy new computers, new teaching materials, and new bandwidth for the testing. At a time when school budgets have been cut in most states and many thousands of teachers have been laid off, school districts across the nation will spend billions to pay for Common Core testing. Los Angeles alone committed to spend $1 billion on iPads for the tests – the money is being taken from a bond issue approved by voters for construction and repair of school facilities. Meanwhile, the district has cut teachers of the arts, class size has increased, and necessary repairs are deferred because the money will be spent on iPads. The iPads will be obsolete in a year or two, and the Pearson content loaded onto the iPads has only a three-year license. The cost of implementing the Common Core and the new tests is likely to run into the billions at a time of deep budget cuts.

Other controversies involve the standards themselves. Early childhood educators are nearly unanimous in saying that no one who wrote the standards had any expertise in the education of very young children. More than 500 early childhood educators signed a joint statement complaining that the standards were developmentally inappropriate for children in the early grades. The standards, they said, emphasize academic skills and leave inadequate time for imaginative play. They also objected to the likelihood that young children would be subjected to standardized testing. And yet proponents of the Common Core insist that children as young as 5 or 6 or 7 should be on track to be college-and-career ready, even though children this age are not likely to think about college, and most think of careers as cowboys, astronauts, or firefighters.

There has also been heated argument about the standards' insistence that reading must be divided equally in the elementary grades between fiction and informational text, and divided 70-30 in favor of informational text in high school. Where did the writers of the standards get these percentages? They relied on the federal National Assessment of Educational Progress (NAEP), which uses these percentages as instructions to test developers. NAEP never intended that these numbers would be converted into instructional mandates for teachers. This idea that informational text should take up half the students' reading time in the early grades and 70% in high school led to outlandish claims that teachers would no longer be allowed to teach whole novels. Somewhat hysterical articles asserted that the classics would be banned while students were required to read government documents. The standards contain no such demands.

Defenders of the Common Core standards said that the percentages were misunderstood. They said they referred to the entire curriculum – math, science, and history, not just English. But since teachers in math, science, and history are not known for assigning fiction, why was this even mentioned in the standards? Which administrator will be responsible for policing whether precisely 70% of the reading in senior year is devoted to informational text? Who will keep track?

The fact is that the Common Core standards should never have set forth any percentages at all. If they really did not mean to impose numerical mandates on English teachers, they set off a firestorm of criticism for no good reason. Other nations have national standards, and I don't know of any that tell teachers how much time to devote to fiction and how much time to devote to informational text. Frankly, I think that teachers are quite capable of making that decision for themselves. If they choose to teach a course devoted only to fiction or devoted only to non-fiction, that should be their choice, not a mandate imposed by a committee in 2009.

Another problem presented by the Common Core standards is that there is no one in charge of fixing them. If teachers find legitimate problems and seek remedies, there is no one to turn to. If the demands for students in kindergarten and first grade are developmentally inappropriate, no one can make changes. The original writing committee no longer exists. No organization or agency has the authority to revise the standards. The Common Core standards might as well be written in stone.

This makes no sense. They were not handed down on Mount Sinai, they are not an infallible Papal encyclical, so why is there no process for improving and revising them?

Furthermore, what happens to the children who fail? Will they be held back a grade? Will they be held back again and again? If most children fail, as they did in New York, what will happen to them? How will they catch up? The advocates of the standards insist that low-scoring students will become high-scoring students if the tests are rigorous, but what if they are wrong? What if the failure rate remains staggeringly high as it is now? What if it improves marginally as students become accustomed to the material, and the failure rate drops from 70% to 50%? What will we do with the 50% who can't jump over the bar? Teachers across the country will be fired if the scores of their pupils do not go up. This is nuts. We have a national policy that is a theory based on an assumption grounded in hope. And it might be wrong, with disastrous consequences for real children and real teachers.

In some states, teachers say that the lessons are scripted and deprive them of their professional autonomy, the autonomy they need to tailor their lessons to the needs of the students in front of them. Behind the Common Core standards lies a blind faith in standardization of tests and curriculum, and perhaps, of children as well. Yet we know that even in states with strong standards, like Massachusetts and California, there are wide variations in test scores. Tom Loveless of the Brookings Institution predicted that the Common Core standards were likely to make little, if any, difference.[52] No matter how high and uniform their standards, there are variations in academic achievement within states, there are variations within districts, there are variations within every school.

It is good to have standards. I believe in standards, but they must not be rigid, inflexible, and prescriptive. Teachers must have the flexibility to tailor standards to meet the students in their classrooms, the students who can't read English, the students who are two grade levels behind, the students who are homeless, the students who just don't get it and just don't care, the students who frequently miss class. Standards alone cannot produce a miraculous transformation.

I do not mean to dismiss the Common Core standards altogether. They could be far better, if there were a process whereby experienced teachers were able to fix them. They could be made developmentally appropriate for the early grades, so that children have time for play and games, as well as learning to read and do math and explore nature.

The numerical demands for 50-50 or 70-30 literature vs. informational text should be eliminated. They serve no useful purpose and they have no justification.

In every state, teachers should work together to figure out how the standards can be improved. Professional associations like the National Council for the Teaching of English and the National Council for the Teaching of Mathematics should participate in a process by which the standards are regularly reviewed, revised, and updated by classroom teachers and scholars to respond to genuine problems in the field.

The Common Core standards should be decoupled from standardized testing, especially online standardized testing. Most objections to the standards are caused by the testing. The tests are too long, many students give up, and the passing marks on the tests were set so high as to create failure.

Yet the test scores will be used to rate students, teachers, and schools.

The standardized testing should become optional. It should include authentic writing assignments that are judged by humans, not by computers. It too needs oversight by professional communities of scholars and teachers.

There is something about the Common Core standards and testing, about their demand for uniformity and standardization, that reeks of early twentieth century factory-line thinking. There is something about them that feels obsolete. Today, most sectors of our economy have standards that are open-sourced and flexible, that rely upon the wisdom of practitioners, that are constantly updated and improved.

In the present climate, the Common Core standards and testing will become the driving force behind the creation of a test-based meritocracy. With David Coleman in charge of the College Board, the SAT will be aligned with the Common Core, so will the ACT. Both testing organizations were well represented in the writing of the standards, and representatives of these two organizations comprised 12 of the 27 members of the original writing committee. The Common Core tests are a linchpin of the federal effort to commit K-12 education to the new world of Big Data. The tests are the necessary ingredient to standardize teaching, curriculum, instruction, and schooling. Only those who pass these rigorous tests will get a high school diploma. Only those with high scores on these rigorous tests will be able to go to college.

No one has come up with a plan for the 50% or more who never get a high school diploma. These days, a man or woman without a high school diploma has meager chances to make their way in this society. They will end up in society's dead-end jobs.

Some might say this is just. I say it is not just. I say that we have allowed the testing corporations to assume too much power in allotting power, prestige, and opportunity. Those who are wealthy can afford to pay fabulous sums for tutors so their children can get high scores on standardized tests and college entrance exams. Those who are affluent live in districts with ample resources for their schools. Those who are poor lack those advantages. Our nation suffers an opportunity gap, and the opportunity gap creates a test score gap.

You may know Michael Young's book *The Rise of the Meritocracy*. It was published in 1958 and has gone through many editions. A decade ago, Young added a new introduction in which he warned that a meritocracy could be sad and fragile. He wrote:

> If the rich and powerful were encouraged by the general culture to believe that they fully deserved all they had, how arrogant they could become, and if they were convinced it was all for the common good,

> how ruthless in pursuing their own advantage. Power corrupts, and therefore one of the secrets of a good society is that power should always be open to criticism. A good society should provide sinew for revolt as well as for power.
>
> But authority cannot be humbled unless ordinary people, however much they have been rejected by the educational system, have the confidence to assert themselves against the mighty. If they think themselves inferior, if they think they deserve on merit to have less worldly goods and less worldly power than a select minority, they can be damaged in their own self-esteem, and generally demoralized.
>
> Even if it could be demonstrated that ordinary people had less native ability than those selected for high position, that would not mean that they deserved to get less. Being a member of the "lucky sperm club" confers no moral right or advantage. What one is born with, or without, is not of one's own doing.

We must then curb the misuse of the Common Core standards. Those who like them should use them, but they should be revised continually to adjust to reality. Stop the testing. Stop the rating and ranking. Do not use them to give privilege to those who pass them or to deny the diploma necessary for a decent life. Remove the high-stakes that policymakers intend to attach to them. Use them to enrich instruction, but not to standardize it.

I fear that the Common Core plan of standards and testing will establish a test-based meritocracy that will harm our democracy by parceling out opportunity, by ranking and rating every student in relation to their test scores.

We cannot have a decent democracy unless we begin with the supposition that every human life is of equal value. Our society already has far too much inequality of wealth and income. We should do nothing to stigmatize those who already get the least of society's advantages. We should bend our efforts to change our society so that each and every one of us has the opportunity to learn, the resources needed to learn, and the chance to have a good and decent life, regardless of one's test scores.

# UNDERSTANDING THE PROPAGANDA CAMPAIGN AGAINST PUBLIC EDUCATION

HUFFINGTON POST, MARCH 11, 2014

*Are you kidding? This is not about improving education. It's not about "the kids." This is the edu-business." – Diane Ravitch's Blog*

A few years ago, when I was blogging at Education Week with Deborah Meier, a reader introduced the term FUD. I had never heard of it. It is a marketing technique used in business and politics to harm your competition. FUD stands for Fear, Uncertainty, and Doubt. The reader said that those who were trying to create a market-based system to replace public education were using FUD to undermine public confidence in public education. They were selling the false narrative that our public schools are obsolete and failing.

This insight inspired me to write *Reign of Error* to show that the "reform" narrative is a fraud. Test scores on NAEP are at their highest point in history for white students, black students, Hispanic students, and Asian students. Graduation rates are the highest in history for these groups. The dropout rate is at an historic low point.

Why the FUD campaign against one of our nation's most treasured democratic institutions? It helps the competition. It makes people so desperate that they will seek out unproven alternatives. It makes the public gullible when they hear phony claims about miracle schools, where everyone graduates and everyone gets high test scores, and everyone goes to a four-year college. No such school exists. The "miracle school" usually has a high suspension rate, a high expulsion rate, a high attrition rate, and such schools usually do not replace the kids they somehow got rid of. Some "miracle schools" have never graduated anyone because they have only elementary schools, but that doesn't stop the claims and boasting.

It turns out that there is actually a scholar studying the phenomenon of the "cultural production of ignorance." He hasn't looked at the attack on public schools, but his work shows how propaganda may be skillfully deployed to confuse and mislead the public. Michael Hiltzik of the *Los Angeles Times* writes about the work of Robert Proctor of Stanford University:[53]

> Robert Proctor doesn't think ignorance is bliss. He thinks that what you don't know can hurt you. And that there's more ignorance around than there used to be, and that its purveyors have gotten much better at filling our heads with nonsense.
>
> Proctor, a professor of the history of science at Stanford, is one of the world's leading experts in agnotology, a neologism signifying the study of the cultural production of ignorance. It's a rich field, especially today when whole industries devote themselves to sowing public misinformation and doubt about their products and activities.
>
> The tobacco industry was a pioneer at this. Its goal was to erode public acceptance of the scientifically proven links between smoking and disease. In the words of an internal 1969 memo legal opponents extracted from Brown & Williamson's files, "Doubt is our product." Big Tobacco's method should not be to debunk the evidence, the memo's author wrote, but

> to establish a "controversy."
>
> When this sort of manipulation of information is done for profit, or to confound the development of beneficial public policy, it becomes a threat to health and to democratic society. Big Tobacco's program has been carefully studied by the sugar industry, which has become a major target of public health advocates.

FUD was pioneered decades ago. Now public education is the target, and privatizing it is the goal. I hope Professor Proctor turns his attention to this issue, where a well-funded propaganda campaign seeks to spread enough doubt to destroy an essential democratic institution.

There is no evidence from any other nation that replacing a public system with a privatized choice system produces anything but social, economic, and racial segregation.

# "WE'VE HAD THESE CHILDREN SINCE KINDERGARTEN" FACT-CHECKING EVA MOSKOWITZ'S CLAIMS

HUFFINGTON POST, MARCH 12, 2014

The battle between NYC Mayor Bill de Blasio and Eva Moskowitz, CEO of the Success Academy charter chain, has blown up into a national controversy, covered on national television, *The New York Times*, and *The Wall Street Journal*.

Mayor de Blasio had the nerve to award the Moskowitz chain only five of the eight charters that it wanted, and Moskowitz has been on the warpath to get all eight, even if it means pushing kids with disabilities out of their public school classrooms.

What is missing from the controversy so far is any interest on the part of the journalists in basic facts. Instead, what is happening is a public relations battle. Moskowitz has attacked Mayor de Blasio in multiple media appearances, and no one in the media has bothered to check any of her claims.

Let's fill that gap.

On MSNBC's *Morning Joe*, Ms. Moskowitz claimed that Success Academy 4 in Harlem is the "highest performing school in New York State in math in fifth grade." This is obviously an odd metric to use in judging a school. Picking out one subject in a single grade should raise suspicion among the media, but it hasn't.

It is also not true:[54]

- On the fifth grade state math test, the students at Success Academy 4 are, in fact, #8 in New York City (tied with another school) and presumably even lower when compared to schools across the state.
- The fourth grade math test scores are #54 in New York City (tied with six other schools).
- The third grade math scores rank #63 in New York City (tied with 6 other schools).

The school's rankings are even worse in English:

- The fifth grade English test scores rank #59 in New York City (tied with seven other schools),
- The fourth grade English test scores rank #81 in New York City (tied with five other schools),
- The third grade English test scores rank #65 in New York City (tied with eight other schools).

The school is not the "highest performing school in the state" in any grade.

Moskowitz's interviewers have said that the students at Success Academy 4 are the "most disadvantaged kids in New York City," to which she assented. She has said "it's a random lottery school. We don't know who they are."

We do, in fact, know who the students at Success Academy are. They are not the most disadvantaged kids in New York City. Harlem Success Academy schools have half the number of English Language Learners as the neighboring public schools in Harlem. The students in Success Academy 4 include 15 percent fewer free lunch students and an economic need index (a measure of students in temporary housing and/or who receive public assistance) that is 35 percent lower than nearby public schools.

Moskowitz's Success Academy 4 has almost none of the highest special needs students as compared to nearby Harlem public schools. In a school with nearly 500 students, Success Academy 4 has zero, or one, such students, while the average Harlem public school includes 14.1 percent such students. With little sense of irony or embarrassment, Moskowitz has attacked Bill de Blasio for preventing the school's expansion inside PS 149. Her school's expansion would have come at the cost of space for students with disabilities.[55] The school has already lost "a fully equipped music room ... A state-mandated SAVE room ... A computer lab ... Individual rooms for occupational and physical therapy ... and the English Language Learners (ELL) classroom," due to earlier Success Academy expansions in the same building.

Moskowitz said, referring to the students in her schools, "we've had these children since kindergarten." But she forgot to mention all the students who have left the school since kindergarten. Or the fact that Harlem Success Academy 4 suspends students at a rate 300 percent higher than the average in the district. Last year's seventh grade class at Harlem Success Academy 1 had a 52.1 percent attrition rate since 2006-07. That's more than half of the kindergarten students gone before they even graduate from middle school. Last year's sixth grade class had a 45.2 percent attrition rate since 2006-07. That's almost half of the kindergarten class gone and two more years left in middle school. In just four years Harlem Success Academy 4 has lost over 21 percent of its students. The pattern of students leaving is not random. Students with low test scores, English Language Learners, and special education students are most likely to disappear from the school's roster. Large numbers of students disappear beginning in 3rd grade, but not in the earlier grades. No natural pattern of student mobility can explain the sudden disappearance of students at the grade when state testing just happens to begin.

Moskowitz made a number of other claims during her *Morning Joe* appearance. She said "we are self-sustaining on the public dollar alone." In fact, Success Academy spends $2,072 more per student than schools serving similar populations.[56]

This additional funding comes from donations by the very same hedge fund moguls who have donated over $400,000 to Governor Cuomo's re-election campaign.[57] Charter supporters in the financial and real estate sector have contributed some $800,000 to Governor Cuomo's campaign.

Moskowitz has said "in terms of cracking the code that's what we've set out to do." But we don't need charter schools to crack the code if the cryptographic key is to keep out the neediest students and kick out students with low test scores. Public schools could do that too. Then they too would have higher test scores and a high attrition rate. They don't do it because it would probably be illegal. And besides, it is the wrong thing to do. Public schools are expected to educate everyone, not just those who are likeliest to succeed.

*This article was co-written with Avi Blaustein*

# THE FATAL FLAW OF THE COMMON CORE STANDARDS

HUFFINGTON POST, MARCH 24, 2014

Across the nation, parents and educators are raising objections to the Common Core standards, and many states are reconsidering whether to abandon them and the federally-funded tests that accompany them. Arne Duncan, Jeb Bush, Bill Gates, the U.S. Chamber of Commerce, and the Business Roundtable vocally support them, yet the unease continues and pushback remains intense.

Why so much controversy?

The complaints are coming from all sides, from Tea Party activists who worry about a federal takeover of education, and from educators, parents, and progressives who believe that the Common Core will standardize instruction and eliminate creativity in their classrooms.

But there is a more compelling reason to object to the Common Core standards.

They were written in a manner that violates the nationally and international recognized process for writing standards. The process by which they were created was so fundamentally flawed that these "standards" should have no legitimacy.

Setting national academic standards is not something done in stealth by a small group of people, funded by one source, and imposed by the lure of a federal grant in a time of austerity.

There is a recognized protocol for writing standards, and

the Common Core standards failed to comply with that protocol.

In the United States, the principles of standard-setting have been clearly spelled out by the American National Standards Institute (ANSI).[58] On its website ANSI describes how standards should be developed in every field:

> ANSI has served in its capacity as administrator and coordinator of the United States private sector voluntary standardization system for more than 90 years. Founded in 1918 by five engineering societies and three government agencies, the Institute remains a private, nonprofit membership organization supported by a diverse constituency of private and public sector organizations.
>
> Throughout its history, ANSI has maintained as its primary goal the enhancement of global competitiveness of U.S. business and the American quality of life by promoting and facilitating voluntary consensus standards and conformity assessment systems and promoting their integrity. The Institute represents the interests of its nearly 1,000 company, organization, government agency, institutional and international members through its office in New York City, and its headquarters in Washington, D.C.

ANSI's fundamental principles of standard-setting are transparency, balance, consensus, and due process, including a right to appeal by interested parties. According to ANSI, there are currently more than 10,000 American national standards, covering a broad range of activities.

The Common Core standards were not written in conformity with the ANSI standard-setting process that is broadly recognized across every field of endeavor.

If the Common Core standards applied to ANSI for recognition, they would be rejected because the process of writing the standards was so deeply flawed and did not adhere to the "ANSI Essential Requirements." ANSI states:

> Due process is the key to ensuring that ANSs are developed in an environment that is equitable, accessible and responsive to the requirements of various stakeholders. The open and fair ANS process ensures that all interested and affected parties have an opportunity to participate in a standard's development. It also serves and protects the public interest since standards developers accredited by ANSI must meet the Institute's requirements for openness, balance, consensus and other due process safeguards.

The Common Core standards cannot be considered standards when judged by the ANSI requirements. According to ANSI, the process of setting standards must be transparent, must involve all interested parties, must not be dominated by a single interest, and must include a process for appeal and revision.

The Common Core standards were not developed in a transparent manner. The standard-setting and writing of the standards included a significant number of people from the testing industry, but did not include a significant number of experienced teachers, subject-matter experts, and other educators from the outset, nor did it engage other informed and concerned interests, such as early childhood educators and educators of children with disabilities. There was no consensus process. The standards were written in 2009 and adopted in 2010 by 45 states and the District of Columbia as a condition of eligibility to compete for $4.3 billion in Race to the Top funding. The process was dominated from start to finish by the Gates Foundation, which funded the standard-setting process. There was no process for appeal or revision, and there is still no process for appeal or revision.

The reason to oppose the Common Core standards is not because of their content – some of which is good, some of which is problematic, some of which needs revision – but because there is no process for appeal or revision.

The reason to oppose the Common Core standards is because they violate the well-established and internationally recognized process for setting standards in a way that is transparent, that recognizes the expertise of those who must implement them, that builds on the consensus of concerned parties, and that permits appeal and revision.

The reason that there is so much controversy and pushback now is that the Gates Foundation and the U.S. Department of Education were in a hurry and decided to ignore the nationally and internationally recognized rules for setting standards, and in doing so, sowed suspicion and distrust. Process matters. According to ANSI, here are the core principles for setting standards:[59]

> The U.S. standardization system is based on the following set of globally accepted principles for standards development:
>
> **Transparency**
>
> Essential information regarding standardization activities is accessible to all interested parties.
>
> **Openness**
>
> Participation is open to all affected interests.
>
> **Impartiality**
>
> No one interest dominates the process or is favored over another.
>
> **Effectiveness and Relevance**
>
> Standards are relevant and effectively respond to regulatory and market needs, as well as scientific and technological developments.
>
> **Consensus**
>
> Decisions are reached through consensus among those affected.
>
> **Performance-based**

Standards are performance based, specifying essential characteristics rather than detailed designs where possible.

**Coherence**

The process encourages coherence to avoid overlapping and conflicting standards.

**Due Process**

Standards development accords with due process so that all views are considered and appeals are possible.

**Technical Assistance**

Assistance is offered to developing countries in the formulation and application of standards.

In addition, U.S. interests strongly agree that the process should be:

**Flexible**

Allowing the use of different methodologies to meet the needs of different technology and product sectors.

**Timely**

So that purely administrative matters do not result in a failure to meet market expectations.

**Balanced among all affected interests**

Lacking most of these qualities, especially due process, consensus among interested groups, and the right of appeal, the Common Core standards cannot be considered authoritative, nor should they be considered standards. The process of creating national academic standards should be revised to accord with the essential and necessary procedural requirements of standard-setting as described by the American National Standards Institute. National standards cannot be created ex nihilo without a transparent, open, participatory consensus process that allows for appeal and revision.

# NEW YORK SCHOOLS: THE ROAR OF THE CHARTERS

## THE NEW YORK REVIEW OF BOOKS - NYR DAILY, MARCH 27, 2014

In his speech at Riverside Church last Sunday, New York Mayor Bill de Blasio tried to end weeks of attacks on his schools policies by striking a conciliatory tone toward the city's privately managed charter schools. He used the charter sector's own rhetoric of "crisis" and "failure" to describe the school system that he inherited from Mayor Bloomberg. He spoke of parents eager to escape failing schools and condemned the "status quo" without noting that it was Bloomberg's status quo. He opposed the idea that public schools and charter schools are competing and called for a new era "in which our charter schools help to uplift our traditional schools." According to *The New York Times,* he called some of the financial leaders on Wall Street, the billionaires who have paid millions of dollars for the ads attacking him, to plead for a truce.

De Blasio decided he could not win this war. The other side had too much money and proved it could drive down his poll numbers. He said that the charter schools could help public schools, but in reality, charter schools could learn a few things from the public schools, like how to teach children with disabilities and second-language English learners. Contrary to popular myth, the charter schools are more racially segregated than public schools, and have performed no better than the public schools on the most recent state tests. But what they have behind them is vast resources, and de Blasio capitulated.

The underlying question remains: How did a privately managed school franchise that serves a tiny portion of New York's students manage to hijack the education reforms of a new mayor with a huge popular mandate?

When Bill de Blasio was running for mayor of New York City last year, he set out an ambitious plan for reforming education. After twelve years of Mayor Bloomberg's obsession with testing, the public was eager for a fresh approach, one that was focused more on helping students than on closing their schools. Bloomberg's haughty indifference to public opinion did not endear him to parents. He displaced tens of thousands of students from their public schools, with never a show of remorse, as he opened hundreds of new small public schools and nearly two hundred privately managed charter schools. Bloomberg's preference for small public schools came at a price; they were unable to offer the full array of advanced courses in math and science, electives, and the choice of foreign languages that larger schools offered. He appointed three chancellors who were not professional educators, one of whom – a publisher – lasted all of ninety days before he removed her. He showed preferential treatment to the hundreds of small public schools that his administration opened, granting them extra resources and allowing them to exclude the neediest students. And he boasted about the explosion of privately managed charter schools, which now enroll 6 percent of the city's children, on whose boards sit titans of Wall Street, the hedge fund managers who belong to Bloomberg's social set.

During the campaign, de Blasio wanted to change the subject from Bloomberg's boutique ideas to a larger vision. He wanted to address the needs of the vast majority of New York City's 1.1 million students. His big idea was to provide universal access to pre-kindergarten, a research-based program that would give a better start to the city's neediest children and after-school activities for adolescents in middle schools. During the campaign, the public widely supported de Blasio's plans,[60] while Bloomberg's education policies usually registered about 25 percent approval.

When asked about charter schools, de Blasio made clear that he felt they had gotten far too much media attention, considering that they serve a small fraction of the population. He pledged that he would charge them rent for use of public space and would not allow any more co-locations – the practice of inserting a new school into a building with an existing school – without community hearings. Co-location happens when a charter school is offered shared space in a building with a public school; it also happens when large schools are divided into four, five, or six small schools operating under the same roof. Public school parents strongly oppose these arrangements. The host public school is often forced to give up its art room, its dance room, its computer room, every room used for any purpose other than classroom instruction, to make way for the unwelcome newcomer. The co-located schools must negotiate over access to the library, the auditorium, the playground. Co-locations cause overcrowding, as well as a competition for space and resources among students and multiple administrators within a single building.

De Blasio's skeptical campaign comments about charter schools unleashed the wrath of New York City's most outspoken charter school leader, Eva Moskowitz. Her Success Academy chain of twenty-two charter schools now enrolls 6,700 students. Because she doesn't have to follow the public school regulations forbidding political activities on school time, she can turn her students and their parents out on short notice for political demonstrations and legislative hearings, dressed in matching t-shirts, carrying posters and banners. A few weeks before last fall's mayoral election, she closed her schools and led a march of students and parents across the Brooklyn Bridge to protest de Blasio's criticism of charter schools. She was accompanied by de Blasio's Republican opponent, Joe Lhota. Voters were unconvinced, however, and de Blasio won in a landslide.

After coming to office, the newly elected mayor focused

his energies on trying to persuade Governor Cuomo and the legislature to enact a new tax in New York City to pay for his goal of universal pre-kindergarten. De Blasio called for a modest tax increase for those who earn over $500,000 a year. It would cost each of them, he said, about $1,000 a year, or less than a cup of soy latte every day at Starbucks. The billionaires were not amused. Nor was Governor Cuomo, who wants to be perceived as a conservative, pro-business Democrat who does not raise taxes.

While de Blasio was pressing for universal pre-kindergarten (or UPK, as it is known), he was faced with a decision about how to handle the dozens of proposals for co-locations and new charter schools that had been hurriedly endorsed by Bloomberg's Panel on Education Policy in the last months of his term. The panel had approved forty-five new schools, seventeen of which were charters. De Blasio decided to approve thirty-six, including fourteen of the seventeen charter school proposals. He did not hold community hearings, as he had promised, so he managed to enrage public school parents whose schools would now suffer the unwanted entry of a new school into their building and, in many cases, an overcrowded building.

The three charter proposals the mayor rejected were part of the Moskowitz charter chain. She had asked for eight new schools – more than any other single applicant – and de Blasio gave her five. Most school leaders would be thrilled to win five new schools. But Eva cried foul and publicly accused the mayor of "evicting" her students. This was despite the fact that two of the three rejected schools did not exist,[61] so no students were affected. The third was Moskowitz's request to expand her elementary school that was already co-located with P.S. 149 in Harlem; Moskowitz wanted to add a middle school. But adding a middle school meant kicking out students with disabilities in P.S. 149, which de Blasio refused to do.

Moskowitz was ready. Her friends on Wall Street and the far-right Walton Family Foundation paid out nearly $5 million for television ads attacking Mayor de Blasio as a heartless, ruthless, possibly racist politician who was at war with charter schools and their needy students. The ads showed the faces of adorable children, all of them being kicked out of "their" school by a vengeful Mayor who hates charter schools. The ads never acknowledged that the Mayor had approved fourteen out of seventeen charter proposals. Moskowitz, whose charter chain pays more than $500,000 a year for the services of for SDK Knickerbocker, a high-powered D.C. public relations firm, also made the rounds of television talk shows, where she got free air time to lash out at de Blasio for allegedly "evicting" her needy students[62] from "the highest performing school in New York State." Meanwhile, the Murdoch-owned media – not only *The New York Post* but also *The Wall Street Journal* and Fox News – kept up a steady barrage of hostile stories echoing Moskowitz's claims against de Blasio.

None of the talking heads checked the facts.[63] None knew or acknowledged that approving the middle school Moskowitz was denied would have meant the *actual* eviction of the neediest students of all – students at P.S. 149 with special needs. Or that her own existing school in that building has *no* students with high levels of disability, in contrast with Harlem's neighborhood public schools, where such students account for 14 percent of the school population. Or that Moskowitz's school has half as many students who are English learners as the neighborhood public schools. Or that her school is not the highest performing school in the state or the city. In English language arts, Moskowitz's Harlem Success Academy 4 ranked eighty-first in the city, with 55 percent of its students passing the latest state test; in math, the school was thirteenth in the city, with 83 percent of students passing the state test. Or that nearly half her students leave within a few years. Or that her schools spend $2,000 more per student than the neighboring schools. Or that Moskowitz is paid $485,000 a year to oversee fewer than seven thousand students.

All of these facts were known by the de Blasio administration. But the new mayor seemed helpless. Somehow this man who had run a brilliant campaign to change the city was left speechless by the charter lobby. His poll numbers took a steep dive. He never called a press conference to explain his criteria for approving or rejecting charter schools, each of which made sense. For example, he would not approve a charter if it displaced students with disabilities, if it placed elementary students in a building with high school students, if it required heavy construction, or if it had fewer than 250 students. Reasonable though his criteria were, they were not enough for the charter lobby. His speech at Riverside Church offered an olive branch, all but conceding that the charter lobby had beaten him. He followed up his conciliatory remarks by creating a committee to review the space needs of the city's schools and appointed to it representatives of the charter sector, which remains hungry for more free space from the Mayor.

Meanwhile, Moskowitz began using political leverage as well. On the same day that de Blasio organized a rally in Albany on behalf of raising taxes on the rich to pay for UPK, she closed her schools and bused thousands of students and parents to Albany for a pro-charter school rally. Governor Andrew Cuomo stood by her side, pledging to "save" charter schools and to protect them from paying rent; his ardent devotion to the charter cause may have been abetted by the $800,000 in campaign contributions he received from charter advocates in the financial industry.[64]

For its part, the Republican-dominated State Senate demonstrated loyalty to Eva Moskowitz by passing a budget resolution with language forbidding the mayor from displacing a co-located charter school and forbidding him from charging rent to a private corporation (a charter school) using public space. Not only had Moskwitz cleverly portrayed herself as a victim, she had managed to make her narrow cause more important than universal prekindergarten and after-school programs for teens. She demonstrated that she was more powerful than the mayor or his schools chancellor. She won the battle of the moment.

But Moskowitz unknowingly taught the public a different lesson, which may be important in the future. Her schools do not operate like public schools. They are owned and managed by a private corporation with a government contract. They make their own rules. They choose their own students, kick out those they don't want, and answer to no one. No public school would be allowed to close its doors and take its students on a political march across the Brooklyn Bridge or bus them to Albany to lobby the statehouse; the principal would be fired instantly.

Consider the court battle initiated by Moskowitz that played out in the midst of the confrontation with the mayor. A judge in New York's State Supreme Court ruled,[65] as Moskowitz hoped, that the State Comptroller has no power to audit her schools, because they are "not a unit of the state." Put another way, her schools are not public schools. And, as the public begins to understand what that means, that lesson may ultimately be the undoing of this stealth effort to transfer public funds to support a small number of privately managed schools, amply endowed by billionaires and foundations, that refuse to pay rent and are devoted to competing with, not helping, the general school population.

What will it mean for New York City to have two school systems, both supported with public money, with one free to choose and remove its students and the other required to accept all students? A recent study found that New York State has the most segregated schools in the nation,[66] and that the charters are even more segregated than the public schools. In 2014, the year that we remember the sixtieth anniversary of *Brown v. Board of Education,* it is passing strange to find that New York City and school districts across the nation are embarked on the re-creation of a dual school system.

# OPT YOUR CHILD OUT OF STATE TESTING: DON'T FEED THE MACHINE

HUFFINGTON POST, MARCH 31, 2014

This week begins the make-or-break, do-or-die standardized testing that will label your child a success or a failure. I urge you not to let your child take the state test.

Opt out.

The best test for students is the test made by their teacher. Teachers know what they taught, they test what the students were taught. They get instant feedback. They can find out immediately which students didn't understand the lesson and need extra help. They can get instant feedback about their own success or lack of success if the students didn't learn what they taught.

The standardized tests are useless for instant feedback. They have no diagnostic value. The test asks questions that may cover concepts that were never introduced in class. The test is multiple-choice, creating an unrealistic expectation that all questions have only one right answer. The tests may have errors, e.g., two right answers or no right answers or a confusing question. The test results are returned months after the test, meaning that the student now has a different teacher. The test scores give no breakdown of what the student did or did not understand, just a score.

These days, the purpose of the tests is to evaluate the

teacher. Most researchers agree that using student scores to evaluate teachers gives inaccurate and unusable results. This year's "effective" teacher may be next year's "ineffective" teacher. "Value-added-measurement" has not proven to work anywhere. Most teachers don't teach tested subjects and they are assigned a rating based on the results of the school as a whole. A music teacher may be found "ineffective" based on the school's math scores. This is madness.

Because the tests have no diagnostic value for students, they are worthless. If they can't be used to help students or to improve instruction, they shouldn't be used at all. We can learn all we need to know about states or cities by sampling like NAEP, which compares states to states, and cities to cities. We can learn all we need to know about individual students by relying on teacher judgment and testing in specific grades, like 4 and 8.

The reason we have so much testing is because our policy-makers don't trust teachers. If we trusted teachers, we would let them teach and trust them to do what is right for their students. The more we distrust teachers, the less appealing is teaching as a job or a profession.

Another reason we test so much is the power of the testing corporations, which pay lobbyists in Washington and the states to push for more testing. This is big business.

Elite private schools rarely use standardized tests. They trust their teachers to evaluate their students' progress.

We are trapped in a machine that is profitable for the few, but demoralizing to teachers and students.

Testing is not teaching. It steals time from instruction. Making it so important leads to schools narrowing the curriculum, cutting funding for the arts, eliminating social workers and counselors, cutting recess and physical education. Making testing so important leads to states and districts gaming the system, to schools shedding low-scoring students, to cheating, to teaching to the test, and to other anti-educational actions.

How to stop the machine?

Opt out.

Don't let your children take the test.

Deny the machine the data on which it feeds. There are corporations ready to mine your child's data. Don't let them have it.

I am reminded of the famous speech by Mario Savio, leader of the Free Speech Movement, during a protest rally at the University of California at Berkeley in 1964. He said:[67]

> There's a time when the operation of the machine becomes so odious, makes you so sick at heart that you can't take part! You can't even passively take part! And you've got to put your bodies upon the gears and upon the wheels, upon the levers, upon all the apparatus – and you've got to make it stop! And you've got to indicate to the people who run it, to the people who own it – that unless you're free, the machine will be prevented from working at all!

Assert your independence. Protect your child. Stop the machine. Opt out.

# NEW YORK'S DUMB STATE BUDGET

HUFFINGTON POST, APRIL 2, 2014

In writing the state budget, New York legislators totally capitulated to the billionaire-funded charter industry. Of course, they were egged on by Governor Cuomo, who now sees himself as a national leader of the school privatization movement. He is even leading a retreat[68] with other prominent figures of the movement to turn public schools over to private management. Please note that the "philosophers" who wrote the invitation to the retreat couldn't manage to spell the name of James Russell Lowell correctly.

The budget deal includes these terms:

- The private corporations that manage charter schools in New York City will never have to pay for using public space.
- The de Blasio administration must offer space to all charters approved in the dying days of the Bloomberg administration. De Blasio had previously approved 14 of 17, now he must approve all 17. Whatever Eva Moskowitz wants, Eva gets.
- The charters located inside public school buildings may expand as much as they wish, and the mayor can't stop them. If this means pushing out children with severe disabilities, so be it. If it means taking control

of the entire building and pushing all of the students out of their public school, so be it.
- If a charter chooses to rent private space, the New York City public schools must pay their rent. Where will the money come from? Well, the public schools can always increase class size, or they can lay off social workers and counselors and psychologists. Or they could cut back on the arts. That's their problem.

In addition, the budget deal includes a provision to authorize merit bonuses of $20,000 for "highly effective" teachers based on the state's highly ineffective educator evaluation system. No one bothered to tell our legislators that merit pay failed in Nashville, where the bonus was $15,000, failed in New York City, where the bonus went to the whole school, failed in Chicago, and has consistently failed for nearly 100 years.

The bottom line is that when billionaires talk, the New York legislature and Governor Cuomo listen. Actually, they sit up, bark, and roll over.

You see, the charter schools say they get higher test scores, but they don't. On the 2013 state tests, the charter schools had the same scores as the public schools. The billionaires believe that students with high test scores deserve more privileges than students with low scores. Sort of like their own world, where those with the most money get to live in bigger houses, drive nicer cars, and have multiple privileges.

How did the legislature capitulate to the billionaires? Ask Paul Tudor Jones, who manages $13 billion and has decided that it is up to him to "save" American education. Ask Dan Loeb, hedge fund manager. Ask Democrats for Education Reform, which is the organization of hedge fund managers that is politically active in many states to promote privatization. Maybe they can explain why a child with high test scores is more deserving than a child with disabilities.

# WHAT DO WE CALL OPPONENTS OF CORPORATE EDUCATION REFORM?

HUFFINGTON POST, APRIL 7, 2014

For the past decade or more, a bevy of very powerful people have savaged our nation's public schools while calling themselves "reformers." It is perfectly clear that they have no desire to "reform" our public schools but to privatize and monetize them. The Bush-Obama era of "measure and punish" has not reformed our public schools, but has plunged them into unending disruption, demoralization, and upheaval.

The so-called reformers have honed their PR message well. They couldn't very well go to the public and say "with the help of some Wall Street billionaires and foundations run by billionaires, we have come to demolish your community's schools and hand them over to corporations." That wouldn't play well. So they sold their goals as "reform," even as they used the power of the federal government through No Child Left Behind and Race to the Top to close community public schools, to demean the teaching profession, and to make pie-in-the-sky promises about the wonders of choice. George Wallace, Strom Thurmond, and other segregationists of their generation (the 1950s and 1960s) must be laughing in their graves to hear our "reformers," even our secretary of education, proclaiming the glories of school choice.

What should we call these people who want to destroy

public education as a civic responsibility? The Status Quo. They control the U.S. Department of Education and most state education departments, and they control federal policy. They control our nation's biggest foundations – Gates, Walton, Broad, Dell, Arnold and others. They have the support of media moguls like Rupert Murdoch, Mortimer Zuckerman, Mark Zuckerberg, and Jeff Bezos, as well as the editorial boards of major newspapers. They own NBC's *Education Nation*. They *are* the Status Quo.

What do we call the millions of parents and teachers, principals, superintendents, school board members, and researchers who fight for democratic control of education? The Resistance.

We cannot be bought off or intimidated. We know that the strategies and mandates of the Status Quo have failed wherever they were tried. We fight for our children. We fight for democracy. We oppose segregation, budget cuts, high-stakes testing, closing public schools, rating teachers by student test scores, and labeling children by test scores. We will resist their bad ideas. We will resist their efforts to destroy public education. We will resist privatization. We will fight for a better future for all the children of our nation. We will not allow the Status Quo to monetize what belongs to all of us.

# NEW REPORT REBUKES CENTRAL FEATURE OF 'RACE TO THE TOP'

HUFFINGTON POST, APRIL 13, 2014

The central feature of the Obama administration's $5 billion "Race to the Top" program was sharply refuted last week by the American Statistical Association, one of the nation's leading scholarly organizations. Spurred on by the administration's combination of federal cash and mandates, most states are now using student test scores to rank and evaluate teachers. This method of evaluating teachers by test scores is called value-added measurement, or VAM. Teachers' compensation, their tenure, bonuses, and other rewards and sanctions are tied directly to the rise or fall of their student test scores, which the Obama administration considers a good measure of teacher quality.

Secretary Arne Duncan believes so strongly in VAM that he has threatened to punish Washington State for refusing to adopt this method of evaluating teachers and principals. In New York, a state court fined New York City $150 million for failing to agree on a VAM plan.

The ASA issued a short but stinging statement that strongly warned against the misuse of VAM.[69] The organization neither condemns nor promotes the use of VAM, but its warnings about the limitations of this methodology clearly demonstrate that the Obama administration has committed the nation's public schools to a policy fraught with error. ASA warns that VAMs are "complex statistical models" that require "high-level statistical expertise" and awareness of their "assumptions and possible limitations," especially when they are used for high-stakes purposes as is now common. Few, if any, state education departments have the statistical expertise to use VAM models appropriately. In some states, like Florida, teachers have been rated based on the scores of students they never taught.

The ASA points out that VAMs are based on standardized tests and "do not directly measure potential teacher contributions toward other student outcomes." They typically measure correlation, not causation. That means that the rise or fall of student test scores attributed to the teacher might actually be caused by other factors outside the classroom, not under the teacher's control. The VAM rating of teachers is so unstable that it may change if the same students are given a different test. The ASA's most damning indictment of the policy promoted so vigorously by Secretary of Education Arne Duncan is:

> Most VAM studies find that teachers account for about one percent to 14 percent of the variability in test scores, and that the majority of opportunities for quality improvement are found in the system-level conditions. Ranking teachers by their VAM scores can have unintended consequences that reduce quality.

The ASA points out:

> This is not saying that teachers have little effect on students, but that variation among teachers accounts for a small part of the variation in scores. The majority of the variation in test scores is attributable to factors outside of the teacher's control such as student and family background, poverty, curriculum, and unmeasured influences.

As many education researchers have explained – including a joint statement by the American Educational Research Association and the National Academy of Education[70] – the VAM ratings of those who teach children with disabilities and English language learners will be low, because these children have greater learning challenges than their peers, as will the ratings of those who teach gifted students, because the latter group has already reached a ceiling. Like the ASA, those two groups agreed that test scores are affected by many factors besides the teacher, not only the family, but the school's leadership, its resources, class size, curriculum, as well as the student's motivation, attendance and health. Yet the Obama administration and most of our states are holding teachers alone accountable for student test scores.

The ASA warns that the current heavy reliance on VAMs for high-stakes testing and their simplistic interpretation may have negative effects on the quality of education. There will surely be unintended consequences, such as a diminishment in the number of people willing to become teachers in an environment where "quality" is so crudely measured. There will assuredly be more teaching to the test. With the Obama administration's demand for VAM:

> ... more classroom time might be spent on test preparation and on specific content from the test at the exclusion of content that may lead to better long-term learning gains or motivation for students. Certain schools may be hard to staff if there is a perception that it is harder for teachers to achieve good VAM scores when working in them. Over-reliance on VAM scores may foster a competitive environment, discouraging collaboration and efforts to improve the educational system as a whole.

For five years, the Obama administration has been warned by scholars and researchers that its demand for value-added assessment is having harmful effects on teachers and students, on the morale of teachers, on the recruitment of new teachers, and on the quality of education, which has been reduced to nothing more than standardized testing. Secretary Duncan has brushed aside all objections and pushed full steam ahead with his disastrous policies, like Captain Ahab in pursuit of the great white whale, heedless to all warnings.

Based on the complementary statements of our nation's most eminent scholarly associations, any teacher who is wrongfully terminated by Duncan's favorite but deeply flawed methodology should sue for wrongful termination. What is not so clear is how the nation can protect our children and our public schools from this administration's obsessive reliance on standardized tests to rank and rate students, teachers, principals and schools.

# WHY DOESN'T THE NEW YORK TIMES UNDERSTAND THE CONTROVERSY OVER COMMON CORE?

## HUFFINGTON POST, APRIL 20, 2014

*"It shows beyond doubt that family income and test scores are tightly correlated. A chart of educational attainment in school districts, arrayed by family income, shows that: "Sixth graders in the richest school districts are four grade levels ahead of children in the poorest districts." That is a huge test score gap."*
*– Diane Ravitch's Blog*

In story after story, *The New York Times* consistently misses the essence of the controversy surrounding Common Core.

Sunday's *New York Times* gives its lead article on page 1, column right, top of the fold,[71] to the battle raging within the Republican Party about the Common Core. On one side is Jeb Bush, standing up for the Common Core standards and presumably a moderate (let's not talk about his fight for vouchers and for the destruction of public education in Florida), while on the other are figures like Ted Cruz and other extremists of the party. Common Core, we are told, is now the "wedge issue" in the Republican party, with sensible people like Jeb Bush fending off the extremists.

A few weeks ago, the newspaper wrote an editorial enthusiastically endorsing the Common Core standards, while giving no evidence for its enthusiasm other than the promises offered by the advocates of Common Core.

Story after story has repeated the narrative invented by Arne Duncan, that the only opponents of the Common Core are members of the Tea Party and other extremists.

Occasionally a story will refer to extremists on the right and the left, as though no reasonable person could possibly doubt the claims made on behalf of the Common Core.

Of course, David Brooks' column on Friday[72] echoed the now familiar trope of *The New York Times* that only extremists could oppose this worthy and entirely laudable endeavor.

Missing is any acknowledgement of the many researchers who have challenged the wacky assumption that standards alone will cause everyone's achievement to rise higher and higher, despite no evidence for this assertion.

Missing is any recognition that there are reputable educators and scholars and parents who are disturbed either by the substance of the standards or by the development process. Anthony Cody, for example, just won the Education Writers Association's first prize award for his series of blogs challenging the claims of the Common Core.

Missing is the pushback from teachers that caused the leaders of the NEA and the AFT to call for a slowdown in implementation of the standards. The media sees this only as teachers' fear of being evaluated by tests.

Missing is the concern of early childhood educators about the developmental inappropriateness of the standards for the early grades, which reflects the fact that no early childhood educator participated in drafting the standards. Also missing from the writing group was any educator knowledgeable about children with disabilities or English language learners.

Missing is any acknowledgement that not a single classroom teacher was included in the small group that wrote the standards, and that the largest contingent on the "working groups" was from the testing industry.

Missing is any suggestion that the writing of the standards was not "state-led," but was the product of a small group of insider organizations inside the Beltway, heavily funded by one organization, the Gates Foundation.

Missing is any recognition that there is no appeals process, no means to revise standards that make no sense when applied in real classrooms with real students.

Missing is any awareness that the Obama administration made eligibility for $4.35 billion in Race to the Top funding contingent on state adoption of "college and career ready" standards, which turned out to be the Common Core standards. How else to explain their rapid adoption by 45 states?

Missing is any acknowledgement that there is very little connection between the quality of any state's standards and its performances on the NAEP, or that some states with standards higher than the Common Core dropped their proven standards so as to be eligible for the new federal funding.

Missing is any recognition that the Common Core standards are an essential ingredient in a Big Data plan that involves a multi-billion dollar investment in new hardware, new software, and new bandwidth for Common Core testing, all of which will be done (for no good reason) online.

Missing is the issue of value-added measurement (VAM) of teachers and school-closings based on test scores, or the fact that major scholarly organizations (the American Educational Research Association, the National Academy of Education, and the American Statistical Association) have pointed out the inaccuracy and instability of VAM. Nor has it ever been reported by *The New York Times* that these same organizations have said that teachers' influence on variation in test scores ranges from 1-15 percent, with the influence of the family, especially family income and education, looming far larger.

Question: How can the nation's "newspaper of record" be so seriously indifferent to or ignorant of the major education issue of our day?

# WHAT POWERFUL AND GREEDY ELITES ARE HIDING WHEN THEY SCAPEGOAT THE SCHOOLS

HUFFINGTON POST,MAY 5, 2014

*"I have nothing against the wealthy. I don't care that some people have more worldly goods than others. I understand that life's not fair. I just harbor this feeling that a person ought to be able to get by on $100 million or so and not keep piling up riches while so many others don't know how they will feed their children tonight." – Diane Ravitch's Blog*

Our economy is changing in ways that are alarming. Income inequality[73] and wealth inequality[74] are at their highest point in many decades, and some say we are back to the age of the robber barons. Most of the gains in the economy since the great recession of 2008 have benefited the 1 percent,[75] or even the 1 percent of the 1 percent. The middle class is shrinking, and we no longer have the richest middle class in the world.[76] The U.S. has the highest child poverty rate of any of the advanced nations of the world – and, no, I don't count Romania as an advanced nation, having visited that nation, which suffered decades of economic plunder and stagnation under the Communist Ceausescu regime.

Forbes reports that there were 442 billionaires in the U.S. in 2013. Nice for them. Taxes have dropped dramatically for the top 1 percent[77] since the 1970s. But don't call them plutocrats. Call them our "job creators," even though they should be called our "job outsourcers."

Now what caused these changing conditions? My guess would be that unbridled capitalism generates inequality. Deregulation benefits the few, not the many. People with vast wealth give large sums to political candidates, who when elected, protect the economic interests of their benefactors. Anyone who wants to run for president must raise $1 billion or so. Where do you raise that kind of money? You go to the super-rich, who have the money to fund candidates of both parties, as well as an agenda to keep their money and make more.

A recent paper[78] by Martin Gilens of Princeton University and Benjamin I. Page of Northwestern University concludes:

> ... economic elites and organized groups representing business interests have substantial independent impacts on U.S. government policy, while mass-based interest groups and average citizens have little or no independent influence. Our results provide substantial support for theories of Economic Elite Domination and for theories of Biased Pluralism, but not for theories of Majoritarian Electoral Democracy or Majoritarian Pluralism.

Recent decisions by the U.S. Supreme Court[79] removing limits on campaign contributions by corporations and individuals reinforce control of our political system by elites. The danger signals for democracy are loud and clear.

We often hear talk of the "hollowing out" of the middle class. We know that many regions in our country are economically depressed because they lost the local industries that provided good jobs for high school graduates. Some of those jobs were lost to new technologies, and some were outsourced to low-wage countries. Free trade sounds good, but did the politicians realize how many millions of jobs and thousands of corporations would move to Mexico, China, Bangladesh, and other countries that do not pay what Americans consider a living wage?

Instead of looking in the mirror, our politicians blame the schools. They say that we lost those jobs because our schools were preparing students poorly, not because the "job creators" wanted to export jobs to countries that pay their workers a few dollars a day.

The politicians say we must send everyone to college so we can be "globally competitive," but how will we compete with nations that pay workers and professionals only a fraction of what Americans expect to be paid and need to be paid to have a middle-class life? How can we expect more students to finish college when states are shifting college costs onto individuals and burdening them with huge debt? How can we motivate students to stay in college when so many new jobs in the next decade[80] – retail clerks, fast-food workers, home health aides, janitors, construction workers, truck drivers, etc. – do not require a college degree? The only job in the top 10 fastest growing occupations that requires a college degree is as a registered nurse.

So here we are, with politicians who could not pass an eighth grade math test blaming our teachers, our schools, and our students for economic conditions that they did not create and cannot control.

In a just and sensible world, our elected officials would change the tax rates, taxing both wealth and income to reduce inequality. There is no good reason for anyone to be a billionaire. When one man or woman is worth billions of dollars, it is obscene. A person can live very handsomely if their net worth is "only" $100 million. How many homes, how many yachts, how many jets, does one person need? In terms of income taxes, consider this. Under President Dwight D. Eisenhower,[81] the marginal tax rate for the very rich was 91 percent, it is now 35 percent. The tax on long-term capital gains has dropped from 25 percent to 15 percent. No wonder that billionaire investor Warren Buffett famously said that there has indeed been class warfare,[82] and that "my class has won." Buffett noticed that secretaries in his office were paying a higher tax rate than he was. He even took to the op-ed page of *The New York Times* to complain that the tax code unfairly spared the richest Americans.[83]

Will the "job creators" lose all ambition if they can't pile up billions and billions? I doubt it very much. Surely there will be even more people yearning to get very rich, even if their wealth has a limit of $100 million or even $200 million.

We need to spend more to reduce poverty. We need to spend more to make sure that all children get a good start in life. We need to reduce class sizes for our neediest children. We need to assure free medical care for those who have none. We have many needs, but we won't begin to address them until we change our tax codes to reduce inequality.

# 60 YEARS AFTER BROWN V. BOARD OF EDUCATION, WILL CONGRESS REVIVE A DUAL SCHOOL SYSTEM?

HUFFINGTON POST, MAY 17, 2014

*"One of ALEC's primary goals is the privatization of public education. Pence has faithfully followed the ALEC script in pushing for charters and vouchers in Indiana." – Diane Ravitch's Blog*

Congress is considering new charter legislation, awarding more money to the charter sector, which will operate with minimal accountability or transparency.

The bill has already passed the House of Representatives with a bipartisan majority and now moves to the Senate.

Make no mistake, on the 60th anniversary of the *Brown v. Board of Education* decision, Congress is set to expand a dual school system. One sector, privately managed, may choose its students, exclude those who might pull down its test scores, and kick out those it doesn't want. The other sector – the public schools – must take in all students, even those kicked out by the charters.

One sector – the charter sector – may enroll no students with profound disabilities, while the public schools are required by federal law to accept them all. The charter sector may accept only half as many English language learners, while the public schools are required to accept them all. Some charter schools push out children who are behavior problems, the public schools must take them all.

This is a dual school system, one bound by laws, the other deregulated. One free to select the "winners", the other bound to accept all.

Will federally-funded charters be allowed to operate for profit, as many charters do? Will they pay their executives exorbitant salaries, of more than $400,000, as some charters do? Will they be exempt from nepotism laws, as many charters are? Will charter leaders be allowed to hire their relatives or give them contracts? Will they be exempt from conflict of interest and self-dealing laws, as they are in some states? Will members of the board be permitted to win profitable contracts from the board?

The growth of the charter sector has been driven by a strange coalition. Charters are supported by wealthy hedge fund managers who give generously to individual charters and to charter chains, and they fund political candidates who support charters. Charters are supported enthusiastically by the Obama administration, which endorses the privatization of public schools. Charters are a favorite of conservative groups like ALEC (the American Legislative Exchange Council) and right-wing governors. Charters receive millions from some of the nation's wealthiest foundations, including the Gates Foundation, the Broad Foundation, and the Walton Family Foundation.

This odd coalition doesn't seem to care that it is reversing the *Brown v. Board of Education* decision of 1954. The fact that charters are highly segregated does not trouble them. The fact that charters undermine public education, an institution that is basic to our democracy, does not trouble them.

The federal courts bore the historic burden of dismantling the long-established institution of legally-enforced racial segregation. Sadly, as new justices were appointed, the federal courts abandoned that role. The U.S. Department of Education also abandoned its once strong dedication to eliminating segregation and ignored its return. Both parties lost interest in integration. Imagine if the Obama administration had dedicated its $5 billion in Race to the Top funds as rewards for districts that increased racial integration. Instead, it initiated a pursuit of higher test scores, and dismissed segregation as yesterday's issue.

Once there was a dream that American children could live and learn together. That was Dr. Martin Luther King's dream. The charter movement says that dream is over, if it ever existed, and that the democratic dream of equal educational opportunity for all in common schools controlled by local communities is history, a relic of the past, replaced by the 21st century reality of a dual school system, separate and unequal.

Should we acquiesce in a social arrangement that we know is wrong? Should we celebrate the official approval of segregated schools? Should we hail Congress for bending to the new realities of segregation and academic apartheid? Should we cheer Congressional support for privately-managed schools that get public funds but are not subject to the same requirements of accountability and transparency as public schools?

The 60th anniversary of the *Brown v. Board of Education* decision is a time to recall how far short we have fallen from our ideals. And a time to plan for the day when we can reclaim them and build the America we want for our children and grandchildren.

# GLENN BECK'S ANGRY AND IGNORANT BOOK ABOUT COMMON CORE

HUFFINGTON POST, MAY 21, 2014

Over the years, we have seen a steady dumbing down of American culture, especially in the mass media. Whether newspapers, radio, or television, we have lost many of our well-educated, cultured, well-informed thinkers. Often they have been replaced by shock jocks, ranting talk show hosts, and an entire cable channel devoted to trashing liberals, liberal social programs, and labor unions.

I miss Walter Cronkite, Dan Rather, and dozens of other smart journalists who brought more than their opinions to their journalism. Bill Moyers is one of that breed. We need more.

Another thing I don't understand is why people on the far right like to paint their own country in the most negative tones while pretending to be patriots. I used to see a lot of this in right-wing think tanks, where people seized gleefully on every negative statistic to prove what a bad country this is, how horrible our public schools are, how dumb our teachers are, how we are doomed. Michelle Rhee's advertisements often make me think she really hates this country, that no one is smart enough or good enough for her.

All of this is a long-winded way of disassociating myself from Glenn Beck's screed against Common Core and public education. It is called *Conform: Exposing the Truth about Common Core and Public Education*.

Here is a review by Hilary Tone of Media Matters[84] that gives you an idea of how false and hysterical this book is. It is clear that Beck did not read *Reign of Error*. I won't be reviewing *Conform*. I am not interested in reading or writing about crazy right-wing attacks on our great American tradition of public education or on our nation.

In the same vein as the one now being mined by Glenn Beck is a video about a Florida legislator[85] denouncing the Common Core because it will make all children gay. Seriously.

This is crazy stuff, and it makes it difficult if not impossible to have a reasonable discussion about the pros and cons of the Common Core. The Common Core is not wicked, evil, or dangerous, nor are those who wrote it.

Perhaps my critique of Common Core is too sophisticated for those who want simplistic answers. I don't condemn those who want to use Common Core. I don't think they are wrong or un-American. If they like it, they should use it.

My advice to states that want to use it, who think it is better than what they do now, is this:

- Convene your best classroom teachers and review CCSS. Fix whatever needs fixing. Recognize that not all students learn at the same pace. Leave time for play in K-3.
- Do not use the federally funded tests. Do not spend billions on hardware and software for testing. Let teachers write their own tests. Use standardized tests sparingly, like a state-level NAEP, to establish trends, not to label or rank children and teachers.
- Do not use results of CCSS to produce ratings to "measure" teacher quality. Study after study, report after report warns that this is a very bad idea that will harm the quality of education by focusing too much on standardized tests, narrowing the curriculum, and

forcing teachers to teach to the tests.

- Do not let your judgment be clouded by people who make hysterical claims about the standards or those who wrote them.

# BUSINESS GROUP PLEDGES $500,000 CAMPAIGN FOR COMMON CORE - WHO WILL IT REALLY BENEFIT?

HUFFINGTON POST, MAY 30, 2014

Who supports Common Core? Who opposes the new national standards? Are the critics right or left?

A new group in New York has been created to spend $500,000 to promote Common Core.[86] This article says the group consists of business organizations but its prominent supporters are the Gates Foundation, the Helmsley Foundation, Michelle Rhee's StudentsFirst, and the Gates-funded Educators for Excellence.

Allegedly, business wants "higher standards" because the CCSS will close the skills gap and produce more qualified workers. Is there any evidence for this belief? No. On the first round of Common Core testing, 70 percent of students in New York failed. The failure rate for minorities, English learners, and students with disabilities was even higher. Among students with disabilities, for example, 95 percent failed the Common Core tests.

Where is the evidence that Common Core will make all students college-ready? There is none.

Would business groups be equally willing to invest in a campaign for equitable school funding, reduced class sizes, universal pre-school, pre-natal care, after-school programs, school nurses, and a raise in the minimum wage? All of these have a solid research base. They are proven strategies for reform.

Do the business leaders think that CCSS makes those investments unnecessary?

It is certainly appealing to fiscal conservatives to believe that higher standards can somehow magically solve the problems of huge economic and social inequality. CCSS, they imagine, can compensate for the fact that nearly one-quarter of our children live in poverty.

Someday, maybe 12 years from now they think, all children will be college-ready, even if they live in squalor or have no home, even if they attend overcrowded classes with inexperienced teachers. Are they gullible? Or do they believe the public can be easily deceived? Remember when the same groups believed that tougher standards, tests, and accountability would raise up all children and "no child" would be "left behind"? We spent billions on tests and consultants, on closing schools and opening schools, and that didn't work out.

Fool me once, shame on you. Fool me twice, shame on me.

# TIME FOR CONGRESS TO INVESTIGATE BILL GATES' COUP

## HUFFINGTON POST, JUNE 9, 2014

The story in *The Washington Post* about Bill Gates' swift and silent takeover[87] of American education is startling. His role and the role of the U.S. Department of Education in drafting and imposing the Common Core standards on almost every state should be investigated by Congress.

The idea that the richest man in America can purchase, and working closely with the U.S. Department of Education impose, new and untested academic standards on the nation's public schools is a national scandal. A Congressional investigation is warranted.

The close involvement of Arne Duncan raises questions about whether the law was broken.

Thanks to the story in *The Washington Post* and to diligent bloggers,[88] we now know that one very rich man bought the enthusiastic support of interest groups on the left and right to campaign for the Common Core.

Who knew that American education was for sale?

Who knew that federalism could so easily be dismissed as a relic of history? Who knew that Gates and Duncan, working as partners, could dismantle and destroy state and local control of education?

The revelation that education policy was shaped by one unelected man, underwriting dozens of groups and allied with the Secretary of Education whose staff was laced with Gates' allies, is ample reason for Congressional hearings.

I have written on various occasions[89] [90] that I could not support the Common Core standards because they were developed and imposed without regard to democratic process. The writers of the standards included no early childhood educators, no educators of children with disabilities, and no experienced classroom teachers. Indeed, the largest contingent of the drafting committee were representatives of the testing industry. No attempt was made to have pilot testing of the standards in real classrooms with real teachers and students. The standards do not permit any means to challenge, correct, or revise them.

In a democratic society, process matters. The high-handed manner in which these standards were written and imposed in record time makes them unacceptable. These standards not only undermine state and local control of education, but the manner in which they were written and adopted was authoritarian. No one knows how they will work, yet dozens of groups have been paid millions of dollars by the Gates Foundation to claim that they are absolutely vital for our economic future, based on no evidence whatever.

Why does state and local control matter? Until now, in education, the American idea has been that no single authority has all the answers. Local boards are best equipped to handle local problems. States set state policy, in keeping with the concept that states are "laboratories of democracy," where new ideas can evolve and prove themselves. In our federal system, the federal government has the power to protect the civil rights of students, to conduct research, and to redistribute resources to the neediest children and schools.

Do we need to compare the academic performance of students in different states? We already have the means to do so with the federally funded National Assessment of Educational Progress (NAEP). It has been supplying state comparisons since

1992.

Will national standards improve test scores? There is no reason to believe so. Brookings scholar Tom Loveless predicted two years ago[91] that the Common Core standards would make little or no difference. The biggest test-score gaps, he wrote, are within the same state, not between states. Some states with excellent standards have low scores, and some with excellent standards have large gaps among different groups of students.

The reality is that the most reliable predictors of test scores are family income and family education. Nearly one-quarter of America's children live in poverty. The Common Core standards divert our attention from the root causes of low academic achievement.

Worse, at a time when many schools have fiscal problems and are laying off teachers, nurses, and counselors, and are eliminating arts programs, the nation's schools will be forced to spend billions of dollars on Common Core materials, testing, hardware, and software.

Microsoft, Pearson, and other entrepreneurs will reap the rewards of this new marketplace. Our nation's children will not.

Who decided to monetize the public schools? Who determined that the federal government should promote privatization and neglect public education? Who decided that the federal government should watch in silence as school segregation resumed and grew? Who decided that schools should invest in Common Core instead of smaller classes and school nurses?

These are questions that should be asked at Congressional hearings.

# VERGARA DECISION IS LATEST ATTEMPT TO BLAME TEACHERS AND WEAKEN PUBLIC EDUCATION

HUFFINGTON POST, JUNE 11, 2014

Judge Rolf M. Treu, who decided the Vergara case, declared that he was shocked, shocked! to learn from Professor Raj Chetty and Professor Thomas Kane of Harvard about the enormous harm that one "grossly ineffective" teacher can do to a child's lifetime earnings or to their academic gains.[92 93]

How did he define "grossly ineffective" teacher? He didn't. How did these dreadful teachers get tenure? Clearly, some grossly incompetent principal must have granted it to them. What was the basis, factual or theoretical, that the students would have had high scores if their teachers did not have the right to due process? He didn't say.

As I see it, the theory behind the case is that low test scores are caused by bad teachers. Get rid of the bad teachers, replace them with average teachers, and all students will get high test scores. You might call it the judicial version of No Child Left Behind – that is, pull the right policy levers, say testing and accountability, or eliminate tenure – and every single child in America will be proficient by 2014. Congress should hang its collective head in shame for having passed that ridiculous law, yet it still sits on the books as the scorned, ineffective, toxic law of the land.

Judge Treu was also regurgitating the unproven claims behind Race to the Top, specifically that using test scores to evaluate teachers will make it possible to weed out "bad teachers," recruit and reward top teachers, and test scores will rise to the top. Given this theory, a concept like tenure (due process) slows down the effort to fire those "grossly ineffective" teachers and delays the day when every student is proficient.

Relying on Chetty and Kane, Judge Treu is quite certain that the theory of universal proficiency is correct. Thus, in his thinking, it becomes a matter of urgency – a civil rights issue – to eliminate tenure and any other legal protection for teachers, leaving principals free to fire them promptly, without delay or hindrance.

Set aside for the moment that this decision lacks any evidentiary basis. Another judge might have heard the same parade of witnesses and reached a different conclusion.

Bear in mind that the case will be appealed to a higher court, and will continue to be appealed until there is no higher court.

It is not unreasonable to believe that the California Teachers Association might negotiate a different tenure process with the legislature, perhaps a requirement of three years probationary status instead of two.

The one thing that does seem certain is that, contrary to the victory claims of hedge fund managers and right-wing editorial writers, no student will gain anything as a result of this decision. Millions more dollars will be spent to litigate the issues in California and elsewhere, but what will students gain? Nothing. The poorest, neediest students will still be in schools that lack the resources to meet their needs. They will still be in schools where classes are too large. They will still be in buildings that need repairs. They will still be in schools where the arts program and nurses and counselors were eliminated by budget cuts.

If their principals fire all or most or some of their teachers, who will take their places? There is no long line of superb teachers waiting for a chance to teach in inner-city schools. Chetty and Kane blithely assume that those who are fired will be replaced by better teachers. How do they know that?

Let's be clear. No "grossly ineffective" teacher should ever get tenure. Only a "grossly ineffective" principal would give tenure to a "grossly ineffective" teacher. Teachers do not give tenure to themselves.

Unfortunately, the Vergara decision is the latest example of the blame-shifting strategy of the privatization movement. Instead of acknowledging that test scores are highly correlated with family income, they prefer to blame teachers and the very idea of public education. If they were truly interested in supporting the needs of the children, the backers of this case would be advocating for smaller classes, for arts programs, for well-equipped and up-to-date schools, for after-school programs, for health clinics, for librarians and counselors, and for inducements to attract and retain a stable corps of experienced teachers in the schools attended by Beatriz Vergara and her co-plaintiffs.

Let us hope that a wiser judicial panel speedily overturns this bad decision and seeks a path of school reform that actually helps the plaintiffs without inflicting harm on their teachers.

# DO TEACHERS' UNIONS HAVE ANY FRIENDS IN THE OBAMA ADMINISTRATION?

HUFFINGTON POST, JULY 1, 2014

We are living in an era when the very idea of public education is under attack, as are teachers' unions and the teaching profession. Let's be clear, these attacks and the power amassed behind them are unprecedented in American history. Sure, there have always been critics of public schools, of teachers, and of unions. But never before has there been a serious and sustained effort to defund public education, to turn public money over to unaccountable private hands, and to weaken and eliminate collective bargaining wherever it still exists. And this effort is not only well-coordinated but is funded by billionaires who have grown wealthy in a free market, and who can't see any need for regulation or unions or public schools.

In the past, Democratic administrations and Democratic members of Congress could be counted on to support public education and to fight privatization. In the past, Democrats supported unions, which they saw as a dependable and significant part of their base.

This is no longer the case. Congress is about to pass legislation to expand funding of charter schools, despite the fact that they get no better results than public schools and despite the scandalous misuse of public funds by charter operators in many states.

The Obama administration strongly supports privatization via charters. One condition of Race to the Top was that states had to increase the number of charters. The administration is no friend of teachers or of teacher unions. Secretary Duncan applauded the lamentable Vergara decision, as he has applauded privatization and evaluating teachers by the test scores of their students. There are never too many tests for this administration. Although the president recently talked about the importance of unions,[94] he has done nothing to support them when they are under attack. Former members of his administration are leading the war against teachers and their unions.

Think Rahm Emanuel, who apparently wants to be known as the mayor who privatized Chicago and broke the teachers' union. Or think Robert Gibbs, the former White House press secretary,[95] who is now leading the public relations campaign against teachers' due process rights.

The National Education Association is meeting now in Denver at its annual conference. The American Federation of Teachers holds its annual convention in Los Angeles in another week or so. Both must take seriously the threat to the survival of public education, not only privatization but austerity and over-testing. These are not different threats. They are connected. Austerity and over-testing set public schools up to fail. They are precursors to privatization. They are intended to make public schools weak and to destroy public confidence in democratically controlled schools. What is needed at this hour is a strong, militant response to these attacks on teachers, public schools, and where they exist, unions.

For sure, unions have their faults. But they are the only collective voice that teachers have. Now is the time to use that voice. The battle for the future of public education is not over.

Supporters of public education must rally and stand together and elect a president in 2016 who supports public schools. This is a time to get informed, to organize, to strategize, and to mobilize. If you are not angry, you have not been paying attention.

# GOOD RIDDANCE TO COMMON CORE TESTING

HUFFINGTON POST, JULY 3, 2014

A few years ago, Arne Duncan, Bill Gates, David Coleman, and a merry band of policy wonks had a grand plan. The non-governmental groups like Achieve, the National Governors Association, the Council of Chief State School Officers, and Coleman's own Student Achievement Partners would write the Common Core standards, paid for by the Gates Foundation. Duncan would require states to agree to adopt them as a condition of eligibility for a share of the billions of Race to the Top funds at a time when states were broke. The Feds would spend $370 million to develop tests for the standards, and within a few short years the U.S. would have a seamless system of standards and assessments that could be used to evaluate students, teachers, and schools.

The reason that the Gates Foundation had to pay for the standards is that federal law prohibits the government from controlling, directing, or supervising curriculum or instruction. Of course, it is ludicrous to imagine that the federally-funded tests do not have any direct influence on curriculum or instruction. Many years ago, I interviewed a professor at MIT about his role in the new science programs of the 1960s, and he said something I never forgot: "Let me write a nation's tests, and I care not who writes its songs or poetry."

So how fares the seamless system? Not so well. Critics of the standards and tests seem to gathering strength and growing bolder. The lack of any democratic process for writing, reviewing, and revising the standards is coming back to bite the architects and generals who assumed they could engineer a swift and silent coup. The claim, often made by Duncan, that the U.S. needs a way to compare the performance of students in different states ignores the fact that the Federal National Assessment of Educational Progress (NAEP) already exists to do precisely that. In addition, critics like Carol Burris and John Murphy have pointed out[96] that the Common Core tests agreed upon a cut score (passing mark) that is designed to fail most students.

Politico reports that support for the federally-funded tests is crumbling[97] as states discover the costs, the amount of time required, and their loss of sovereignty over a basic state function. The federal government pays about 10 percent of the cost of education, while states and localities pay the other 90 percent. Why should the federal government determine what happens in the nation's schools? What happened to the long-established tradition that states are "laboratories of democracy"? Why shouldn't the federal government stick to its mandate to fund poor schools and to defend the civil rights of students, instead of trying to standardize curriculum, instruction, and testing?

So far, at least 17 states have backed away from using the federal tests this spring, and some are determined not to use them ever. Another half-dozen may drop out. In many, legislators are appalled at the costs of adopting a federal test. Both the NEA and the AFT, which have supported the standards, have balked at the tests because teachers are not ready, nor are curriculum, teaching resources, and professional development. As Politico reports, time and costs are big issues for the federal exams:

- The Partnership for Assessment of Readiness for College and Careers (PARCC) estimates its exams will take eight hours for an average third-grader and nearly 10 hours for high school students – not counting optional midyear assessments to make sure students and teachers are on track.

- PARCC also plans to develop tests for kindergarten, first- and second- graders, instead of starting with third grade as is typical now. And it aims to test older students in 9th, 10th and 11th grades instead of just once during high school.
- Cost is also an issue. Many states need to spend heavily on computers and broadband so schools can deliver the exams online as planned. And the tests themselves cost more than many states currently spend – an estimated $19 to $24 per student if they're administered online and up to $33 per student for paper-and-pencil versions.
- That adds up to big money for testing companies. Pearson, which won the right to deliver PARCC tests, could earn more than $1 billion over the next eight years if enough states sign on.

One of the two federally-funded testing consortia, PARCC, is now entangled in a legal battle in New Mexico, which was sued by the American Institutes for Research (AIR) for failing to take competitive bids for the lucrative testing contract. This could lead to copycat suits in other states whose laws require competitive bidding but ignored the law to award the contract to Pearson.

Frankly, the idea of subjecting third graders to an eight-hour exam is repugnant, as is the prospect of a 10-hour exam for high school students, as is the absurd idea of testing children in kindergarten, first, and second grades. All of these tests will be accompanied by test preparation and interim exams and periodic exams. This is testing run amok, and the biggest beneficiary will be the testing industry, certainly not students.

Students don't become smarter or wiser or more creative because of testing. Instead, all this testing will deduct as much as a month of instruction for testing and preparation for testing. In addition, states will spend tens of millions, hundreds of millions, or even more, to buy the technology and bandwidth necessary for the Common Core testing. Los Angeles – just one district – plans to spend a cool $1 billion to buy the technology for the Common Core tests. The money spent for Common Core testing means there will be less money to reduce class sizes, to hire arts teachers, to repair crumbling buildings, to hire school nurses, to keep libraries open and staffed, and to meet other basic needs. States are cutting the budget for schools at the same time that the Common Core is diverting huge sums for new technology, new textbooks, new professional development, and other requirements to prepare for the Common Core.

Common Core testing will turn out to be the money pit that consumed American education. The sooner it dies, the sooner schools and teachers will be freed of the Giant Federal Accountability Plan hatched in secret and foisted upon our nation's schools. And when it does die, teachers will have more time to do their job and to use their professional judgment to do what is best for each student.

# THE EXCELLENT BUT FALSE MESSAGING OF THE COMMON CORE STANDARDS

HUFFINGTON POST, JULY 11, 2014

Have you ever wondered about the amazingly effective campaign to sell the Common Core standards to the media, the business community, and the public? How did it happen that advocates for the standards used the same language, the same talking points, the same claims, no matter where they were located?

The talking points sounded poll-tested because they were. The language was the same because it came from the same source. The campaign to have "rigorous," "high standards" that would make ALL students "college and career-ready" and "globally competitive" was well planned and coordinated. There was no evidence for these claims but repeated often enough in editorials and news stories and in ads by major corporations, they took on the ring of truth. Even the new stories that reported on controversies between advocates and opponents of the Common Core used the rhetoric of the advocates to describe the standards.

This was no accident.

Lyndsey Layton of *The Washington Post* reported[98] that the Hunt Institute in North Carolina received more than $5 million from the Gates Foundation to organize support for the brand-new, unknown, untested Common Core standards. Organizing support meant creating the message as well as mobilizing messengers, many of whom were also funded by the Gates Foundation.

In Layton's blockbuster article about how the Gates Foundation underwrote the rapid adoption of "national standards" by spreading millions of dollars strategically, this remarkable story was included:

> The foundation, for instance, gave more than $5 million to the University of North Carolina-affiliated Hunt Institute, led by the state's former four-term Democratic governor, Jim Hunt, to advocate for the Common Core in statehouses around the country.
>
> The grant was the institute's largest source of income in 2009, more than 10 times the size of its next largest donation. With the Gates money, the Hunt Institute coordinated more than a dozen organizations – many of them also Gates grantees – including the Thomas B. Fordham Institute, National Council of La Raza, the Council of Chief State School Officers, National Governors Association, Achieve and the two national teachers unions.
>
> The Hunt Institute held weekly conference calls between the players that were directed by Stefanie Sanford, who was in charge of policy and advocacy at the Gates Foundation. They talked about which states needed shoring up, the best person to respond to questions or criticisms, and who needed to travel to which state capital to testify, according to those familiar with the conversations.
>
> The Hunt Institute spent $437,000 to hire GMMB, a strategic communications firm owned by Jim Margolis, a top Democratic strategist and veteran of both of Obama's presidential campaigns. GMMB conducted polling around standards, developed fact sheets, iden-

> tified language that would be effective in winning support and prepared talking points, among other efforts.
>
> The groups organized by Hunt developed a "messaging tool kit" that included sample letters to the editor, op-ed pieces that could be tailored to individuals depending on whether they were teachers, parents, business executives or civil rights leaders.

And that, ladies and gentlemen, is why the advocates for the Common Core standards have the same rhetoric, the same claims, no matter where they are, because the campaign was well organized and well messaged.

What the campaign did not take into account was the possibility of push-back, the possibility that the very lack of public debate and discussion would sow suspicion and controversy. What the advocates forgot is that the democratic way of making change may be slow and may require compromise, but it builds consensus. The Common Core standards, thanks to Gates' largesse, skipped the democratic process, imposed new standards on almost every state, bypassed the democratic process, and is now paying the price of autocratic action in a democratic society.

# WHAT'S AT STAKE IN PUBLIC EDUCATION?

HUFFINGTON POST, JULY 18, 2014

Jeff Bryant notes that many in the national media were stunned when the NEA called for Secretary Arne Duncan's resignation.[99] For years they believed the secretary's press releases, instead of investigating the festering discontent against his ill-informed policies. Many journalists are oblivious to the protests by teachers – like the one at Garfield High school in Seattle – against the use of student test scores to judge their quality. Many journalists never noticed growing protests by students against obsessive testing in cities like Providence. Many never heard about parents groups objecting to profiteering by test publishers or dismissed them as publicity stunts. Many have been oblivious to the devastating effects of budget cuts by state legislatures, while at the same time they open unsupervised charter schools that impoverish community public schools. With some notable exceptions, like the *Detroit Free Press* and the *Akron Beacon Journal*, the mainstream media has simply ignored a widespread assault on the principle of free public education, democratically controlled, open to all. Instead, they print press releases written by corporations about "miracle schools," where every child graduates and goes to college, without bothering to check facts.

Reporters quote spokespeople from right-wing think tanks that support privatization, or from groups like Democrats For Education Reform (DFER), which represents hedge fund managers, even though they are neither teachers nor parents nor have any other claim to authority. DFER recently referred to NEA as "the lunatic fringe" in *The New York Times* for denouncing Duncan, even though NEA speaks for three million teachers and DFER speaks for a handful of fabulously wealthy equity speculators.

What is most astonishing is to see the almost total indifference or ignorance of the mainstream media to an unprecedented and well-coordinated effort to privatize public education. Reporters don't care that certain individuals and corporations are accumulating millions of dollars in taxpayer funding, while schools are cutting their budgets and closing their libraries and increasing class sizes. Reporters don't care that state authorities are allowing schools to open whose founders are not educators and may even be high school dropouts. Nor do they care when charter corporations claim to be "public schools," yet refuse to permit the state to audit their expenditures, and in some states, refuse to share financial information with their own board. Has anyone tried to explain how a school can be "public" if its financials are not? Reporters know, but don't care, that major charter chains contribute millions of dollars to state legislatures to make sure that no one investigates their use of public funds. A few reporters in Ohio, Michigan, Pennsylvania, and Florida have dared to pry into the cozy relationship between the charters and the legislature, but their exposes are followed by silence and inaction.

If present trends continue, in another decade the U.S. will have a dual system of education. Some cities will have few public schools, only charters that choose their students and exclude those with disabilities and those who can't speak English. The few remaining public schools in urban districts will enroll the charter school rejects. The great irony is that on average, privately managed schools don't get better results than public schools for poor students, yet they are a gold mine for their founders. What is at stake is the great tradition of public schools, open to all, supported by all, and controlled by the public, not by corporations. This is a principle worth fighting for, yet the public cannot fight if they are uninformed. It is up to a free press to sound the alarm when private interests seek to undermine, exploit, monetize, and control our democratic institutions. To date, with rare exceptions, the press has not sounded the alarm.

# TO FIGHT FOR PUBLIC SCHOOLS IS TO FIGHT FOR DEMOCRACY

HUFFINGTON POST, JULY 24, 2014

Friends, when a small group of parents and educators formed the Network for Public Education (NPE) in 2013, we had a singular goal – to mobilize the allies of public education against the powerful forces supporting privatization and high-stakes testing. To advance that goal, we hoped to create a force to counter the large amounts of money that were being dumped into state and local school board races to undermine public education, to demoralize teachers, and to promote an agenda of choice, testing, and sanctions.

We knew we were up against some of the wealthiest people in the nation. We knew they included a bunch of billionaires, and we could never match their spending.

But we put our faith in democracy. We put our faith in the simple idea that we are many, and they are few. We believed, and continue to believe, that an informed public will not give away its public schools to amateurs, hedge fund managers, rock stars, for-profit corporations, athletes, fly-by-night entrepreneurs, and religious groups. Our goal is to inform the public, assuming that they would not willingly abandon or give away what rightfully belongs to the entire community.

We believed that we could exert influence if we established

our credibility as genuine supporters of children, parents, teachers, administrators, and real education, as opposed to the data-driven, high-stakes testing policies that degrade education, and the consumer-oriented choice programs that divide communities and harm public schools.

Our budget can't match the budgets of those who want to turn our schools into profit centers. But we believe in the power of our message. During our short existence, we have proven on several occasions that our message can beat Big Money. We have seen candidates in state and local races triumph over well-funded adversaries. We think that our support gave them added visibility and contributed to their astonishing victories.

We supported Sue Peters for the school board in Seattle, and she won. We supported Monica Ratliff in a race for the Los Angeles school board, and she won. We supported Ras Baraka in his race for Mayor of Newark, and he won. This past week, we supported Valarie Wilson in the runoff for the Democratic nomination for state superintendent in Georgia, and she won. All of these candidates were outspent, sometimes by multiples of numbers.

Some candidates we endorsed lost their races. But our message has been consistent and powerful. All credit goes to the candidates themselves, of course, but we are proud that we gave them support and hope when they needed it most, and that our endorsement may have helped their fundraising and campaigning.

We urge you to join us as we promote the principles that will improve our public schools and repel those who seek to monetize them. We want our children to have a childhood. We want our teachers and principals to be highly respected professionals. We want parents and educators to stand together on behalf of their children and their community.

We oppose the status quo. We seek better schools for all children. We will work diligently with like-minded allies until we can turn the tide away from those who seek silver bullets or profits, and turn the tide towards those who work to restore public education as the public institution dedicated to spreading knowledge and skills, advancing equality of educational opportunity, and improving the lives of children and communities, while encouraging collaboration and a commitment to democratic values.

Join us! With your help, we will build better schools and better communities for all children.

*Diane Ravitch, President, The Network for Public Education*

*Anthony Cody, Treasurer, The Network for Public Education*

*Robin Hiller, Executive Director, The Network for Public Education*

# WILL A FLORIDA COUNTY'S BOLD DECISION TO OPT OUT OF STATE TESTING CATCH FIRE?

HUFFINGTON POST, AUGUST 29, 2014

Does Palm Beach County, Florida, have the nerve to follow the example set by Lee County, Florida, which just last week voted to opt the entire district out of state testing? The Palm Beach County school board is weighing that decision, according to the *Sun-Sentinel*:[100]

> Palm Beach County School Board members want to opt out of state-required testing, a controversial move that could jeopardize funding, athletics and students' ability to graduate.
>
> They say testing has gotten out of control and creates too much pressure for students and teachers. After discussing the opt-out idea at a recent meeting, board members asked their lawyers for further study. They will discuss it again at a workshop in the next few weeks.
>
> "Sometimes it takes an act of civil disobedience to move forward," School Board member Karen Brill

> said. "We must explore the consequences, but we cannot allow fear to hold us back."
>
> This week, the Lee County school board made history by becoming the first district in the Florida to opt out, after hundreds of parents pushed them to do so.
>
> But Joe Follick, a spokesman for the Florida Department of Education, said opting out would create chaos. The tests help determine a school's letter grade and can affect school enrollment, teacher pay and even the prices of homes.
>
> "There's no way to know how you're doing if you don't take a test every year," he said.

The state warned that it could suspend funding to punish the district.

"Imagine," as John Lennon sang. Imagine if many districts opted out. Imagine if most districts opted out. Imagine if every district opted out. Maybe then the state bureaucrats would remember that they work for the public, not the other way around. Maybe then the legislators would listen to their constituents.

Imagine schools where children were tested every three or four years, at transition points, as in the world's top-performing nations. Imagine schools where teachers wrote their own tests and used their professional judgment. Imagine schools that did not insist on giving tests to children in hospice care.

Imagine.

# SUCCESS ACADEMY, THE NEW YORK TIMES MAGAZINE, AND PUBLIC EDUCATION

HUFFINGTON POST, SEPTEMBER 7, 2014

*"Yes. It is time to remind Republicans – and Democrats – that charters are a conservative strategy. They sacrifice community to competition. They get rid of unions. They make teachers at-will employees." – Diane Ravitch's Blog*

*The New York Times Magazine* has a long article[101] about Eva Moskowitz and her chain of charter schools in New York City. The charter chain was originally called Harlem Success Academy, but Moskowitz dropped the word "Harlem" when she decided to open new schools in gentrifying neighborhoods and wanted to attract white and middle-class families.

I spent a lot of time on the phone with the author, Daniel Bergner. When he asked why I was critical of Moskowitz, I said that what she does to get high test scores is not a model for public education or even for other charters. The high scores of her students are due to intensive test prep and attrition. She gets her initial group of students by holding a lottery, which in itself is a selection process because the least functional families don't apply. She enrolls small proportions of students with disabilities and English language learners as compared to the neighborhood public school. And as time goes by, many students leave.

The only Success Academy school that has fully grown to

grades 3-8 tested 116 third graders but only 32 eighth graders. Three other Success Academy schools have grown to sixth grade. One tested 121 third graders but only 55 sixth graders, another 106 third graders but only 68 six graders, and the last 83 third graders but only 54 sixth graders. Why the shrinking student body? When students left the school, they were not replaced by other incoming students. When the eighth grade students who scored well on the state test took the admissions test for the specialized high schools like Stuyvesant and Bronx Science, not one of them passed the test.[102]

I also told Bergner that Success Academy charters have among the highest rates of teacher turnover every year, which would not happen if teachers enjoyed the work. Helen Zelon wrote in City Limits:[103]

> In Harlem Success Academies 1-4, the only schools for which the state posted turnover data, more than half of all teachers left the schools ahead of the 2013-14 school year. In one school, three out of four teachers departed.

I also told Bergner about a website called Glass Door,[104] where many former teachers at Success Academy charters expressed their candid views about an "oppressive" work climate at the school. As more of these negative reviews were posted, a new crop of favorable reviews were added, echoing the chain's happy talk but not shedding light on why teachers don't last long there.

Bergner argued every issue with me. He reiterated Success Academy's talking points. He said that public schools lose as many students every year as Success Academy charters. I replied that public schools don't close their enrollment to new students. Again, defending Success Academy, he said that closing new enrollments made sense because Moskowitz was "trying to build a culture," and the culture would be disrupted by accepting new students after a certain grade. I responded that public schools might want to "build a culture" too, but they are not allowed to refuse new students who want to enroll in fourth grade or fifth grade or sixth grade, or even in the middle of the year.

He did not think it mattered that none of her successful eighth grade students was able to pass the test for the specialized high schools, and he didn't mention it in the article. Nor was he interested in teacher turnover or anything else that might reflect negatively on Success Academy charters.

Subsequently I heard from his editor, who called to check the accuracy of the quotes by me. I had to change some of the language he attributed to me. For example, he quoted me defending "large government-run institutions," when what I said was "public schools." He was using Success Academy's framing of my views. I asked whether Bergner had included my main point about attrition, and the editor said no. I explained it to her and sent her supporting documentation.

This is the paragraph that appeared in Bergner's article, which understates the significance of selective attrition while not mentioning Success Academy's policy of not accepting new students after a certain grade:

> On the topic of scores, the U.F.T. and Ravitch insist that Moskowitz's numbers don't hold up under scrutiny. Success Academy (like all charters), they say, possesses a demographic advantage over regular public schools, by serving somewhat fewer students with special needs, by teaching fewer students from the city's most severely dysfunctional families and by using suspensions to push out underperforming students (an accusation that Success Academy vehemently denies). These are a few of the myriad factors that Mulgrew and Ravitch stress. But even taking these differences into account probably doesn't come close to explaining away Success Academy's results.

This minimizes the stark differences in demographics when comparing her schools to neighborhood public schools. The Success Academy charters in Harlem have half as many English language learners as the Harlem public schools. The Harlem Success Academy 4 School, which has 500 students, has zero students with the highest special needs as compared to an average of 14.1 percent in Harlem public schools. This disparity is not accurately described as "somewhat fewer." It is a very large disparity. Attrition rates are high, which would not be happening if the school was meeting the needs of students. As I wrote earlier this year:[105]

> Moskowitz said [on the Morning Joe show on MSNBC], referring to the students in her schools, "we've had these children since kindergarten." But she forgot to mention all the students who have left the school since kindergarten. Or the fact that Harlem Success Academy 4 suspends students at a rate 300 percent higher than the average in the district. Last year's seventh grade class at Harlem Success Academy 1 had a 52.1 percent attrition rate since 2006-07. That's more than half of the kindergarten students gone before they even graduate from middle school. Last year's sixth grade class had a 45.2 percent attrition rate since 2006-07. That's almost half of the kindergarten class gone and two more years left in middle school. In just four years Harlem Success Academy 4 has lost over 21 percent of its students. The pattern of students leaving is not random. Students with low test scores, English Language Learners, and special education students are most likely to disappear from the school's roster. Large numbers of students disappear beginning in third grade, but not in the earlier grades. No natural pattern of student mobility can explain the sudden disappearance of students at the grade when state testing just happens to begin.

I have no personal grudge against Eva Moskowitz. On the few occasions when we have appeared together, we have had very cordial conversation. What I deeply oppose – and this is what I stressed to Bergner and he deliberately ignored – is that Success Academy is not a model for public education. No one expects that Bronx Science is a model because it does not have open doors, it admits only those who meet its standards and they are high. Eva Moskowitz pretends that her schools get superior results with exactly the same population because of her superior methods, when in reality the success of her schools is built on a deliberate policy of winnowing out low-performing and nonconformist students.

Why did Bergner insist on obscuring this crucial difference between Success Academy charter schools and public schools? Public schools can't remove students with low scores. They can't refuse to enroll students with severe disabilities and students who can't read English. They can't close their enrollment after a certain grade. Unless they have a stated policy of selective admissions, they must accept everyone who seeks to enroll, even if they arrive in February or March. Their doors must be open to all, without a lottery. It is not honest to pretend that public schools can imitate Moskowitz's practice of selective attrition. And it is not honest to overlook that difference.

# WHAT MATTERS MORE THAN TEST SCORES

HUFFINGTON POST, OCTOBER 15, 2014

As a nation, we worry far too much about PISA scores, which rank and rate students according to standardized tests. Many nations have higher average scores than we do, yet we are the most powerful nation on earth – economically, technologically, and militarily. What do the PISA scores mean?

In his book, *Who's Afraid of the Big Bad Dragon? Why China Has the Best (and Worst) Education System in the World,* Yong Zhao says that the East Asian nations have the top scores because they do heavy-duty test prep. One thing is clear – the PISA scores do not predict the future of our economy. They never have. Our students have never had high scores on international tests, not since the first international test of math was administered in 1964, and our seniors scored last among 12 nations. We went on over the half-century since then to outcompete the other 11 nations who had higher test scores.

Let's look at some other international measures, those that reflect the well-being of children. According to a UNICEF survey,[106] we lead the industrialized nations of the world in child poverty. Actually, UNICEF finds that Romania has even higher child poverty than we do, but anyone who has been to that nation would not rank the mighty, rich, and powerful U.S. in the same league with Romania, still struggling to overcome 50 years of Communist misrule and impoverishment. When it comes to child poverty, we are number 1.

While we obsess over test scores, we ignore other important indicators – for example, the proportion of children who are enrolled in a quality preschool program. *The Economist* magazine published an international survey of 45 nations,[107] in relation to quality and availability, and the United States ranked 24th, tied with the United Arab Emirates. The Nordic countries led the survey with near universal high-quality preschool.

Another number reflects our government's failure to invest in what works. The March of Dimes in partnership with other organizations conducted an international survey[108] of the availability of good prenatal care programs for pregnant women. Preterm births are the leading cause of death among newborns, and are also a significant cause of cognitive and developmental disabilities. Of 184 nations surveyed, we ranked 131, tied with Thailand, Turkey, and Somalia. This problem could easily be solved by just a few of our billionaire philanthropists.

So what do you think matters most? The test scores of 15-year-old students, or the health and well-being of our young children? Might there be a connection?

Standardized tests are an accurate predictor of family income and education. Reduce poverty, and scores will rise. Scores on the SAT college admission test, for example, mirror a student's family background. Students from the poorest families score the lowest, and students from the richest families score the highest. The gap between those at the bottom and those at the top is 400 points. As one *Wall Street Journal* blogger put it,[109] the SAT might just as well be known as the Student Affluence Test.

Our policymakers' obsession with test scores is unhealthy and counter-productive. They think the way to raise scores is to make the standards and curriculum harder and to test more. Today, little children are taking 8 or 9 hours of tests, and as the standards grow "harder," the failure rate goes higher. We are the most over-tested nation in the world, and the benefits accrue to testing corporations like Pearson and McGraw-Hill, not to children. The tests themselves are a dubious measure. There are better ways to know whether children are learning than standardized tests. Why else would our elites send their children to schools that seldom use them? What's good enough for the children of Bill Gates and Barack Obama should be good enough for other people's children.

We should stop obsessing about test scores and start obsessing about the health and well-being of children and their families. The gains would be far more valuable than a few points on a standardized test. That is the only way we will assure children a good start in life and a fair chance to succeed in our society.

# THE MOST IMPORTANT BOOK OF THE YEAR: BOB HERBERT'S "LOSING OUR WAY"

HUFFINGTON POST, NOVEMBER 6, 2014

Bob Herbert's book *Losing Our Way: An Intimate Portrait of a Troubled America* is one of the most important, most compelling books that I have read in many years. For those of us who have felt that something has gone seriously wrong in our country, Herbert connects the dots. He provides a carefully documented, well-written account of what went wrong and why. As he pulls together a sweeping narrative, he weaves it through the personal accounts of individuals whose stories are emblematic and heartbreaking.

Herbert reminds us of a time when America's policymakers had great visions for the future and acted to make them real, whether it was the building of the Erie Canal or the transcontinental rail system, Franklin D. Roosevelt's TVA, or Dwight D. Eisenhower's national highway system. He reminds us that the American dream was to create a nation where there were good jobs for those who wanted to work, where there was increasing equality, and a growing middle class.

What we have today is a nation dominated by plutocrats and corporations, which are allowed by the U.S. Supreme Court's *Citizens United* decision to dump unlimited amounts of money into elections and to write legislation that favors plutocrats and corporations. What we have is historic levels of wealth inequality and income inequality, where corporations outsource good jobs and many people are slipping from the middle class into minimum wage jobs or even poverty. Herbert explains that our failure to invest in rebuilding the nation's infrastructure has left us with crumbling bridges, tunnels, water mains, sewers, and gas lines, which are dangerous and sometimes fatal to citizens who happen to be in the wrong place at the wrong time, as bridges collapse, levees fall, and gas lines explode.

He goes into detail about the corporate assault on public education, fueled by the plutocrats' desire to turn education into a free market. He points out that the plutocrats' favorite reform – charter schools – enroll a tiny percentage of students and have on average an unimpressive record. Their relentless attacks on the teaching profession will damage that profession for many years into the future. Herbert spent time in Pittsburgh, meeting the activists and parent leaders there. He saw at ground-level the harm inflicted by massive cuts in the state budget and the determination of parents to fight back. He describes the emptiness of the reformers' boast that they can close the achievement gap by privatization and by union-busting. Having talked to teachers, parents, and principals, he knows the harm that poverty inflicts on children, and the pain caused by living without adequate food, shelter, and medical care.

Herbert writes movingly about the endless wars in the Middle East of the past decade. Did the policymakers know what they were doing when they launched the wars in Iraq and Afghanistan? Did they have a strategy for victory? No, they did not. They launched wars with a goal (victory) but not a plan. He quotes Secretary of Defense Donald Rumsfeld, who assured the American public that our invasion of Iraq would not last longer than five months. Herbert writes about a remote sector in Afghanistan called "the valley of death," where American troops struggled to establish a base. It was portrayed in an award-winning documentary called *Restrepo*. Many young Americans died there, but no one could explain why our troops were sent there. Eventually, the disaster ended, and we abandoned that forlorn valley. Herbert cites economists who calculate that the wars of the past decade will cost trillions of dollars, as well as thousands of American lives and the lives of hundreds of thousands of lives of people in the countries we went to "save." There is no end in sight. Does anyone still believe that Iraq or Afghanistan are on their way to becoming stable democracies or even a country that will no longer harbor terrorists?

Herbert pulls all these events and issues into a coherent whole. We have lost our way. Our elected officials dream no big dreams. They have little or no concept of major public works programs to rebuild our nation's infrastructure, which would put millions of people to work and invigorate our economy. They willingly waste blood and treasure on wars in distant lands, yet they cannot bring themselves to invest in our nation and create jobs by rebuilding the vital roads, tunnels, bridges, sewers, and other public assets that are now in disrepair, rusting, crumbling, threatening lives. We have money aplenty for war, but no money to put people to work fixing our infrastructure. Plutocrats buy politicians to protect their fortunes and reduce their taxes. Corporations buy politicians who will deregulate their activities and cut their taxes. The stock market rewards corporations that cut their payroll, firing experienced employees who had served those corporations loyally for decades. Men like Jack Welch of GE and "Chainsaw Al" Dunlap became famous as business leaders who coolly and heartlessly fired tens of thousands of workers to increase shareholder value in their corporations. Herbert writes:

> How did things go so wrong? How is it that so many millions were finding it so difficult to get ahead, to emerge from the terrible, demoralizing rut of joblessness and underemployment? In a country as rich as the United States, why were so many being left behind?
>
> The biggest factor by far was the toxic alliance forged by government and America's mega corporations

> and giant banks. That alliance of elites, fueled by endless greed and a near-pathological quest for power, reshaped the rules and regulations of the economy and the society at large to heavily favor the interest of those who were already well-to-do. In the process they trampled the best interests of ordinary Americans.

Herbert's book comes alive through his account of the experiences of two individuals – one a woman in Minnesota who was driving across a bridge that spanned the Mississippi River when it collapsed in 2007, the other a young man who was grievously wounded in Afghanistan and struggled to regain the ability to walk. In these and many other accounts of individuals and families, Herbert uses his superb journalistic skills to bring major issues to life. Along with the data and the documentation to make his arguments, Herbert vividly portrays what matters most, the human impact of political decisions.

If you read only one book this year, make it Bob Herbert's *Losing Our Way*. It will change you. It will make you want to get involved, take action, make a difference. As he says at the end of the book, it doesn't have to be this way. Changing it depends on us.

# A NEW PARADIGM FOR ACCOUNTABILITY: THE JOY OF LEARNING

HUFFINGTON POST, NOVEMBER 12, 2014

Now that we have endured more than a dozen long years of No Child Left Behind and five fruitless, punitive years of Race to the Top, it is clear that they both failed. They relied on carrots and sticks and ignored intrinsic motivation. They crushed children's curiosity instead of cultivating it.* They demoralized schools. They disrupted schools and communities without improving children's education.

We did not leave no child behind. The same children who were left behind in 2001-02 are still left behind. Similarly, Race To The Top is a flop. The Common Core tests are failing most students, and we are nowhere near whatever the "Top" is. If a teacher gave a test, and 70% of the students failed, we would say she was not competent, tested what was not taught, didn't know her students. The Race turns out to be NCLB with a mask. NCLB on steroids. NCLB 2.0.

Whatever you call it, RTTT has hurt children, demoralized teachers, closed community schools, fragmented communities, increased privatization, and doubled down on testing.

I have an idea for a new accountability system that relies on different metrics. We begin by dropping standardized test scores as measures of quality or effectiveness. We stop labeling, ranking, and rating children, teachers, and schools. We use tests only when needed for diagnostic purposes, not for comparing children to their peers, not to find winners and losers. We rely on teachers to test their students, not corporations.

The new accountability system would be called No Child Left Out. The measures would be these:

- How many children had the opportunity to learn to play a musical instrument?
- How many children had the chance to play in the school band or orchestra?
- How many children participated in singing, either individually or in the chorus or a glee club or other group?
- How many public performances did the school offer?
- How many children participated in dramatics?
- How many children produced documentaries or videos?
- How many children engaged in science experiments? How many started a project in science and completed it?
- How many children learned robotics?
- How many children wrote stories of more than five pages, whether fiction or nonfiction?
- How often did children have the chance to draw, paint, make videos, or sculpt?
- How many children wrote poetry? Short stories? Novels? History research papers?
- How many children performed service in their community to help others?
- How many children were encouraged to design an invention or to redesign a common item?
- How many students wrote research papers on historical topics?

Can you imagine an accountability system whose purpose

is to encourage and recognize creativity, imagination, originality, and innovation? Isn't this what we need more of?

Well, you can make up your own metrics, but you get the idea. Setting expectations in the arts, in literature, in science, in history, and in civics can change the nature of schooling. It would require far more work and self-discipline than test prep for a test that is soon forgotten.

My paradigm would dramatically change schools from Gradgrind academies to halls of joy and inspiration, where creativity, self-discipline, and inspiration are nurtured, honored, and valued.

This is only a start. Add your own ideas. The sky is the limit. Surely we can do better than this era of soul-crushing standardized testing.

**Kudos to Southold Elementary School in Long Island, where these ideas were hatched as I watched the children's band playing a piece they had practiced.*

# THE MYTH OF CHINESE SUPER SCHOOLS

### THE NEW YORK REVIEW OF BOOKS, NOVEMBER 20, 2014

On December 3, 2013, Secretary of Education Arne Duncan announced yet again that American students were doing terribly when tested, in comparison to students in sixty-one other countries and a few cities like Shanghai and Hong Kong. Duncan presided over the release of the latest international assessment of student performance in reading, science, and mathematics (called the Program for International Student Assessment, or PISA), and Shanghai led the nations of the world in all three categories.

Duncan and other policymakers professed shock and anguish at the results, according to which American students were average at best, nowhere near the top. Duncan said that Americans had to face the brutal fact that the performance of our students was "mediocre" and that our schools were trapped in "educational stagnation."

He had used virtually the same rhetoric in 2010, when the previous PISA results were released. Despite the Bush administration's No Child Left Behind (NCLB) law, which mandated that every child in every school in grades 3–8 would be proficient in math and reading by 2014, and despite the Obama administration's $4.35 billion Race to the Top program, the scores of American fifteen-year-old students on these international tests were nearly unchanged since 2000. Both NCLB and Race to the

Top assumed that a steady diet of testing and accountability, of carrots for high scores and sticks for low scores, would provide an incentive for students and teachers to try harder and get higher test scores. But clearly, this strategy was not working. In his public remarks, however, Duncan could not admit that carrots and sticks don't produce better education or even higher test scores. Instead, he blamed teachers and parents for failing to have high expectations.

Duncan, President Obama, and legislators looked longingly at Shanghai's stellar results and wondered why American students could not surpass them. Why can't we be like the Chinese? they wondered. Why should we be number twenty-nine in the world in mathematics when Shanghai is number one? Why are our scores below those of Estonia, Poland, Ireland, and so many other nations? Duncan was sure that the scores on international tests were proof that we were falling behind the rest of the world and that they predicted economic disaster for the United States. What Duncan could not admit was that, after a dozen years, the Bush–Obama strategy of testing and punishing teachers and schools had failed.

One response of the Obama administration was to support an initiative called the Common Core standards, which set demands so high for students in every grade from kindergarten to senior year that most of those who have taken the tests associated with the standards have failed them. In New York State, for example, nearly 70 percent of students failed to reach "proficient" in reading, including 95 percent of students with disabilities, 97 percent of English-as-a-second-language learners, and more than 80 percent of black and Hispanic students.

Although the federal government is barred by law from influencing or controlling curriculum or instruction, the Common Core tests are federally funded. Without doubt, tests influence and control curriculum and instruction. The Common Core standards are a gamble, because no one knows if they will raise test scores or even if they will improve education. But what they will certainly do is require many tens of billions in new spending on technology, because the new federal tests will be delivered online, meaning that every school district must have new computers, new bandwidth, and training for staff to use the new technology. It is no surprise that the testing industry – dominated by the British corporation Pearson – and the technology industry both love the new standards. However, recent polls show that a growing majority of parents and teachers oppose the Common Core standards. They have become a political lightning-rod, drawing fire from those on the right who see them as federal evisceration of local control, and from those on the left who dislike standardization and loss of professional autonomy.

Policymakers and legislators are convinced that the best way to raise test scores is to administer more standardized tests and to make them harder to pass. This love affair with testing had its origins in 1983, when a national commission on education released a report called "A Nation at Risk."

President Ronald Reagan had hoped his commission would recommend vouchers and school prayers, but that did not happen. Instead, the report recommended a stronger curriculum, higher graduation requirements, more teacher pay, and longer school hours, as well as standards and testing at transitional points, like high school graduation. The main effect of the report was caused by its alarmist rhetoric, which launched a three-decade-plus obsession with the idea that American public schools are failing and that the way to fix them is to raise test scores.

The report warned that "the educational foundations of our society are presently being eroded by a rising tide of mediocrity that threatens our very future as a Nation and a people." It said ominously, "If an unfriendly foreign power had attempted to impose on America the mediocre educational performance that exists today, we might well have viewed it as an act of war." But no, we did it to ourselves. We were careless. "We have, in effect, been committing an act of unthinking, unilateral educational disarmament." The commission complained that on nineteen different international academic tests, completed a decade earlier, American students never placed first or second, and were last on seven occasions.

This academic "disarmament," the commission believed, was undercutting our industrial might. Other nations were overtaking us. The Japanese were making automobiles more efficiently, and their government was subsidizing their development and export. South Koreans had built the world's most efficient steel mill. German products were replacing American machine tools. In the thirty years since "A Nation at Risk," American students have typically scored no better than average – and sometimes worse – on the international tests.

It is worth noting that American students have never received high scores on international tests. On the first such test, a test of mathematics in 1964, senior year students in the U.S. scored last of twelve nations, and eighth-grade students scored next to last. But in the following fifty years, the U.S. outperformed the other eleven nations by every measure, whether economic productivity, military might, technological innovation, or democratic institutions. This raises the question of whether the scores of fifteen-year-old students on international tests predict anything of importance, or whether they reflect that our students lack motivation to do their best when taking a test that doesn't count toward their grade or graduation.

Nonetheless, the militaristic rhetoric of "A Nation at Risk" created a sense of crisis. States convened study groups, task forces, and committees to devise plans to confront this threat to the nation. All agreed that students needed more testing, and the public schools needed new accountability measures to prove their worth. States adopted new tests for promotion and graduation, and stronger graduation requirements. In 1989, President George H.W. Bush convened a summit of the nation's governors in Charlottesville, Virginia, to set national education goals for the year 2000. The governors and the Bush administration adopted six national goals. By the year 2000, for example, students in the U.S. would be first in the world in mathematics and science; by the year 2000, all children would start school ready to learn.

The federal government actually had limited means of

bringing any of the goals to fruition, since education was traditionally a state and local function, and the federal portion of funding was typically about 10 percent. What the federal government did have was a testing program called the National Assessment of Educational Progress (NAEP), which monitored achievement regionally. In 1992, in response to demands by governors, mainly in the South, the NAEP began reporting test scores not just by region, but by state. Anyone who wanted to know how students in Mississippi compared to students in Maine or Oregon could look at NAEP scores and find out.

There was no educational problem, it seemed, that could not be cured by more testing.

A few critics questioned the testing craze and wondered whether there was any crisis at all. David Berliner and Bruce Biddle belittled the claims of the politicians and pundits in *The Manufactured Crisis* (1995). Gerald Bracey wrote numerous columns and several books debunking the crisis talk. What did the test scores of high school students have to do with the growth of the Japanese automobile industry? Why blame high school students for the American automakers who continued to produce gas-guzzlers even after the oil-producing nations formed a cartel in the late 1970s to drive up the price of fuel? How could any of the industrial shifts to which the commission pointed be blamed on elementary and secondary teachers and students? Why hold them accountable for the outsourcing of manufacturing to low-wage countries in Latin America and Asia (with lower test scores than ours)? When the U.S. economy improved, would any of the politicians thank the schools? Of course not.

No matter. The demand for test scores became insatiable. Starting with President George H.W. Bush in 1988, every president wanted to be remembered as "the education president." His plan was called America 2000, and its purpose was to encourage the American people to strive to reach the national goals set by the governors at Charlottesville. Stymied by a Democratic Congress, Bush was unable to pass any legislation, and America 2000 soon faded into obscurity.

Then came Bill Clinton, who also wanted to be remembered as "the education president." He believed in the national goals and added two more to the original six (one about teacher training, another about parent involvement). Congress passed Goals 2000, Clinton's program, in 1994. It awarded money to states to devise their own standards and tests. Then came President George W. Bush, and his education program, No Child Left Behind, became law early in 2002. It was an audacious federal intrusion into education policy. It directed every state to test every child in reading and math every year from grades 3 through 8, while requiring that children be proficient in those two basic subjects by the year 2014.

This was an impossible goal, one that no nation in the world has ever met. Any school that did not make steady progress toward that goal was at risk of being closed, taken over by the state, or handed over to private management. With the passage of NCLB, the nation's public schools became obsessed with test scores. Failure to raise test scores every year jeopardized the survival of the school and the jobs of its staff. Many hundreds, possibly thousands, of public schools have been closed since the passage of NCLB, due to low test scores.

With the election of Barack Obama in 2008, educators expected that he would repudiate NCLB and help them cope with rising costs, budget cuts, and growing levels of poverty and non-English-speaking students. But the Obama administration was as fixated on test scores as its predecessors. In 2009, Obama and his Education Secretary Duncan unveiled the administration's own plan, Race to the Top. The very terminology signaled that this administration wanted test scores that were at the top of the world.

Race to the Top offered states a chance to win a share of $4.35 billion in federal funds if they agreed to open more privately managed charter schools, intervened aggressively to "turn around" their lowest-performing schools (for instance, by firing and replacing their staff), adopted rigorous standards (i.e., the Common Core) to demonstrate that students are "college-

and career-ready," and evaluated their teachers in relation to the test scores of their students. The Obama administration also favored "merit pay," paying teachers more if their students have higher test scores. Far from being a fresh initiative, Race to the Top reaffirmed the bipartisan consensus that scores on standardized tests are the ultimate decider of the fate of schools and teachers.

Obama and Duncan used the latest international test scores as proof that more testing, more rigor, was needed. The Obama administration, acting out the script of "A Nation at Risk," repeatedly treats our scores on these tests as a harbinger of economic doom, rather than as evidence that more testing does not produce higher test scores. Now, a dozen years after the passage of George W. Bush's NCLB, it is clear that testing every child every year does not produce better education, nor does it raise our standing on the greatly overvalued international tests.

At this juncture comes the book that Barack Obama, Arne Duncan, members of Congress, and the nation's governors and legislators need to read. Yong Zhao's *Who's Afraid of the Big Bad Dragon? Why China Has the Best (and Worst) Education System in the World.* Zhao, born and educated in China, now holds a presidential chair and a professorship at the University of Oregon. He tells us that China has the best education system because it can produce the highest test scores. But, he says, it has the worst education system in the world because those test scores are purchased by sacrificing creativity, divergent thinking, originality, and individualism. The imposition of standardized tests by central authorities, he argues, is a victory for authoritarianism. His book is a timely warning that we should not seek to emulate Shanghai, whose scores reflect a Confucian tradition of rote learning that is thousands of years old. Indeed, the highest-scoring nations on the PISA examinations of fifteen-year-olds are all Asian nations or cities: Shanghai, Hong Kong, Chinese Taipei, Singapore, Korea, Macao (China), and Japan.

Zhao explains that China has revered a centrally administered examination system for at least two thousand years as the sure path to professional esteem and a career in government. A system called *keju* lasted for thirteen hundred years, until 1905, when it was abolished by the emperor of the Qing dynasty. This system maintained Chinese civilization by requiring knowledge of the Confucian classics, based on memorization and writing about current affairs. There were local, provincial, and national examinations, each conferring privileges on the lucky or brilliant few who passed. Exam scores determined one's rank in society. The *keju* was a means of social mobility, but for the ruling elite, it produced the most capable individuals for governing the country.

*Keju*, writes Zhao, was China's fifth great invention, "along with gunpowder, the compass, paper, and movable type." Because it was seen as meritocratic, the *keju* system was adopted in other East Asian nations such as Japan, Korea, and Vietnam. It "shaped East Asia's most fundamental, enduring educational values." Zhao holds *keju* responsible for China's inability to evolve into a modern scientific and technological nation:

> For example, the Chinese used their compass mainly to help find building locations and burial sites with good *fengshui* – not to navigate the oceans and expand across the globe as the West did. Gunpowder stopped at a level good enough for fireworks, but not for the modern weaponry that gave the West its military might.

China had all the elements necessary for an industrial revolution at least four hundred years before Great Britain, but *keju* diverted scholars, geniuses, and thinkers away from the study or exploration of modern science. The examination system, Zhao holds, was designed to reward obedience, conformity, compliance, respect for order, and homogeneous thinking, and for this reason it purposefully supported Confucian orthodoxy and imperial order. It was an efficient means of authoritarian social control. Everyone wanted to succeed on the highly competitive exams, but few did. Success on the *keju* enforced orthodoxy, not innovation or dissent. As Zhao writes, emperors came and went, but China had "no Renaissance, no Enlightenment, no Industrial Revolution."

Zhao says that China's remarkable economic growth over the past three decades was due not to its education system, which still relies heavily on testing and rote memorization, but to its willingness to open its markets to foreign capital, to welcome Western technology, and to send students to Western institutions of higher education. The more that China retreats from central planning, the more its economy thrives. To maintain economic growth, he insists, China needs technological innovation, which it will never develop unless it abandons its test-based education system, now controlled by *gaokao*, the all-important college entrance exams. Yet this test-based education system is responsible for the high performance of Shanghai, Hong Kong, and East Asian nations on the international tests.

China has a problem, however, that is seldom discussed – cheating and fraud. When the government rewards the production of patents for new products, the number of patents soars, but most of them are worthless. High school students get extra points for college admission if they receive patents for their proposals. Zhao points to a school where a ninth-grade class had received over twenty patents – the school as a whole had registered over five hundred patents in three years. Even middle school students had collected national patents. A large proportion of these patents, writes Zhao, are "junk patents" or demonstrations of "small cleverness." When the government requires the publication of scientific papers for professional advancement, the number of scientific papers increases dramatically, but a high proportion of those papers are fraudulent. Zhao says there is a billion-dollar industry in China devoted to writing "scientific" papers for sale to students and professionals who lack the research skills to write their own.

The quality of China's patents and research publications, Zhao says, is "abysmal," because of the circumstances under which they are produced and the ubiquity of fraud. Any criticism of the authoritarian culture that produces cheating and fraud is "viewed as un-Chinese and anti-Chinese" and might lead to "political and legal troubles."

Zhao quotes Zheng Yefu, a professor at Peking University and the author of a popular book in 2013 titled *The Pathology of Chinese Education*, who wrote:

> No one, after 12 years of Chinese education, has any chance to receive a Nobel Prize, even if he or she went to Harvard, Yale, Oxford or Cambridge for college....
>
> Out of the one billion people who have been educated in Mainland China since 1949, there has been no Nobel Prize winner....
>
> This forcefully testifies [to] the power of education in destroying creativity on behalf of the [Chinese] society.

This was written after officials who administer the PISA examinations had hailed Shanghai for its remarkably high test scores. Zhao says this is what Chinese students, even in rural areas, are best at – high test scores. Chinese students regularly win any competition that depends on test performance. Where they fall short is creativity, originality, and divergence from authority. The admirers of Chinese test scores never point out that what makes it the "best" education system is also what makes it the worst education system. Zhao writes that:

> The most damaging aspect of Chinese education is its effectiveness in eliminating individual differences, suppressing intrinsic motivation, and imposing conformity. The Chinese education system is a well-designed and continuously perfected machine that effectively and efficiently transmits a narrow band of predetermined content and cultivates prescribed skills. Moreover, the system determines people's livelihood. Because it is the only path to social mobility, people follow it eagerly.
>
> China is trapped by Western praise. Its education leaders,

Zhao writes, would like to break free of the exam-based orthodoxy that limits creativity, but they dare not abandon the methods that produce the results that Westerners admire.

China is accustomed to hierarchy and ranking, and the education system delivers both. As the only path to success, students are ranked according to their performance, and very few will win the race. Competition is fierce for the top spots in the top schools and universities. Not surprisingly, wealthy parents resort to cheating and bribery to give their children advantages, such as extra lessons, the best teachers, and the best schools. Chinese educators complain that the competition makes children unhappy and unhealthy, and that it is unfair and inequitable.

Zhao describes the lengths to which students go to get high scores. Many of the courses they take are specifically geared for test preparation, not learning. Schools exist to prepare for the tests:

> Teachers guess possible items, companies sell answers and wireless cheating devices to students, and students engage in all sorts of elaborate cheating. In 2013, a riot broke out because a group of students in Hubei Province were stopped from executing the cheating scheme their parents purchased to ease their college entrance exam.

Zhao quotes the British newspaper *The Daily Telegraph* as reporting that an angry mob of two thousand people smashed cars and chanted, "We want fairness. There is no fairness if you do not let us cheat." He goes on to note that in the last year of high school, many schools do nothing but test preparation – "No new content is taught.... A large proportion of publications for children in China are practice test papers."

The most shocking story that Zhao tells is about a rural township in Anhui province that is known as Asia's largest test-prep machine. It is home to Maotanchang or Mao Zhong, a residential secondary school devoted to test preparation. More than 11,000 students from this school took the college entrance exam in 2013, and 82 percent scored high enough to gain admission to a four-year college. Tuition is about $6,000, the same as the average annual income for residents of Shanghai. Parents pay for a year's living expenses in addition to tuition. Students come to this school from across China to prepare for the tests. The workload is three times what it is in the typical Chinese school. Students are in class by 6:30 AM and finish for the day at 10:30 PM, with homework yet to do. Zhao describes that:

> The school has become a legend in China. The national TV network, CCTV, sent a drone to capture the send-off for more than ten thousand students, traveling in seventy buses, escorted by police cars, to take the exam on June 5, 2013.

Leading Chinese educators have attempted to reduce the importance of examinations, but thus far have failed. Zhao calls testing "the witch that cannot be killed." No matter how often they issue directives to reduce homework and academic pressure, the pressure remains, enforced by schools and parents. Zhao wrote his book to warn Americans not to abandon their historic values of creativity and innovation, not to be lured by China's high test scores, and not to be corrupted by authoritarian standards and tests. Americans mistake "China's miseries as secrets to success." China, he writes, is "a perfect incarnation of authoritarian education." It is no model for the United States:

> As traditional routine jobs are offshored and automated, we need more and more globally competent, creative, innovative, entrepreneurial citizens – job creators instead of employment-minded job seekers.
>
> To cultivate new talents, we need an education that enhances individual strengths, follows children's passions, and fosters their social-emotional development. We do *not* need an authoritarian education that aims to fix children's deficits according to externally prescribed standards.

> If the West is concerned about being overtaken by China, then the best solution is "to avoid becoming China."

The United States is already ensnared in the testing obsession that has trapped China. It is not too late to escape. Parents and educators across the nation are up in arms about the amount of instructional time now devoted to test preparation and testing. Yong Zhao offers wise counsel. We should break our addiction to standardized testing before we sacrifice the cultural values that have made our nation a home to innovation, creativity, originality, and invention.

Zhao believes that the two major changes that should shape education policy are globalization and technology. Students need to understand the world that they will live in, and to master technology. Repelled by test-based accountability, standardization, and authoritarianism, he advocates for the autonomy of well-prepared teachers and the individual development of their students. He strongly urges that the U.S. equalize the funding of schools, broadly redefine the desired outcomes of schooling beyond test scores, and eliminate the opportunity gaps among students of different racial groups.

He rejects the current "reforms" that demand uniformity and a centrally controlled curriculum. He envisions schools where students produce books, videos, and art, where they are encouraged to explore and experiment. He imagines ways of teaching by which the individual strengths of every student are developed, not under pressure, but by their intrinsic motivation. He dreams of schools where the highest value is creativity, where students are encouraged to be, as he wrote in his last book, *World Class Learners,* "confident, curious, and creative." Until we break free of standardized testing, this ideal will remain out of reach.

# AN OPEN LETTER TO LAMAR ALEXANDER: DON'T FORGET RULE #84 IN THE LITTLE PLAID BOOK

HUFFINGTON POST, JANUARY 20, 2015

*"I hate to criticize Texas, because it is my native state. On the other hand, Texas brought us NCLB and promoted testing as the answer to all our ills. And frankly, it has always been nutty when it comes time to adopt textbooks." – Diane Ravitch's Blog*

Senator Lamar Alexander
U.S. Senate
Washington, D.C.

Dear Lamar,

I wish I could be in Washington for the hearings about the reauthorization of NCLB. I can't make it for two reasons: I wasn't invited, and I have a date to speak to parents at P.S. 3 in Manhattan who are outraged about all the testing imposed on their children.

I learned a lot about education policy and federalism after you chose me to serve as your Assistant Secretary of Education in charge of research and improvement and as counsel to the Secretary of Education (you). I am imagining that I am still advising you, as I did from 1991 to 1993 (remember that you and every other top administrator in the Department left a day before the inauguration of Bill Clinton, and you told me I was Acting Secretary for the day?). What I always admired about you was your deliberateness, your thoughtfulness, your ability to listen to discordant voices, and your respect for federalism. You didn't think you were smarter than everyone else in the country just because you were a member of the President's Cabinet. You understood federalism. You didn't think it was your job to impose what you wanted on every school in America. You respected the ability of local communities to govern their schools without your supervision or dictation.

NCLB was not informed by your wisdom. It set impossible goals, then established punishments for schools that could not do the impossible. I remember a panel discussion in early 2002 at the Willard Hotel soon after NCLB was signed. You were on the panel. I was in the audience, and I stood up and asked you whether you truly believed that 100% of all children in grades 3-8 would be "proficient" by 2014. You answered, "No, Diane, but we think it is good to have goals." Well, based on goals that you knew were out of reach, teachers and principals have been fired, and many schools – beloved in their communities – have been closed.

NCLB has introduced an unprecedented level of turmoil into the nation's public education system. Wearing my conservative hat, I have to say that it's wrong to disrupt the lives of communities, schools, families, and children to satisfy an absurd federal mandate, based on a false premise and based too on the non-existent "Texas miracle." Conservatives are not fire-breathing radicals who seek to destroy community and tradition. Conservatives conserve, conservatives believe in incremental change, not in upheaval and disruption.

I urge you to abandon the annual mandated federal testing in grades 3-8. Little children are sitting for 8-10 hours to take the annual tests in math and reading. As a parent, you surely understand that this is madness. This is why the Opt Out movement is growing across the nation, as parents protest what feels like federally-mandated child abuse.

Do we need to compare the performance of states? NAEP does that already. Anyone who wants to know how Mississippi compares to Massachusetts can look at the NAEP results, which are released every two years. Do we want disaggregated data? NAEP reports scores by race, gender, English language proficiency, and disability status. How will we learn about achievement gaps if we don't test every child annually? NAEP reports that too. In short, we already have the information that everyone says they want and need.

NCLB has forced teachers to teach to the test. That once was considered unethical and unprofessional, but now it is an accepted practice in schools across the country. NCLB has caused many schools to spend more time and resources on test prep, interim assessments, and testing. That means narrowing the curriculum: when testing matters so much, there is less time for the arts, physical education, foreign languages, civics, and other valuable studies and activities. Over this past dozen years, there have been numerous examples of states gaming the system and educators cheating because the tests determine whether schools will live or die, and whether educators will get a bonus or be fired.

I urge you to enact what you call "option one," grade span testing, and to abandon annual testing. If you keep annual testing in the law, states and districts will continue to engage in the mis-education that NCLB incentivized. Bad habits die hard, if at all.

Just say no to annual testing. No high-performing nation does it, and neither should we. We are the most over-tested nation in the world, and it's time to encourage children to sing, dance, play instruments, write poetry, imagine stories, create videos, make science projects, write history papers, and discover the joy of learning.

As I learned from you, the U.S. Department of Education should not act as a National School Board. The Secretary of Education is not the National Superintendent of Schools. The past dozen years of centralizing control of education in Washington, D.C., has not been good for education or for democracy.

The law governing the activities of the U.S. Department of Education states clearly that no federal official should attempt to "exercise any direction, supervision, or control over the curriculum, program of instruction, [or] administration … of any educational institution." When I was your Assistant Secretary and Counselor, I was very much aware of that prohibition. For the past dozen years, it seems to have been forgotten. Just a few years ago, the current administration funded tests for the Common Core standards, which will most assuredly exert control over the curriculum and program of instruction. The federal tests will determine what is taught.

The nation has seen a startling expansion of federal

power over local community public schools since the passage of NCLB. There is certainly an important role for the federal government in ensuring equality of educational opportunity and informing the American people about the progress of education. But the federal role today is taking on responsibilities that belong to states and local districts. The key mechanism for that takeover is annual testing, the results of which are used to dictate other policies of dubious legality and validity, like evaluating teachers and even colleges of education by student test scores.

Sir, please revise the federal law so that it authorizes the federal government to do what it does best: protecting the rights of children, gathering data, sponsoring research, encouraging the improvement of teaching, funding special education, and distributing resources to the neediest districts to help the neediest students (which was the original purpose of the Elementary and Secondary Education Act of 1965).

In closing, may I remind you of something you wrote in your book of advice?

No. 84: Read anything Diane Ravitch writes about education.

**Lamar Alexander**, *Little Plaid Book*, page 44

I agree with you.

Yours truly,
Diane Ravitch

# THE LOST PURPOSE OF SCHOOL REFORM

## THE NEW YORK REVIEW OF BOOKS - NYR DAILY, APRIL 2, 2015

*"I wonder why our policymakers in Washington, D.C., love euphemisms. Ten years ago, Congress passed No Child Left Behind, and by now, is there anyone in the United States who takes seriously the idea that "No Child" has been "Left Behind"? Since Congress can't agree on how to change the law, maybe they could just rename it and call it "Many Children Left Behind" (MCLB) or "No Child Left Untested" (NCLU). When the name of a federal law is so clearly at odds with its actual results, either we must rename the law or declare it a failure or both. But, please, no euphemisms, no flowery predictions in the title of the legislation." – Diane Ravitch's Blog*

Fifty years ago, Congress passed a federal education law to help poor children get a good public education – the Elementary and Secondary Education Act (ESEA) of 1965. Revised many times, it is still the basis for federal education policy today. When it was last reauthorized in 2001, it was named "No Child Left Behind," which was President George W. Bush's signature education initiative. Both the House and the Senate are now debating a reauthorization of the law, which has been pending since 2007. Since the law gives Congress the power to determine how federal dollars will be spent, it is crucial to understand its origins and how it has evolved over time. Much is at stake.

ESEA was originally conceived as part of President Lyndon B. Johnson's "war on poverty." It had one overriding purpose – to send federal funding to schools that enrolled large numbers of children living in poverty. The schools that stood to benefit most were mainly in the South and in big cities.

Advocates of federal aid to public schools had been trying without success to persuade Congress to approve it since the 1870s. Their efforts consistently failed because neither party trusted the other to control the nation's schools. Over the years, there were other complicating issues. Southern members of Congress (all of whom were white) feared that federal aid might be used to interfere with racially segregated schools, urban members of Congress opposed federal aid unless it also served children in Catholic schools, and in the mid-twentieth century, far-right conservatives suspected that the federal bureaucracy might push Communist ideas into school curriculums.

President Johnson was a master persuader, and he assuaged everyone's concerns. The purpose of the law, he insisted, was to help poor children get a better education, and everyone could agree on that. The South could no longer preserve its segregated system, not only because of the *Brown v. Board of Education* decision of 1954, but because Congress had passed the Civil Rights Act of 1964, giving the federal government the power it needed to demand desegregation of southern schools. Catholics were mollified because they were included in ESEA's funding (a Supreme Court decision later removed them). And by 1965, the Red Scare had subsided and was no longer an obstacle to federal aid to education. The bill was funded with $1 billion, and the federal government was at last committed to policies aimed at providing minorities and the poor with the same quality of education as everyone else. That funding, however, was far from sufficient, because public schools are typically underwritten by property taxes, which favor those who live in affluent areas.

Over the years, federal education funding for poor children has steadily grown but has never been enough to overcome the vast inequities between rich and poor. The United States is one of the few advanced nations in the world that spends more public money on rich children than on poor children.[110]

With the passage of time, new federal programs were added to ESEA, such as funding for bilingual education, anti-drug programs, and charter schools. But the major shift in its purpose occurred in 1994, when the Clinton administration renamed it the Improving America's Schools Act and required states to write academic standards and develop state tests for at least reading and mathematics. This was the first codification in federal law of the idea that uniform standards and testing were necessary to ensure equal access to education.

Seven years later, when Congress again reauthorized the ESEA, and the Bush administration renamed it No Child Left Behind (NCLB), President George W. Bush and his advisors touted what was known at the time as "the Texas miracle." This was subsequently discredited as campaign overstatement. The Bush team claimed that the mere act of testing children every year and publishing the results created an incentive for teachers and students to produce higher test scores and better graduation rates. The new federal law became a mandate for annual testing of all children in grades 3 to 8 in reading and mathematics. States could use their own tests, but schools had to improve their passing rates every year or face increasingly onerous sanctions.

NCLB decisively changed the purpose of the law. What had once been a means of sending additional resources to schools enrolling poor students was turned into a testing mandate. By law, all students, regardless of disability or language proficiency, had to be "proficient" on state tests by 2014. Congress and the Bush administration believed that their mandate could produce universal success in school, akin to passing a law proclaiming that all crime should cease by a date certain. Note to Congress: if wishes (or congressional mandates) were horses, then beggars would ride.

Not surprisingly, it didn't work. Very few schools reached 100 percent proficiency, and the nation's entire public education system "failed," by the law's definition. Had the law been followed to the letter, almost every public school by now would be closed or handed over to private management. NCLB was chaos by design. It was a giant death star for public education.

President Obama's secretary of education, Arne Duncan, offered waivers to allow states to avoid some of the dire consequences of the law, but states had to accept his conditions if they wanted them. He demanded more upheaval, more chaos. They had to agree to open more charter schools, to evaluate teachers to a significant degree by the test scores of their students, and to take drastic action to change low-performing schools – like closing the school, privatizing it, or firing the entire staff. None of these "remedies" was supported by research or experience, but almost every state eagerly sought a waiver. When Washington State refused to judge its teachers by test scores, a practice decisively refuted by the American Statistical Association,[111] Duncan withdrew the state's waiver, and subsequently, every superintendent in the state was compelled by NCLB to inform parents that their child was attending a failing school.

Now Congress is struggling to reauthorize NCLB. Since Republicans took control of both houses of Congress in the last election, they are in charge of this process. Lamar Alexander of Tennessee, chairman of the Senate Committee on Health, Education, Labor, and Pensions, is leading the reauthorization process in that chamber. His proposal is called "Every Child Ready for College or Career Act of 2015." In the House, the NCLB revision is led by Minnesota Congressman John Kline, whose proposal is called "the Student Success Act." Notice the difference from 1965, when the law was simply called the Elementary and Secondary Education Act. Now, every law is given an aspirational title (like No Child Left Behind) that bears little relation to its actual effects.

Both of the Republican-led revisions under consideration have a single goal, and that is to reduce the federal government's heavy-handed involvement in education since the passage of NCLB. Secretary Duncan has been especially intrusive, as he promoted the untested Common Core State Standards, advocated on behalf of privately managed charter schools, weakened student privacy laws, applauded school closings, and allocated $360 million to create tests aligned with the Common Core standards. Federal law already says clearly that no federal official should seek to control or direct curriculum and instruction, and Duncan disingenuously claims that he has kept his hands off those areas. But standardized tests have a decisive influence on curriculum and instruction, and he knows it. Educators often say, "What gets tested is what gets taught." The Common Core standards, funded entirely by the Bill and Melinda Gates Foundation, directly affect curriculum and instruction, and they have been avidly promoted by Duncan, despite the law's strictures.

As negotiations proceed, there are two major sticking points – the NCLB requirement for annual tests, and the Republicans' demand to make federal funding "portable," enabling students to take "their" money and enroll in a private school or a charter school.

The annual testing mandated by the federal government has changed public schools in dramatic ways because they are now used to determine the fate of students, teachers, principals, and schools. More time for testing means less time for instruction. Students are the losers. The testing industry has benefited, especially the British giant Pearson. Not only did Pearson win the contract to write one of the federally-funded tests, it also now sells curriculum and textbooks aligned with the Common Core, owns the GED (which awards high school diplomas to students who did not graduate with their class), and has gained control of the teacher-certification process as well through a program called edTPA.

Parents and educators have noisily opposed the annual testing mandate, which they think places too much emphasis on standardized tests and causes schools to cut funding for the arts, physical education, foreign languages, history, and other subjects. Even now, many thousands of parents are refusing to allow their children to sit for the Common Core tests to protest them. The Common Core tests are not like tests that adults took many years ago – they require anywhere from eight to eleven hours and are "delivered" online. In the past, teachers wrote their own tests to find out what students had or had not learned. They could tailor instruction to help students who had fallen behind. But results from the new standardized tests are not reported until four to six months after the tests, and teachers are not permitted to see how students answered specific questions. Thus, everyone ends up with a grade – the student, the teacher, the principal, and the school – but the tests have no diagnostic value because teachers cannot learn from them about the needs of their students.

Despite widespread parent and teacher opposition to the law's testing mandate, Congress seems determined to retain annual testing as part of federal law. Senator Alexander considered the idea of grade span testing – that is, tests offered once in elementary school, once in middle school, and once in high school. But President Obama and Secretary Duncan insist on annual testing, as does Senator Patty Murray of Washington State, the leading Democratic on the Senate committee. And civil rights groups demand it as well, even though minority children have overwhelmingly failed the new Common Core tests. Apparently, the Obama administration has convinced them that their children will be overlooked unless their failure is demonstrated repeatedly by the tests.

Ironically, it is Democrats who are most determined to preserve President George W. Bush's legacy of high-stakes testing. It is worthy of note that none of the world's highest-performing nations – such as Finland, Japan, China, Korea, Canada, Poland, Estonia, and Singapore – tests every child every year. In that burdensome and expensive practice, the United States stands alone.

The second issue holding up reauthorization is the "portability" of federal funding. Republicans have long embraced the principle of school choice, which has more to do with ideology than evidence. They assert that federal money should follow the child to any school his family selects, whether it is public, private, charter, or religious. Democrats have typically opposed this argument, noting that federal aid can then be used to weaken public education and spur the privatization of elementary and secondary schools. Vouchers have nowhere been more successful than public schools, and the public has rejected them whenever they were on the ballot. Charter schools have a spotty record. A few charter chains post high test scores, but most charters perform no better – and often much worse – than public schools.

This is a useful time to remember that the original Elementary and Secondary Education Act had one purpose – to send additional resources to schools enrolling large numbers of poor children. Over the past two decades, ESEA has become a vehicle for those who believe that standards and testing will cure poverty and low performance, a strategy that has failed to attain its goal after two decades of trying. With the Republican ascendancy, ESEA has become a vehicle for those who want to replace public education with a choice system, inserting their political goals into a program where they do not belong. All of the partisans are substituting their ideology for the commonsense understanding of Lyndon B. Johnson that poverty is the major obstacle to equal education. To overcome that obstacle requires not only investing greater resources in the education of poor children, but creating economic opportunity and jobs for their parents.

# I BELIEVE IN FREEDOM OF CHOICE

HUFFINGTON POST, JUNE 11, 2015

Parents should be able to send their children to the school of their choice, and they do, but the public should not be expected to pay for their private choices.

The public has a civic obligation to support public education. Even if you don't have children, you pay taxes to educate the children of the community. Even if your children are grown, you pay school taxes. Even if you send your children to private school, you pay school taxes. Public schools are a public responsibility.

If you don't like the public schools, you are free to choose a private school, a charter school, a religious school, or home school. That's your choice. But you must pay for it yourself.

We all pay for police and firefighters. If you want a private security guard, pay for it yourself. We all pay for public schools, even if we don't patronize them. They belong to the community. We do so to invest in the future of our society. It is a civic obligation.

We all pay to support public libraries. If you never use the local library, you still have to pay the taxes to support it. If you prefer to buy books instead of using the free public library, don't ask taxpayers to subsidize your private choice. Buy your own books. Pay for it yourself.

The taxes you pay support the common good, not your private preferences. They pay for highways you may never drive on, fire departments you may never call on, beaches open to all that you may never set foot on, public parks, and a range of services and facilities open to all without fee.

When it comes to education, there is a simple rule. Public money for free, democratically controlled schools, private money for private, privately-controlled, and religious schools.

# ARNE DUNCAN'S LEGACY

## HUFFINGTON POST, JULY 9, 2015

Lyndsey Layton of *The Washington Post* has written a sympathetic article[112] about Arne Duncan and the waning of his powers as Secretary of Education. He is a nice guy. He is a close friend of the president. He cares about individual children that he met along the way. The pending reauthorization of the Elementary and Secondary Education Act will prohibit him and future Secretaries from interfering in state decisions about standards, curriculum and assessment. His family has already moved back to Chicago. But he will stay on the job to the very end.

When Obama was elected, many educators and parents thought that Obama would bring a new vision of the federal role in education, one that freed schools from the test-and-punish mindset of George W. Bush's No Child Left Behind. But Arne Duncan and Barack Obama had a vision no different from George W. Bush and doubled down on the importance of testing, while encouraging privatization and undermining the teaching profession with a $50 million grant to Teach for America to place more novice teachers in high-needs schools. Duncan never said a bad word about charters, no matter how many scandals and frauds were revealed.

During Duncan's tenure in office:

- He used his control of billions of dollars to promote a dual school system of privately managed charter schools operating alongside public schools.

- He has done nothing to call attention to the fraud and corruption in the charter sector or to curb charters run by non-educators for profit or to insist on charter school accountability or to require charters to enroll the neediest children.
- He pushed to require states to evaluate teachers by the test scores of their students, which has caused massive demoralization among teachers, raised the stakes attached to testing, and produced no positive results.
- He used federal funds and waivers from NCLB to push the adoption of Common Core standards and to create two testing consortia, which many states have abandoned.
- The Common Core tests are so absurdly "rigorous" that most students have failed them, even in schools that send high percentages of students to four-year colleges. The failure rates have been highest among students who are English language learners, students with disabilities, and students of color.
- He has bemoaned rising resegregation of the schools but has done nothing to reduce it.
- He has been silent as state after state has attacked collective bargaining and due process for teachers.
- He has done nothing in response to the explosion of voucher programs that transfer public funds to religious schools.
- Because of his policies, enrollments in teacher education programs, even in Teach for America, have plummeted, and many experienced teachers are taking early retirement.
- He has unleashed a mad frenzy of testing in classrooms across the country, treating standardized test scores as the goal of all education, rather than as a measure.

- His tenure has been marked by the rise of an aggressive privatization movement, which seeks to eliminate public education in urban districts, where residents have the least political power.
- He loosened the regulations on the federal student privacy act, permitting massive data mining of the data banks that federal funds created.
- He looked the other way as predatory for-profit colleges preyed on veterans and minorities, plunging students deep into debt.
- Duncan has regularly accused parents and teachers of "lying" to students. For reasons that are unclear, he wants everyone to believe that our public schools are terrible, our students are lazy, not too bright, and lacking ambition. If he were a basketball coach, he would have been encouraging the team to try harder and to reach for greater accomplishment, but instead he took every opportunity to run down the team and repeat how dreadful they are. He spoke of "respect" but he never showed it.

This era has not been good for students. Nearly a quarter live in poverty, and fully 51% live in low-income families.

This era has not been good for teachers, who feel disrespected and demeaned by governors, legislatures, and the U.S. Department of Education.

This era has not been good for parents, who see their local public schools lose resources to charter schools and see their children subjected to endless, intensive testing.

It will take years to recover from the damage that Arne Duncan's policies have inflicted on public education. He exceeded the authority of his office to promote a failed agenda, one that had no evidence behind it.

The next president and the next Secretary of Education will have an enormous job to do to restore our nation's public education system from the damage done by Race to the Top. We need leadership that believes in the joy of learning and in equality of educational opportunity. We have not had either for 15 years.

# SOLVING THE MYSTERY OF THE SCHOOLS

THE NEW YORK REVIEW OF BOOKS, MARCH 24, 2016

In recent years, American public education has been swamped by bad ideas and policies. Our national leaders, most of whom were educated at elite universities and should know better, have turned our most important domestic duty into a quest for higher scores on standardized tests. While it is true that students must do well on standardized tests to enter universities, few of the better universities judge students' knowledge and ability solely by such flimsy measures. Thus it is puzzling why public officials have made test scores the purpose of education.

The heavy reliance on standardized tests in schools began with the passage of George W. Bush's No Child Left Behind legislation in 2001. The law mandated that every child in every school would take standardized tests in reading and math from grades three through eight and would achieve "proficiency" by the year 2014. No excuses. Even children who could not read English and children with significant cognitive handicaps would be expected to reach "proficiency." Every state was left to define "proficiency" as it wished.

The punishments for not achieving higher test scores every year were increasingly onerous. A school that fell behind in the first year would be required to hire tutors. In the second year, it would have to offer its students the choice to move to a different school. By the end of five years, if it was not on track to achieve

100 percent proficiency, the school might be handed over to a private manager, turned into a charter school, taken over by the state, or closed. In fact, there was no evidence that any of these sanctions would lead to better schools or higher test scores, but no matter.

With these sanctions in mind, schools made intense efforts to prepare children to take the all-important tests. In some places, like Atlanta, Washington, D.C., and El Paso, Texas, teachers, principals, and superintendents cheated, changing the scores to save their jobs or their schools. Schools across the nation spent more time and money on preparing materials to help students pass tests and reduced the time for the arts, science, history, physical education, and even recess. Some states, such as New York and Illinois, manipulated the passing scores on the tests by lowering the definition of proficiency needed in order to demonstrate progress.

After Bush left office and was replaced by Barack Obama, the obsession with testing grew even more intense. Congress gave Secretary of Education Arne Duncan $5 billion in economic stimulus funds to encourage education reforms. Duncan released a plan in 2009 called Race to the Top, pledging that American students would be "racing to the top" of the international tables of comparative scores if they followed his policies.

In order to be eligible to compete for a share of that money at a time of deep economic distress, states had to adopt Duncan's strategies. They had to expand the number of privately managed charter schools in the state, and they had to agree to adopt "college-and-career-ready standards" – which were the not-yet-completed Common Core State Standards. They had to agree, moreover, to evaluate teachers in relation to the rise or fall of the test scores of their students, and they had to agree to "turn around" schools with low test scores by firing the principal, or firing all or half of the staff, or doing something equally drastic.

The standardized tests immediately became more important than ever. Some states introduced standardized testing as early as kindergarten to begin getting children ready for the big standardized tests that would consume their time in school from grades three through eight. The competition among the states was keen, everyone needed more money. Forty-six states and the District of Columbia changed their laws to make themselves eligible for Race to the Top funding, but only eighteen states and D.C. won the money.

Duncan endorsed the premise of the No Child Left Behind Act that standardized tests are the best measure of student achievement, but he was upset that the fifty states each had its own standards and tests. Thus when several Washington-based groups (the National Governors Association, Achieve, the Council of Chief State School Officers, and Student Achievement Partners) began work on national standards, Duncan cheered them on. Federal law bars any federal official from seeking to influence or control curriculum or instruction, and Duncan drew a fine line between his outspoken advocacy for the Common Core standards and his funding of Race to the Top. However, he did allocate $360 million to two consortiums of testing experts to prepare new tests for the Common Core State Standards.

As it happened, the Bill and Melinda Gates Foundation spent at least $200 million to pay for the writing and distribution of the standards. It also awarded millions of dollars to practically every influential national education organization to encourage them to support the standards, including the two major teachers' unions, think tanks on the right and left, and civil rights organizations. Advocates for the standards claimed that they would make America globally competitive, and would close the gaping test score gaps between white and Asian students on one hand, and African-American and Latino students on the other.

They didn't know that this was true because the standards had just been written and never tried out, but they dutifully carried this message to the mass media and the public. Before long, a public backlash developed against both the Common Core standards and testing, in large measure because they were imposed with minimal public awareness, consultation, and engagement.

Educators were overwhelmed in a short period of time by the mandates raining down on them from the state and federal governments. Early childhood experts complained that the Common Core standards were too academic for young children and that they squelched play and socialization. Kindergartners are expected to learn to read, experts say that it doesn't matter when children start reading, whether at four, five, six, even seven. The five-year-olds are also supposed to master the conventions of capitalization and punctuation, even though many are just beginning to learn how to hold a pencil.

The standards created unnecessary controversy by setting an artificial division between the percentage of time students read either literature or "informational text." In fourth grade, students are supposed to spend 50 percent of instructional time reading literature and 50 percent on informational text. By twelfth grade, only 30 percent of student readings should consist of literature, and the remaining 70 percent of informational text. No other nation in the world, to my knowledge, tells teachers what proportion of their reading assignments should be literature or nonfiction.

Independent researchers contended that the standards were two grade levels above the capacity of the students for whom they were written. No efforts were made to field-test the standards in order to see how they worked in real classrooms with real students, and to learn whether they would disproportionately affect the test scores of students who were already at the bottom. The tests were designed with an absurdly high passing score, and in every state, a majority of students failed to meet the test-makers' definition of "proficiency."

In New York State, 220,000 students refused to take the state tests in 2015. This is called "opting out" of the test. A survey conducted by the Council of the Great City Schools, which represents sixty-eight urban districts, reported that the average student takes 112 standardized tests from pre-kindergarten to the end of high school, most of which are mandated by the federal government. The new online tests for the Common Core require children in grades three to eight to sit for fifteen to twenty hours over a two-week period to measure their reading and math skills. National opinion polls showed that a majority of parents thought there was too much testing in schools.

In response to such expressions of parental opposition, the Obama administration announced in late October that it was taking action to reduce the burden of standardized testing. Secretary Duncan issued a statement saying that testing was consuming too much instructional time and "causing undue stress for students and educators." The one concrete proposal in the Obama "Testing Action Plan" was advice to states and districts to limit tests to no more than 2 percent of class time. Since most schools are in session 180 days a year for at least six hours a day, the limit translates to twenty-one hours of testing time. In other words, the 2 percent "limit" merely confirmed the status quo, while giving the appearance that the administration was making genuine changes. Nothing in the administration's plan allowed states to drop the failed practice of evaluating the quality of teachers by the test scores of their students.

In early December 2015, Congress passed and President Obama signed a new federal law, replacing Bush's No Child Left Behind. It is called the Every Student Succeeds Act, or ESSA, which is another way of saying "no child left behind" – why Congress feels the need to put an unrealistic prediction into the title of legislation is baffling. Like NCLB, the new law requires annual testing of students in grades three to eight in reading and mathematics, but it turns this responsibility over to the states. ESSA prohibits future secretaries of education from meddling in states' decisions and contracts the federal role in education. It also eliminates federal punishments for schools and teachers with low test scores, leaving those decisions to the states. What is not abandoned is the core belief that standardized testing and accountability are the right levers to improve education.

The best metaphor for education reform today is Dr. Seuss's children's book *Yertle the Turtle*. Yertle, the master turtle, forced all the other turtles to pile themselves into a very high stack so that he could survey his kingdom. From where Yertle sat, perched on top, everything looked grand and glorious. Those on the bottom were not experiencing anything but pain and frustration. When the pile collapsed, Yertle was brought back to earth and got his comeuppance. This will likely be the fate of the politicians, economists, and business leaders who decided to reform the nation's schools, at a distance, without consulting working educators.

And thus we have two new books – Dale Russakoff's *The Prize: Who's in Charge of America's Schools?* and Kristina Rizga's *Mission High: One School, How Experts Tried to Fail It, and the Students and Teachers Who Made It Triumph* – that give readers the view from the top and the view from the bottom. They are both excellent. By sheer coincidence, the authors each spent four years embedded in the stories they report. Each learned different but not conflicting lessons.

Russakoff's *The Prize* is a gripping story about a plan hatched by Mayor Cory Booker of Newark and newly elected Governor Chris Christie of New Jersey to turn Newark into a national model of education reform. Central to this hoped-for miraculous transformation was a gift of $100 million by Facebook founder Mark Zuckerberg, matched by donations of another $100 million by other philanthropists who wanted to take part in a great adventure.

Russakoff was for many years a political reporter at *The Washington Post*, and she writes with wonderful clarity about a complex story that above all concerns politics – Newark politics, New Jersey politics, the politics of extracting large sums of money from very rich donors, the politics of rich white people imposing change on a suspicious African-American community. This is not to say that Russakoff neglects education, but the focal points of her story are the struggle for control of Newark's $1 billion budget ("the prize") and the struggle between would-be reformers like Cory Booker and the people of Newark, who wanted some say in what happened to their children.

Newark is the largest city in New Jersey, but one of the

poorest. Its population contracted after the riots of the 1960s, and turned from majority-white to majority-black. Enrollment in its public schools dropped dramatically, as Russakoff shows. In 1967, there were about 77,000 students; currently, there are about 30,000, with another 13,000 in charter schools. More than 70 percent of families are headed by a single parent, 42 percent of children live below the poverty level, and the median income for families with children is less than $30,000. Newark's public schools had abysmal test scores and graduation rates and were generally considered a failure, despite high annual expenditures.

Newark had one major attraction for the reformers. Its schools have been under state control since 1995. The governor had total control of the district, its budget, and its leadership. The district had been taken over by the state because of poor academic performance and pervasive corruption. But in the next fifteen years, the state had not gotten better results than the regime it displaced. Newark's mayor since 2006, Cory Booker, wanted to uproot the school system and start over.

Booker had been raised in the nearly all-white suburb of Harrington Park, New Jersey, and had graduated from Stanford, Oxford, and Yale. He was a frequent guest on national television shows, and he moved easily among the rich, the powerful, and the famous. Russakoff describes a ride that Booker took with Governor-Elect Christie through Newark one night in December 2009, when they agreed to create a plan for a radical transformation of the Newark public schools. The confidential draft of the plan that Booker sent to Christie proposed turning Newark into "the charter school capital of the nation," weakening seniority and tenure, recruiting new teachers and principals from outside Newark, and building "sophisticated data and accountability systems."

In July 2010, Booker attended an invitation-only meeting in Sun Valley, where he mingled with fabulously wealthy hedge fund managers and high-tech entrepreneurs. There he met Mark Zuckerberg. Booker knew that venture philanthropists were looking for a "proof point," a city where they could demonstrate the success of their business-style school reforms. He persuaded Zuckerberg that Newark was that city. Booker believed that a great education would set every child on the road out of poverty, and he also believed that it would be impossible to do this in the Newark public schools because of their bureaucracy and systems of tenure and seniority. That's why he wanted to spend money turning the city into an all-charter district, without unions, where like-minded reformers could impose the correct reforms, like judging teachers by test scores, firing teachers at will, and hiring whomever they wanted.

That September, Zuckerberg, Booker, and Christie announced the gift of $100 million on *The Oprah Winfrey Show*, to tumultuous applause. When Winfrey asked Zuckerberg why Newark, he responded, "I believe in these guys…. We're setting up a $100 million challenge grant so that Mayor Booker and Governor Christie can have the flexibility they need to…turn Newark into a symbol of educational excellence for the whole nation."

As Russakoff points out, "What Booker, Christie, and Zuckerberg set out to achieve in Newark had not been accomplished in modern times – turning a failing urban school district into one of universally high achievement." Like other reformers, Booker earnestly believed that "We know what works." Zuckerberg's money would give him the chance to prove it. But while the media saw Booker as the "rock star mayor," he faced a growing budget deficit and soaring violent crime when he returned from his frequent fund-raising travels.

Inevitably there was a popular backlash against Booker, who was perceived by many locals as spending too much time with his famous and rich white allies. The anti-Booker figure was Ras Baraka, son of the poet and playwright Amiri Baraka. Ras, a teacher and principal at Central High School, went to a black university, not the Ivy League.

In one of the classes Russakoff visited at Central, a young English teacher wrote a word on the whiteboard and invited students to write "whatever came to mind." When he wrote the word "hope," some of the responses were recorded by Russakoff:

Fourteen-year-old Tyler read his poem to the class:

*We hope to live,*

*Live long enough to have kids*

*We hope to make it home every day*

*We hope we're not the next target to get sprayed...*

*We hope never to end up in Newark's dead pool*

*I hope, you hope, we all hope.*

A boy named Mark wrote, "My mother has hope that I won't fall victim to the streets./I hope that hope finds me."

Khalif: "I hope to make it to an older age than I am."

Nick: "Living in Newark taught me to hope to get home safe."

Tariq: "Hope – that's one thing I don't have."

After Booker and Christie accepted the gift from Zuckerberg, they began the search for matching funds and for a superintendent who shared their ideas about "reform." It took them nearly a year before they found Cami Anderson, who had all the right qualifications. Although she was white and blond, she had grown up in a multiracial home. Her domestic partner was African-American as was her child, she had worked for Teach for America, and she was a rising star under Chancellor Joel Klein in the New York City Department of Education. Booker and Christie were particularly impressed with her toughness, a quality that was necessary in the job ahead of her.

Russakoff describes Anderson's struggle to take control of the school district and impose reforms that outsiders loved and locals did not. The locals perceived her as an agent of the white philanthropists who had put up the money. She never won their confidence. In a city of deep poverty, she was making close to $300,000 a year, and she hired pricey consultants. Newark had a powerless elected school board, and locals insulted Anderson at school board meetings. She stopped attending them.

Christie persuaded the Democratic legislature to weaken tenure but not seniority rules. Anderson's biggest accomplishment was negotiating a new contract with the teachers, which included performance pay and a new teacher evaluation system, as well as $31 million in back pay for teachers.

The most difficult time of Anderson's tenure came when she imposed a reorganization of the school system that wiped out neighborhood schools and reassigned students across the district. The residents' outrage boiled over as their children were assigned to distant schools instead of the one across the street. One father of five, accustomed to walking them to school every day, was furious when his children were assigned to five different schools in three different wards.

By the end of the story, Cory Booker has been elected to the U.S. Senate, and Chris Christie is running for president. Ras Baraka has been elected mayor, after using Cami Anderson's reforms as his major campaign issue, and Anderson has resigned. There are now more charter schools in Newark. None of the reformers gave much thought to the majority of children who are not in charter schools, and not all of the charter schools are successful.

Mark Weber, an experienced teacher and graduate student at Rutgers, criticized Russakoff's book for "creating a false picture of the reality of schooling in Newark." Weber challenges her claim that Newark's public school system "suffers from budgetary bloat." He shows that charter schools spend more money on administration than public schools, and he also disputes her belief that charter schools have more social workers than public schools. He commends Russakoff, however, for recognizing that the charter schools in Newark enroll a different, more advantaged student population than public schools, making test scores comparisons between them invalid.

The only one who seems to have learned from the experience is Mark Zuckerberg, who watched as his $100 million was drained away by consultants, labor costs, and new charter schools. The Newark experiment did not produce a "proof point" or a replicable national model. He must have recognized a cautionary tale about the importance of working with local residents and not treating them and their children as objects to be moved around heedlessly by outsiders. Russakoff writes that Zuckerberg and his wife, the pediatrician Priscilla Chan, determined to concentrate their future philanthropy on schools with comprehensive community-based social, medical, and mental services for children, beginning before kindergarten.

Unfortunately, Zuckerberg and Chan did not learn as much as Russakoff believed. They recently announced that they would celebrate the birth of their daughter Max by pledging 99 percent of their Facebook stock (worth about $45 billion) to a new limited liability corporation, with "personalized learning" as one of its goals. In the world of education jargon, "personalized learning" means computerized instruction, every child learning on a computer that recognizes and responds to the child's strengths and weaknesses. This is actually impersonalized, machine-based instruction, and the research to date shows that it is not helpful to children.

The most valuable education emerges from live interactions between teachers and students, not from the algorithms built into computers to deliver scripted lessons. As a pediatrician who has worked in poor communities, and a graduate of Quincy High School in Massachusetts, Priscilla Chan should know better. Perhaps she will persuade her husband to redirect their fortune to the goals described by Russakoff.

Kristina Rizga is a journalist who covered education for *Mother Jones* (and has returned to its staff). After writing about education for several years, she decided to embed herself in a struggling school over a long period of time so that she could understand the issues better. The school that gave her permission to be a "fly on the wall" was Mission High School in San Francisco. It has 950 students with passports from more than forty different countries. Latino, African-American, and Asian-

American students make up the majority of the students. 75 percent are poor, and nearly 40 percent are learning English.

Mission is a "failing school" because it has low test scores. When Rizga first entered Mission in 2009, it was one of the lowest-performing schools in the nation, as judged by standardized test scores. And yet, contrary to the test scores, 84 percent of its graduates were accepted to college, and other indicators were positive.

One of the six students Rizga followed closely, an immigrant from El Salvador named Maria, asked her, "How can my school be flunking when I'm succeeding?" Maria arrived at Mission High School knowing no English. After only one year in the U.S. she had to take the same state tests as other students. Rizga writes:

> By eleventh grade she was writing long papers on complex topics like the war in Iraq and desegregation. She became addicted to winning debates in class.... In March 2012 Maria and her teachers celebrated her receiving acceptance letters to five colleges, including the University of California at Davis, and two prestigious scholarships.

But she received low scores on the standardized tests mandated by law, because of her weak English skills. Rizga saw Maria's remarkable intellectual, social, and emotional development during her four years as an observer at Mission High. She often failed standardized tests, which seldom reflected her ability or potential. Eventually, as her familiarity with English improved, she scored well enough on the college entrance examinations to gain admission to a good college.

Rizga devotes chapters to the students she gets to know well, who blossom, as Maria did, as a result of their interactions with dedicated Mission teachers. She also devotes chapters to teachers who devote themselves to their students with intense enthusiasm. What the teachers understand that reformers like Booker, Christie, and Anderson do not is that human relationships are the key to reaching students with many economic and social problems.

In contrast to Newark, Mission is a good example of bottom-up reform, where teachers work together and lead the changes that benefit the students. The principal of Mission, Eric Guthertz, has twenty-eight years of experience in urban schools. He encourages his teachers not to "teach to the test," but to use a rich curriculum, hands-on projects, field trips, art and music classes, elective courses, and student clubs. In view of the diversity of the students, Guthertz believes in the value of such clubs as well as after-school programs, and extracurricular activities that teach important skills, like getting along with students from different cultures.

And yet Mission High School was said to be failing.

What Rizga learned is worth sharing. For one, she discovered that "there are too many politicians, powerful bureaucrats, management and business experts, economists, and philanthropists making decisions about the best solutions for schools." In short, the people in charge don't know nearly as much about schooling as the students and teachers they are trying to "fix."

Rizga realized that standardized test scores are not the best way to measure and promote learning. Typically, what they measure is the demographic profile of schools. Thus, schools in affluent white suburbs tend to be called "good" schools. Schools that enroll children who are learning English and children who are struggling in their personal lives have lower scores and are labeled "failing" schools. Hundreds, if not thousands, of such schools have closed in the past decade. Rahm Emanuel, mayor of Chicago, closed fifty schools in a single day, despite the protests of parents, students, and teachers. Rizga writes:

> Some of the most important things that matter in a quality education – critical thinking, intrinsic motivation, resilience, self-management, resourcefulness, and relationship skills – exist in the realms that can't be easily measured by statistical measures and computer algorithms, but they can be detected by teachers using human judgment. America's business-

> inspired obsession with prioritizing "metrics" in a complex world that deals with the development of individual minds has become the primary cause of mediocrity in American schools.

Rizga used to believe that education reform happens when struggling schools adopt models based on the experience and "best practices" of similar schools with high test scores, or of other nations whose test scores are high. But she saw "firsthand how copying and pasting blueprints from other places doesn't work." Every school has a "unique ecosystem" and all children have individual personalities, interests, and needs.

Her advice should have been taken by Booker, Christie, Anderson, Zuckerberg, and the other Newark reformers:

> Educational reforms won't succeed unless there is greater inclusion of the voices of students and teachers and the use of more complex, school-based markers [instead of standardized tests] that can give us a much deeper insight into what quality education means and how sustainable change can happen in all struggling schools.

The authors of these two books demonstrate that grand ideas cannot be imposed on people without their assent. Money and power are not sufficient to improve schools. Genuine improvement happens when students, teachers, principals, parents, and the local community collaborate for the benefit of the children. But a further lesson matters even more – improving education is not sufficient to "save" all children from lives of poverty and violence. As a society, we should be ashamed that so many children are immersed in poverty and violence every day of their lives.

# EDUCATION IN CRISIS AND THE THREAT OF PRIVATIZATION

## HUFFINGTON POST, MARCH 29, 2016

*"The Walton family has made billions of dollars as owners of Walmart. Some family members use this vast wealth to promote privatization of public education and union-busting in U.S. schools. The Walton family could find better uses for its wealth." –*
*Diane Ravitch's Blog*

It has become conventional wisdom that "education is in crisis." I have been asked about this question by many interviewers. They say something like: "Do you think American education is in crisis? What is the cause of the crisis?" And I answer:

> Yes, there is a crisis, but it is not the one you have read about. The crisis in education today is an existential threat to the survival of public education. The threat comes from those who unfairly blame the school for social conditions, and then create a false narrative of failure. The real threat is privatization and the loss of a fundamental democratic institution.

As we have seen again and again, the corporate education industry is eager to break into U.S. public education and turn it into a free marketplace, where they can monetize the schools and be assured of government subsidization. On the whole, these privatized institutions do not produce higher test scores than regular public schools, except for those that cherry-pick their students and exclude the neediest and lowest performing students. The promotion of privatization by philanthropies, by the U.S. Department of Education, by right-wing governors, by a few Democratic governors like Cuomo of New York and Malloy of Connecticut, by the hedge fund industry, and by a burgeoning education equities industry, poses a danger to our democracy. In some communities, public schools verge on bankruptcy as charters drain their resources and their best students. Nationwide, charter schools have paved the way for vouchers by making "school choice" non-controversial.

Yes, education is in crisis. The profession of teaching is threatened by the financial powerhouse Teach for America, which sells the bizarre idea that amateurs are more successful than experienced teachers. TFA, and the belief in amateurism, has also facilitated the passage of legislation to strip teachers of their basic rights to due process, and of salaries tied to experience and credentials.

Education is in crisis because of the explosion of testing and the embrace by government of test scores as both the means and the end of education. The scores are treated as a measure of teacher effectiveness and school effectiveness, when they are in fact a measure of the family income of the students enrolled in the school. The worst consequence of the romance with standardized testing is that children are ranked, sorted, and assigned a value based on scores that are not necessarily scientific or objective. Children thus become instruments, tools, objects, rather than unique human beings, each with his or her own potential.

Education is in crisis because of the calculated effort to turn it into a business with a bottom line. Schools are closed and opened as though they were chain stores, not community institutions. Teachers are fired based on flawed measures. Disruption is considered a strategy rather than misguided and inhumane policy. Children and educators alike are simply data points, to be manipulated by economists, statisticians, entrepreneurs, and dabblers in policy.

Education has lost its way, lost its purpose, lost its definition. Where once it was about enlightening and empowering young minds with knowledge, exploring new worlds, learning about science and history, and unleashing the imagination of each child, it has become a scripted process of producing test scores that can supply data.

Education is in crisis. And we must organize to resist, to push back, to fight the mechanization of learning, and the standardization of children.

# WHY EVERY CHILD SHOULD OPT OUT OF THE STANDARDIZED TESTS

HUFFINGTON POST, APRIL 11, 2016

Want to end the obsession with standardized testing? Opt your children out of the state tests.[113]

Ignore the threats from state and federal officials. The tests today have taken over too much of the school year. Teachers should prepare and give tests that cover what they taught.

What if all students opted out of testing? That's democracy in action. The elected officials who mandate these tests would take notice. They might even discover that no high-performing nation in the world tests every child every year.

The tests today are pointless and meaningless.

The tests are meaningless because the results are returned months after the test, when the student has a different teacher. The tests are meaningless because the scores provide no information about what the students learned and didn't learn. The teacher is not allowed to find out what students got wrong.

Officials claim that the tests help students and teachers and inform instruction. Balderdash. The tests rank and rate students. Worse, the developers of the Common Core tests selected a passing mark so high that the majority of children are expected to fail. The passing mark is a subjective judgment. What exactly is the value of telling children they are failures when they are in third grade?

Schools have cut back on the arts, civics, science, history, and physical education because they are not on the test.

The tests are given online because it is supposed to be cheaper. But many states and districts have had technological breakdowns, and the testing period starts all over again. Students who take pencil and paper tests get higher scores than similar children who take online tests. It may be cumbersome to scroll up and down or sideways, wasting time.

In some states and districts, children with disabilities are expected to take exactly the same tests as children their age, regardless of the nature of their disability. Florida became famous for trying to force a test on a dying child. He cheated the state by dying before they could test him.

When students write essays online, most will be graded by computer. The computer understands sentence length, grammar, and syntax. But the computer does not understand MEANING. A ridiculous essay that is complete gibberish can get a high score.

The testing regime is destroying education. It is driven by politicians who think that tests make students smarter and by educrats who fear to think an independent thought.

There are two ways to stop this madness. One would be to require legislators and policymakers in the states and federal government to take the tests they mandate and publish their scores. This would prove the value of the tests. Why shouldn't they all be able to pass the 8th grade math test?

Since this is unlikely to happen, the best way to restore common sense to American education is to stop taking the tests. Parents should discuss the issues of testing with their children. Explain to them that the tests can't measure what matters most – kindness, integrity, honesty, responsibility, humor, creativity, wisdom, thoughtfulness. The best and only way to send a message to the politicians is to let your children refuse the tests. Do you really care how their scores compare to those of children in other states? If you want to know how they are doing, ask the teachers who see them every day.

# THAT DUMB BATHROOM BILL IN NORTH CAROLINA

### HUFFINGTON POST, APRIL 22, 2016

Did you know that one of the biggest issues in American politics today is not terrorism, not climate change, not the economy, but... whether transgender people should be allowed to go to the bathroom that matches their gender identity?

Yes, it is true. North Carolina passed HB2, which requires transgender people to use the bathroom that corresponds to the gender of their birth certificate. Fear of transgender women (born male) entering women's bathrooms has spurred legislation in South Carolina, Georgia (vetoed by the governor), Mississippi, Minnesota and other states.

The issue has now entered the Presidential race. Ted Cruz warns that women and young girls will be in danger if men who consider themselves female are allowed to use the women's bathroom. Donald Trump says we can't waste money building new bathrooms for transgender people, and the decision should be left to the states.

What's behind all this nonsense? I am old enough to remember a similar fear back in the 1950s. At that time, southern politicians warned that racial desegregation would put white women at risk. If white women, idealized as symbols of purity (even when reality suggested the contrary), came into contact with black men, they warned, rapes would surely follow. Behind much of the resistance to desegregation was sexual panic.

Southern politicians used race-baiting skillfully to divert attention from their corruption and their failure to produce any social or economic gains for the people who elected them. Picking on powerless, disenfranchised blacks kept many a southern politician in power.

The game now is to pick on the last remaining minority that is small in number, mostly hidden, and politically isolated. Who cares about the tiny number of people who are transgender?

It turns out that America's major corporations care. Many, perhaps all of them, have gay employees, and they let Governor Pat McCrory of North Carolina know that HB2, the "bathroom bill," was offensive to them. PayPal canceled a plan to expand its operations in North Carolina, costing the state 400 good jobs. Deutsche Bank canceled its expansion plans. An Internet porn site announced it was cutting off service to its many North Carolina customers. Ouch! Other corporations, entertainment companies, and sports organizations, including the National Basketball Association, are mulling similar actions.

The bathroom bill is especially stupid for several reasons. For one, transgender people have been using public restrooms for years, with no one aware of it and no complaints. For another, the law is unenforceable. Who will monitor whether those who enter women's bathrooms have the "right" genitals?

Some North Carolina politicians have worried that women might emerge from the shower wearing only a towel, unaware that the woman in the room was born male. But where are the public bathrooms that have showers? When women go to the bathroom in an airport, a restaurant, or a hotel, the bathroom has stalls with locks. Each one is completely private.

A week ago, I was in Raleigh, North Carolina. There were gender-neutral bathrooms (called "family bathrooms") in the Marriott Hotel, the Raleigh Convention Center, and the airport.

Governor McCrory's wife has used bathrooms for years with transgender women. North Carolina faces a choice. It can hire bathroom guards to inspect genitalia in every public bathroom, thus creating a jobs program to make up for all the jobs lost as national companies abandon the state, or repeal HB2.

North Carolina may not get to make that choice. A federal appeals court just ruled that a transgender boy in Virginia could use the boy's bathroom and that efforts to compel him to go to the girls' bathroom violate federal anti-discrimination law. In other words, the courts will throw out HB2. North Carolina's Tea Party government sacrificed all those jobs and made the state a laughing stock for nothing.

# TRYING TO EDUCATE THE EDUCATION REFORMERS, WITHOUT SUCCESS

HUFFINGTON POST,MAY 20, 2016

*"The testing monster is coming for our children." – Diane Ravitch's Blog*

Peter Cunningham, former deputy to Arne Duncan, accused Carol Burris and me of "attacking" Campbell Brown. He says we "attack" anyone who disagrees with us. Peter now runs a website called Education Post, where he received $12 million from various billionaires (including Walton and Bloomberg) to defend the corporate reform movement of high stakes testing, evaluating teachers by tests scores, and privatization of public schools.

Anyone who reads my post about Campbell will see that there was no attack. I was doing my level best to educate her about what grade level means and why NAEP proficient is not and should not be used as a "passing mark." Campbell mistakenly said that 2/3 of American students were "below grade level." What the national test calls "proficiency" is equivalent to an "A". No one expects the majority of students to score an "A". If they did, we would call it grade inflation.

Carol Burris, executive director of the Network for Public Education and a former award-winning principal, tweeted with Campbell, hoping to set her straight. So did Tom Loveless of

Brookings, who told her that she was wrong and urged her to correct her error. For some reason, Peter Cunningham did not include Tom in the list of people who were "attacking" Campbell.

Obviously, neither Campbell nor Peter bothered to read the links to scholarly studies and government websites included in my post. They should. They might learn something and stop bashing American public schools and their teachers. I served seven years on the NAEP governing board. I could help them if they are willing to learn.

As for calling Campbell "telegenic," that's no insult, that's a compliment. If you call me telegenic, I would say thank you.

# DON'T USE TEST SCORES TO JUDGE TEACHER QUALITY

THE BOSTON GLOBE, JUNE 30, 2016

The Massachusetts Senate passed a bill repealing the mandate to use test scores in evaluating teacher quality. The approval of the House is needed to enact the bill. The Legislature should act promptly to endorse this bill. Test-based teacher evaluation has been discredited everywhere it has been tried and has been rejected by knowledgeable scholars. Massachusetts should abandon this harmful policy, as Oklahoma, Hawaii, and Houston recently did. The public needs to learn more about why this policy consistently fails.

The idea that teachers should be evaluated by the test scores of their students was a central tenet in former Secretary of Education Arne Duncan's Race to the Top program. Massachusetts won a federal grant of $250 million in 2011 and agreed to follow Duncan's wishes, including this untried method of evaluating teachers. The U.S. Department of Education handed out $5 billion to states to promote privately managed charter schools and test-based evaluation of teachers. In addition, the Gates Foundation gave away hundreds of millions of dollars to five urban districts to use test scores to evaluate teachers.

Evaluating teachers by test scores has not raised scores significantly anywhere. Good teachers have been fired by this flawed method. A New York judge ruled this method "arbitrary and capricious" after one of the state's best teachers was judged ineffective.

Test-based evaluation has demoralized teachers because they know it is unfair to judge them by student scores. Many believe it has contributed to a growing national teacher shortage and declining enrollments in teacher education programs.

A major problem with test-based evaluation is that students are not randomly assigned. Teachers in affluent suburbs may get higher scores year after year, while teachers in urban districts enrolling many high-need students will not see big test score gains. Teachers of English-language learners, teachers of students with cognitive disabilities, and teachers of children who live in poverty are unlikely to see big test score gains, even though they are as good as or even better than their peers in the suburbs. Even teachers of the gifted are unlikely to see big test score gains, because their students already have such high scores. Test scores are a measure of class composition, not teacher quality.

Seventy percent of teachers do not teach subjects that have annual tests. Schools could develop standardized tests for every subject, including the arts and physical education. But most have chosen to rate these teachers by the scores of students they don't know and subjects they never taught.

Scholarly groups like the American Educational Research Association and the American Statistical Association have warned against using test scores to rate individual teachers. There are too many uncontrolled variables, as well as individual differences among students, to make these ratings valid. The biggest source of variation in test scores is not the teacher, but students' family income and home environment.

The American Statistical Association said that teachers affect 1 percent to 14 percent of test score variation. The ASA is an impeccable nonpartisan, authoritative source, not influenced by the teachers' unions.

The Gates Foundation gave a grant of $100 million to the schools of Hillsborough County, Florida (Tampa), to evaluate their teachers by gains and losses in student test scores. It was an abject failure. The district drained its reserve funds, spending nearly $200 million to implement the foundation's ideas. The Gates Foundation refused to pay the last $20 million on its $100 million pledge. The superintendent who led the effort was fired and replaced by one who promised a different direction.

Should Massachusetts cling to a costly, failed, and demoralizing way to evaluate teachers? Should it ignore evidence and experience?

Common sense and logic say no.

Should teachers be judged "subjectively"? Of course. That is called human judgment. Is it perfect? No. Can it be corrected? Yes. Most professionals are judged subjectively by their supervisors and bosses. Standardized tests are flawed instruments. They are normed on a bell curve, guaranteeing winners and losers. They often contain errors – statistical errors, human errors, random errors, scoring errors, poorly worded questions, two right answers, no right answers. No one's professional career should hinge on the answers to standardized test questions.

Massachusetts is widely considered the best state school system in the nation. The hunt for bad teachers who were somehow undetected by their supervisors is fruitless. The Legislature is right to return the decision about which teachers are effective and which are not to the professionals who see their work every day.

# WHY THE OPT OUT MOVEMENT IS CRUCIAL FOR THE FUTURE OF PUBLIC EDUCATION

## HUFFINGTON POST,JULY 7, 2016

*"Parent power beat corporate power!" – Diane Ravitch's Blog*

Many parents and educators are outraged by the over-testing and misuse of testing that has been embedded in federal policy since the enactment of No Child Left Behind in 2002. No high-performing nation in the world tests every child every year in grades 3-8, as we have since the passage of NCLB.

Young children sit for exams that last up to 15 hours over two weeks. The fate of their teachers rests on their performance. Parents remember taking tests in school that lasted no more than one class period for each subject. Their tests were made by their teachers, not by a multinational corporation. Parents can't understand how testing became an endurance trial and the goal of education.

Politicians claim that the tests are necessary to inform parents and teachers and the public how children in one state are doing as compared to their peers in other states. But this information is already reported by the federal test, the National Assessment of Educational Progress (NAEP). Parents have figured out that the tests don't serve any purpose other than to rank their child. No one is allowed to see the test questions after the test.

No child receives a diagnosis of what they know and don't know. They receive only a score. In every state, the majority of children have been ranked as "failures" because the test makers adopted a passing mark that was guaranteed to fail close to 70 percent of children. Parents have learned that the passing mark is not objective, it is arbitrary. It can be set to pass everyone, pass no one, or pass some percentage of children.

In the past 14 years, parents have seen the destruction of neighborhood schools, based on their test scores. They have seen beloved teachers fired unjustly, because of their students' test scores. They have seen the loss of time for the arts, physical education, and anything else that is not tested. They have seen a change in their local public schools that they don't like, as well as a loss of control to federal mandates and state authorities.

In the past, testing companies warned that tests should be used only for the purpose for which they were designed. Now, these corporations willingly sell their tests without warning about misuse. A test of fourth grade reading tests fourth grade reading. It should not be used to rank students, to humiliate students, to fire teachers and principals, or to close schools. But it is.

Communities have been devastated by the closing of their neighborhood schools.

Communities have seen their schools labeled "failing," based on test scores, and taken over by the state or national corporate charter chains.

Based on test scores, punishments abound – for students, teachers, principals, schools, and communities.

This is madness!

What can we as citizens do to stop the destruction of our children, their schools, and our dedicated educators?

Opt out of the tests.

Use the power of the powerless. Say NO. Do not participate. Withdraw your consent from actions that harm your child. Withdrawal of consent in an unjust system. That's the force that brought down Communist regimes in Eastern Europe. Vaclav Havel and Lech Wałęsa said no. They were not alone. Hundreds of thousands stood with them, and the regimes with their weapons and tanks and heavy armor folded. Because the people said no.

Opting out of the tests is the only tool available to parents, other than defeating the elected officials of your state – which is also a good idea, but will take a very long time to bear fruit. One person can't defeat the governor and the local representatives. But one person can refuse to allow their child to take the toxic tests.

The only tool and the most powerful tool that parents have to stop this madness is to refuse to allow their children to take the tests.

Consider New York. A year ago, Governor Andrew Cuomo was in full attack mode against teachers and public schools, while showering praise on privately managed charters. He vowed to "break the monopoly" known as public education. The New York State Board of Regents was controlled by members who were in complete sympathy with Cuomo's agenda of Common Core, high-stakes testing, and evaluating teachers by test scores.

But in 2015, about a quarter million children refused the state tests. Albany went into panic mode. Governor Cuomo convened a commission to re-evaluate the Common Core, standards, and testing. Almost overnight, his negative declarations about education changed in tone, and he went silent. The legislature appointed new members, who did not share the test-and-punish mentality. The chair of the New York State Board of Regents decided not to seek re-appointment after a 20-year career on that board. The Regents elected Dr. Betty Rosa, a veteran educator who was actively supported by the leaders of the opt out movement.

Again in 2016, the opt out movement showed its power. While official figures have not yet been released, the numbers evidently match those of 2015. More than half the students in Long Island opted out. Federal and state officials have issued warnings about sanctions, but it is impossible to sanction huge numbers of schools in middle-class and affluent communities. The same officials have no problem closing schools in poor urban districts, treating citizens there as chess pawns, but they dare not offend an organized bloc in politically powerful communities.

The opt out movement has been ridiculed by critics, treated by the media as a front for the teachers' union, belittled by the former Secretary of Education as "white suburban moms" who were disappointed that their child was not so bright after all, stereotyped as privileged white parents with low-performing children, etc. There are indeed black and Hispanic parents who are part of the opt out movement. Their children and their schools suffer the greatest penalties in the current testing madness. In New York City, where opt out numbers were tiny, parents were warned that their children would not be able to enter the middle school or the high school of their choice if they opted out.

Thus far, the opt out movement has not been discouraged or slowed by these tactics of ridicule and intimidation. The conditions have not changed, so the opt out movement will continue.

The reality is that the opt out movement is indeed a powerful weapon. It is the one weapon that makes governors, legislators, and even members of Congress afraid of public opinion and public action. They are afraid because they don't know how to stop parents from opting out. They can't control opt out parents, and they know it. They offer compromises, promises for the future, but all of this is sham. They have not let go of the testing hammer. And they will not until opt out becomes the norm, not the exception.

In some communities in New York, opting out is already the norm. If politicians and bureaucrats continue on their reckless course of valuing test scores more than children, the opt out movement will not be deterred.

Save your child. Save your schools. Stop the corporate takeover of public education. You have the power. Say no. Opt out.

# THE COMMON CORE COSTS BILLIONS AND HURTS STUDENTS

THE NEW YORK TIMES, JULY 23, 2016

For 15 years, since the passage of George W. Bush's No Child Left Behind act, education reformers have promoted standardized testing, school choice, competition and accountability – meaning punishment of teachers and schools – as the primary means of improving education. For many years, I agreed with them. I was an assistant secretary of education in George H. W. Bush's administration and a member of three conservative think tanks.

But as I watched the harmful effects of No Child Left Behind, I began to have doubts. The law required that all schools reach 100 percent proficiency as measured by state tests or face harsh punishments. This was an impossible goal. Standardized tests became the be-all and end-all of education, and states spent billions on them. Social scientists have long known that the best predictor of test scores is family income. Yet policy makers encouraged the firing of thousands of teachers and the closing of thousands of low-scoring public schools, mostly in poor black and Hispanic neighborhoods.[114]

As the damage escalated, I renounced my support for high-stakes testing and charter schools. Nonetheless, I clung to the hope that we might agree on national standards and a national curriculum. Surely, I thought, they would promote equity since all children would study the same things and take the same tests. But now I realize that I was wrong about that, too.

Six years after the release of our first national standards, the Common Core, and the new federal tests that accompanied them, it seems clear that the pursuit of a national curriculum is yet another excuse to avoid making serious efforts to reduce the main causes of low student achievement – poverty and racial segregation.

The people who wrote the Common Core standards sold them as a way to improve achievement and reduce the gaps between rich and poor, and black and white. But the promises haven't come true. Even in states with strong common standards and tests, racial achievement gaps persist. Last year, average math scores[115] on the National Assessment of Educational Progress declined for the first time since 1990.[116] Reading scores were flat or decreased compared with a decade earlier.

The development of the Common Core was funded almost entirely by the Bill and Melinda Gates Foundation.[117] It was a rush job, and the final product ignored the needs of children with disabilities, English-language learners and those in the early grades. It's no surprise that there has been widespread pushback.

In 2009 President Obama announced Race to the Top, a competition for $4.35 billion in federal grant money. To qualify, states had to adopt "college and career ready standards," a requirement that was used to pressure them into adopting national standards. Almost every state applied, even before the specifics of the Common Core were released in June 2010.

The federal government, states and school districts have spent billions of dollars to phase in the standards, to prepare students to take the tests and to buy the technology needed to administer them online. There is nothing to show for it. Race to the Top demoralized teachers, caused teacher shortages, and led to the defunding of the arts and other subjects that were not tested. Those billions would have been better spent to reduce class sizes, especially in struggling schools, to restore arts and physical education classes, to rebuild physically crumbling schools, and to provide universal early childhood education.

Children starting in the third grade may spend more than 10 hours a year taking state tests – and weeks preparing for them. Studies show that students perform better on written tests than on online tests, yet most schools across the nation are assessing their students online, at enormous costs, because that is how the Common Core tests are usually delivered. Computer glitches are common. Sometimes the server gets overloaded and breaks down. Entire states, like Alaska,[118] have canceled tests because of technical problems. More than 30 states have reported computer testing problems since 2013, according to FairTest,[119] a testing watchdog.

Standardized tests are best at measuring family income. Well-off students usually score in the top half of results, and students from poor homes usually score in the bottom. The quest to "close achievement gaps" is vain indeed when the measure of achievement is a test based on a statistical norm. If we awarded driver's licenses based on standardized tests, half the adults in this country might never receive one. The failure rates on the Common Core tests are staggeringly high for black and Hispanic children, students with disabilities, and English-language learners. Making the tests harder predictably depresses test scores, creating a sense of failure and hopelessness among young children.

If we really cared about improving the education of all students, we would give teachers the autonomy to tailor instruction to meet the needs of the children in front of them and to write their own tests. We would insist that students in every school had an equal opportunity to learn in well-maintained schools, in classes of reasonable size, taught by expert teachers. Anyone who wants to know how students in one state compare with students in other states can get that information from the N.A.E.P., the existing federal test.

What is called "the achievement gap" is actually an "opportunity gap." What we need are schools where all children have the same chance to learn. That doesn't require national standards or national tests, which improve neither teaching nor learning, and do nothing to help poor children at racially segregated schools. We need to focus on that, not on promoting failed ideas.

# AN OPEN LETTER TO MARK ZUCKERBERG AND DR. PRISCILLA CHAN

HUFFINGTON POST, AUGUST 19, 2016

Recently, Checker Finn of the Thomas B. Fordham Institute wrote an open letter to you,[120] proposing that you stay the course with the failed reforms of the past fifteen years. Marc Tucker wrote an open letter to you,[121] disagreeing with Checker. He said that all of Checker's proposals were tinkering at the margins (Teach for America, New Leaders, scholarships, charter schools), and he recommended that you invest in improving the education system with an eye to the high-performing nations of the world. If Marc was thinking about Finland, my personal favorite, I endorse what he says. Finland emphasizes highly educated teachers, minimal testing, pre-school education, medical care, no charters, no vouchers, and lots of emphasis on creativity and play.

You may be tired of receiving open letters. But I want to put in my open letter now that it is open-letter season.

Dear Mark and Priscilla,

I hope you won't mind some unsolicited advice from someone you don't know. I am writing you because you have the resources and the energy to make a real difference in the lives of millions of children and families, as well as their teachers and schools. Your great wealth can be squandered – as it was in Newark, where your $100 million gift disappeared down a very dark hole and did nothing for the children of that city. Or your great wealth can be used to strengthen the one institution that touches the lives of most children – their public school.

I am a historian of American education. I used to be part of the "reform movement," but after too many years, I recognized that the reforms popular among policy makers are useless and counterproductive. I defected from the reform movement, because it has the wrong diagnosis and the wrong solutions. I didn't want to be on the wrong side of history. I hope you too want to use your influence to make a genuine difference in the lives of children, instead of fattening the vast self-serving reform machine, which is already awash in millions and millions of dollars, all chasing the same failed ideas.

You need to understand that reformers live in an echo chamber. They talk to one another, they tell one another the same stories, they learn nothing new. They are sure that American public schools are failing, that public school teachers are ineffective, and that the steady application of standards, tests, punishments, and rewards will transform the lives of children. They believe that schools with low test scores should be privatized, turned into charters, and one day soon, there will be no more poverty. These assumptions are untethered to reality. Standards and tests will not help the children who typically score in the bottom half. Reformers slander a vital democratic institution and the millions of teachers who work for low pay because they have a sense of mission.

Despite what you may have heard, the test scores of American students are at their highest point ever. High school graduation rates are at an all-time high. Dropout rates are at an all-time low.

Why the continuing despair about the state of the schools? Some of it comes from elites who never set foot in a public school. They attended the best private schools, and they look down on public schools and their teachers with condescension.

I am not suggesting that all is well. In fact, the great crisis in our society, reflected in our schools, is a direct result of the high rates of childhood poverty. To our shame, we have the highest rate of child poverty of any advanced nation. Nearly one-quarter of our nation's children are growing up without food security, without assurance of a decent home, without access to regular medical care.

Surely you are aware of the work of Nadine Powell Harris, who has gathered powerful evidence of the lasting effects of childhood trauma. The trauma she describes is closely correlated with extreme poverty and the stress of poverty. And yet reformers blame the public schools and their teachers for the failure of our society! Why have other countries made successful efforts to reduce childhood poverty, but we have not?

Priscilla, I have read that you attributed your personal success to public school teachers who encouraged you. Today, there are millions of teachers working to encourage and inspire children just like you, working to convince them to believe in themselves. These teachers do so despite the vilification that reformers continually direct at them.

Here is my advice to you:

Please join the fight to preserve and strengthen public schools.

Please do not contribute to the movement to privatize public schools.

Please support efforts to create community schools, which are equipped to meet the needs of children.

Please support efforts to establish medical clinics in every school, where children can receive dental care, routine check-ups, and be tested for vision problems, hearing problems, and lead in their blood.

Please insist that schools have the resources to meet the emotional and psychological needs of children.

Please use your influence to assure that every school has a library with a librarian and lots of books and computers.

Please support the right of teachers to bargain collectively. Unions built our middle class, and that middle class is now feeling stressed and under siege.

Please do not support efforts to eliminate the due process rights of teachers. Schools need stability, and teachers need to know that their academic freedom is protected.

Please understand that the expansion of charter schools harms public schools, which enroll the vast majority of children. Charter schools are not better than public schools. Those that get high test scores often do so by keeping out the children who might get low scores. Charter schools, including those that cherry-pick their students, take resources away from public schools, as well as their best students.

Mark and Priscilla, we are at a critical juncture – the

very survival of public education is at risk.

Public schools welcome all students – those with disabilities, those who don't speak English, those who have low test scores. They teach us to live with others who are different from ourselves and our family. They are a basic, essential democratic institution. Schools are not businesses. They are a public service, a part of our common inheritance as citizens.

Do no harm. Strengthen democracy. Strengthen the public schools whose doors are open to all. Stand with the parents and educators who say no to privatization.

The privatizers don't need you. They have a herd of billionaires in their fold.

We need you. Please help us transform our public schools into the great instrument of democracy and social justice that they must be.

Join the Network for Public Education and support the parents and educators across the nation who are trying, often with bare hands, to roll back the deluge of money dedicated to high-stakes testing and privatization.

We need you. Bill Gates and Eli Broad do not.

Diane Ravitch

# WHEN PUBLIC GOES PRIVATE AS TRUMP WANTS WHAT HAPPENS?

## THE NEW YORK REVIEW OF BOOKS, DECEMBER 8, 2016

*"In Los Angeles, charter schools drain $600 million every year from public schools. Real Democrats support public schools and unions, not private management of schools. Real Democrats do not make alliances with the Waltons, the Koch brothers, and DeVos. Every Democratic candidate for president in 2020 should join the UTLA picket line and show: Which side are you on?" – Diane Ravitch's Blog*

*The New York Times* recently published a series of articles about the dangers of privatizing public services, the first of which in June 2016 was called "When You Dial 911 and Wall Street Answers."[122] Over the years, *The New York Times* has published other exposés of privatized services, like hospitals, health care, prisons, ambulances, and preschools for children with disabilities. In some cities and states, even libraries and water have been privatized. No public service is immune from takeover by corporations that say they can provide comparable or better quality at a lower cost. In the June 2016 article, *The New York Times* said that, "Since the 2008 financial crisis, private equity firms ... have increasingly taken over a wide array of civic and financial services that are central to American life."

Privatization means that a public service is taken over

by a for-profit business, whose highest goal is profit. Investors expect a profit when a business moves into a new venture. The new corporation operating the hospital or the prison or the fire department cuts costs by every means to increase profits. When possible it eliminates unions, raises prices to consumers – even charging homeowners for putting out fires – cuts workers' benefits, expands working hours, and lays off veteran employees who earn the most. The consequences can be dangerous to ordinary citizens. Doctors in privatized hospitals may perform unnecessary surgeries to increase revenues or avoid treating patients whose care may be too expensive.

The Federal Bureau of Prisons recently concluded that privatized prisons were not as safe as those run by the bureau itself and were less likely to provide effective programs for education and job training to reduce recidivism. Consequently, the federal government has begun phasing out privately managed prisons, which hold about 15 percent of federal prisoners. That decision was based on an investigation by the Justice Department's inspector general, who cited a May 2012 riot at a Mississippi correctional center in which a score of people were injured and a correctional officer was killed. Two hundred and fifty inmates participated in the riot to protest the poor quality of the food and medical care. Since the election, the stock price of for-profit prisons has soared.

There is an ongoing debate about whether the Veterans Administration should privatize health care for military veterans. Republicans have proposed privatizing Social Security and Medicare. President George W. Bush used to point to Chile as a model nation that had successfully privatized Social Security, but *The New York Times* recently reported that privatization of pensions in Chile was a disaster, leaving many older people impoverished.

For the past fifteen years, the nation's public schools have been a prime target for privatization. Unbeknownst to the public, those who would privatize the public schools call themselves "reformers" to disguise their goal. Who could be opposed to "reform"? These days, those who call themselves "education reformers" are likely to be hedge fund managers, entrepreneurs, and billionaires, not educators. The "reform" movement loudly proclaims the failure of American public education, and seeks to turn public dollars over to entrepreneurs, corporate chains, mom-and-pop operations, religious organizations, and almost anyone else who wants to open a school.

In early September, Donald Trump declared his commitment to privatization of the nation's public schools. He held a press conference at a low-performing charter school in Cleveland run by a for-profit entrepreneur. He announced that if elected president, he would turn $20 billion in existing federal education expenditures into a block grant to states, which they could use for vouchers for religious schools, charter schools, private schools, or public schools. These are funds that currently subsidize public schools that enroll large numbers of poor students. Like most Republicans, Trump believes that "school choice" and competition produce better education, even though there is no evidence for this belief. As president, Trump will encourage competition among public and private providers of education, which will reduce funding for public schools. No high-performing nation in the world has privatized its schools.

The motives for the privatization movement are various. Some privatizers have an ideological commitment to free-market capitalism; they decry public schools as "government schools," hobbled by unions and bureaucracy. Some are certain that schools need to be run like businesses, and that people with business experience can manage schools far better than educators. Others have a profit motive, and they hope to make money in the burgeoning "education industry." The adherents of the business approach oppose unions and tenure, preferring employees without any adequate job protection and with merit pay tied to test scores. They never say, "We want to privatize public schools." They say, "We want to save poor children from failing schools." Therefore, "We must open privately managed charter schools to give children a choice," and "We must provide vouchers so that poor families can escape the public schools."

The privatization movement has a powerful lobby to advance its cause. Most of those who support privatization are political conservatives. Right-wing think tanks regularly produce glowing accounts of charter schools and vouchers along with glowing reports about their success. The American Legislative Exchange Council (ALEC) – a right-wing organization funded by major corporations and composed of two thousand or so state legislators – drafts model charter school legislation, which its members introduce in their state legislatures. Every Republican governor and legislature has passed legislation for charters and vouchers. About half the states have enacted voucher legislation or tax credits for nonpublic schools, even though in some of those states, like Indiana and Nevada, the state constitution explicitly forbids spending state funds on religious schools or anything other than public schools.

If the privatization movement were confined to Republicans, there might be a vigorous political debate about the wisdom of privatizing the nation's public schools. But the Obama administration has been just as enthusiastic about privately managed charter schools as the Republicans. In 2009, its own education reform program, Race to the Top, offered a prize of $4.35 billion that states could compete for. In order to be eligible, states had to change their laws to allow or increase the number of charter schools, and they had to agree to close public schools that had persistently low test scores.

In response to the prodding of the Obama administration, forty-two states and the District of Columbia currently permit charter schools. As thousands of neighborhood public schools were closed, charter schools opened to take their place. Today, there are about seven thousand publicly funded, privately managed charter schools, enrolling nearly three million students. Some are run for profit. Some are online schools, where students sit at home and get their lessons on a computer. Some operate in shopping malls. Some are run by fly-by-night characters hoping to make money. Charters open and close with disturbing frequency – from 2010 to 2015, more than 1,200 charters closed due to academic or financial difficulties, while others opened.

Charters have several advantages over regular public schools. They can admit the students they want, exclude those they do not want, and push out the ones who do not meet their academic or behavioral standards. Even though some public schools have selective admissions, the public school system must enroll every student, at every point in the school year. Typically, charter schools have smaller numbers of students whose native language is not English, and smaller numbers of students with serious disabilities as compared to neighborhood public schools. Both charters and vouchers drain away resources from the public schools, even as they leave the neediest, most expensive students to the public schools to educate. Competition from charters and vouchers does not improve public schools, which still enroll 94 percent of all students, it weakens them.

Charter schools often call themselves "public charter schools," but when they have been challenged in federal or state court or before the National Labor Relations Board, charter corporations insist that they are private contractors, not "state actors" like public schools, and therefore are not bound to follow state laws. As private corporations, they are exempt from state labor laws and from state laws that govern disciplinary policies. About 93 percent of charter schools are non-union, as are virtually all voucher schools. In most charter schools, young teachers work fifty, sixty, or seventy hours a week. Teacher turnover is high, given the hours and intensity of the work.

Over the past twenty years, under Presidents Clinton, Bush, and Obama, the federal government has spent billions of dollars to increase the number of privately managed charter schools. Charter schools have been embraced by hedge fund managers, and very wealthy financiers have created numerous organizations – such as Democrats for Education Reform, Education Reform Now, and Families for Excellent Schools – to supply many millions of dollars to support the expansion of charter schools. The elites who support charters also finance political campaigns for sympathetic candidates and for state referenda increasing charters. In the recent election, out-of-state donors, including the Waltons of Arkansas, spent $26 million in Massachusetts in hopes of expanding the number of charter schools – the ballot question was defeated by a resounding margin of 62–38 percent. In Georgia, the Republican governor sought a change in the state constitution to allow him to take over low-scoring public schools and convert them to charters – it too was defeated, by a vote of 60–40 percent.

In addition to spending on political campaigns, some of the same billionaires have used their philanthropies to increase the number of charter schools. Three of the nation's biggest foundations subsidize their growth – the Bill and Melinda Gates Foundation, the Walton Family Foundation, and the Edythe and Eli Broad Foundation. In addition to these three, charters have also received donations from the Bloomberg Family Foundation, the Susan and Michael Dell Foundation, the Laura and John Arnold Foundation (ex-Enron), the Fisher Family Foundation (The Gap stores), Reed Hastings (Netflix), Jonathan Sackler (Purdue Pharmaceutical, manufacturer of Oxycontin), the DeVos family of Michigan (Amway), and many more of the nation's wealthiest citizens. Eli Broad is financing a program to put half the students in Los Angeles – the nation's second-biggest school district – into privately managed charters.

The Walton Family Foundation alone spends $200 million annually for charters, and claims credit for launching one of every four charter schools in the nation. The Walton family of Arkansas is worth about $130 billion, thanks to the Walmart stores, and they are vehemently antiunion. For them, charters are a convenient way to undermine teachers' unions, one of the last and largest remaining pillars of the organized labor movement. Bill Gates has personally spent money to pass charter legislation in his home state of Washington. Three state referenda on charters failed in Washington, and the fourth passed by less than 1.5 percent of the vote in 2012. Gates's goal was stymied, however, when the state's highest court ruled that charter schools are not public schools because their boards are not elected. In the recent election, Gates and his allies supported opponents who ran against justices of the state Supreme Court who ruled against public funding of privately managed charter schools, but the voters reelected them.

Given the near-complete absence of public information and debate about the stealth effort to privatize public schools, this is the right time for the appearance of two new books on the subject. Samuel E. Abrams, a veteran teacher and administrator, has written an elegant analysis of the workings of market forces in education in his book *Education and the Commercial Mindset.* Abrams is now director of the National Center for the Study of Privatization in Education at Teachers College, Columbia University. The other book, *School Choice: The End of Public Education*, was written by Mercedes K. Schneider, a high school teacher in Louisiana with a doctorate in research methods and statistics who left college teaching to teach adolescents.

*Education and the Commercial Mindset* looks deeply into the history of the Edison Project, an ambitious business plan created by the entrepreneur Chris Whittle. Whittle announced his program in 1991 at the National Press Club in Washington, D.C. He said he intended to revolutionize public education by opening a chain of private schools across the nation in which tuition would be less than the government's cost of public schools, but student performance would be superior. The schools would contain costs by putting students to work as tutors, office aides, and cafeteria workers. The schools would have the latest technology and would be open eight hours a day, eleven months a year. Abrams writes, "Whittle forecasted dramatic growth: 200 schools with 150,000 students by 1996 and 1,000 schools with 2 million students by 2010." The Edison Project was supposed to be the leading edge of a booming new education industry. Whittle turned to private investors to raise the $2.5 to $3 billion that he said he needed for startup funds.

The unspoken premise of the Edison Project was that Congress would authorize vouchers for student tuition. Without vouchers, the plan wouldn't work. Why would parents pay

$8,000 to send their child to an Edison school when they could go to the local public school for free? Whittle pledged to turn education into a business and to measure student learning with precision just as Federal Express tracks its packages. He wooed Benno Schmidt, who was the president of Yale University, to be the CEO of the Edison Project, and he gathered a "design team" of seven people to plan the curriculum and program of the prototype school, only one of whom had ever been a K–12 educator, Abrams points out.

Whittle immediately encountered two roadblocks. President George H.W. Bush was defeated by Bill Clinton in 1992, and there would be no vouchers for students to pay for Edison schools. When Whittle began to raise money from investors, his expectations of billions were dashed. Time Warner invested $22.5 million, Phillips Electronics of Holland invested $15 million, a British newspaper group added $14.4 million, and Whittle and his friends added $8.1 million. This was less than 10 percent of what he had hoped for.

Whittle dropped the original plan of opening private schools and switched to subcontracting with local school districts to run troubled schools and charter schools. For a time, this looked promising. By 1999, Edison operated sixty-one schools with 37,500 students in seventeen states. That year, it received nearly $250 million from investors, and it went public. Its stock opened at $18 a share, two years later, it traded at $38.75 a share. Merrill Lynch was bullish on the future of educational privatization, predicting a booming, profitable industry. Independent analysts predicted that Edison would be the McDonald's of education.

But as it expanded, Edison faced two nagging problems – it didn't achieve the predicted profits, and it didn't achieve the predicted test score gains. Whittle continued to promise that results were just a few years off. Profit margins were so slim that Edison turned to philanthropists friendly to privatization to subsidize its operations. Being a publicly traded company created other problems for Edison. When financial analysts revealed that

Edison was overstating its revenues, its stock plummeted to $1.01 a share in late June 2002.

Edison had a rocky run in Baltimore, where it eventually lost its contract to manage schools. And it had an even harder time in Philadelphia. The governor of Pennsylvania, Tom Ridge, gave Edison a contract of $2.7 million to study the needs of the district. Its biggest need was money – the largely black and poor district was dramatically underfunded by the state, and still is. Edison expected that it would be hired to manage the district as well as to control forty-five schools. Instead, the privatization experiment ran into a wall of opposition by local civil rights groups, clergy, and the teachers' union. Edison did not win the contract to run the district, and it took charge of only twenty schools.

While Edison was battling protesters in Philadelphia, school officials in Georgia, Texas, Massachusetts, and Michigan terminated Edison contracts early because of lackluster performance. With each setback, Edison's stock price plunged. In October 2002, it dropped to fourteen cents a share and was nearly delisted by NASDAQ. The following July the company went private, buying back its stock. It turned its attention to making profits from after-school and summer programs, as well as services like professional development and computer software.

Whittle's dream of revolutionizing American public education by applying market discipline was over. In 2012 the Edison team raised $75 million in private financing to open elite for-profit private schools around the world, with a goal of twenty campuses. Its first school, Avenues, opened in the Chelsea neighborhood of New York City in a large space renovated at a cost of $60 million, with the latest technology and a staff hired from some of the nation's best private schools. For unexplained reasons, Chris Whittle exited this venture in the spring of 2015.

Abrams also looks at the Knowledge Is Power Program (KIPP), a major charter chain that operates as a nonprofit. It has two hundred schools across the nation, which mostly get high marks on standardized tests. Thanks to President George W.

Bush's No Child Left Behind law, standardized testing is considered the only measure of education, although such tests are poor proxies for genuine education. KIPP schools impose strict behavioral standards and teach unquestioning compliance. They are called "no excuses" schools, since there can be "no excuse" for failure. Many other charters try to replicate KIPP's methods and test scores. The drawback of schools like KIPP, Abrams points out, is that they have high turnover as teachers burn out, and high rates of attrition as students leave who can't meet their expectations.

KIPP also has a large financial advantage. In 2011, Abrams shows, KIPP raised nearly $130 million to supplement federal, state, and local funding. This amounts to an additional $3,800 per student, as compared to public schools. KIPP continues to be the recipient of large grants from foundations sympathetic to privatization. The philanthropists apparently believe that strict discipline will enable poor children to gain the attitudes and values to lift themselves out of poverty. However, a recent study of graduates of Texas charter schools by the economists Will Dobbie and Roland Fryer – both friendly to "choice" – found that these youth gained no advantage in post-school earnings.

Abrams reviews the experiences of Sweden and Chile, which embraced school privatization under conservative leadership. In both countries school performance declined, and segregation by race, class, religion, and income grew. The result of school choice was not increased school quality, but increased social inequity.

In his final chapters, Abrams offers Finland as a nation that has chosen a different path and avoided school choice. It performs well on international tests, even though its students seldom encounter standardized tests. Its national goal is to make every school a good school. Teaching is a highly respected profession, requiring five years of education and preparation. While many American schools have abandoned recess to make more time for testing, Finnish schools offer recess after every class. While American students begin learning their letters and numbers in kindergarten or even in pre-kindergarten, Finnish students do not begin formal instruction in reading and mathematics until they reach the age of seven. Until then, the focus in school is on play. The schools emphasize creativity, joy in learning, the arts, and physical education. Child poverty is low, and children get free medical care. Teachers are trusted to write their own tests. Critics say that American society is too diverse to copy a nation that is homogeneous, but it is hard to see why racial and social diversity cancels out the value of anything done in Finnish schools to make children healthier, happier, and more engaged in learning.

Mercedes Schneider's book examines the contradictions of school choice, which is now the rallying cry for those who call themselves reformers. She documents the history of this idea, beginning with economist Milton Friedman's 1955 essay advocating school vouchers. It appeared by happenstance in the immediate aftermath of the 1954 U.S. Supreme Court's *Brown v. Board of Education* decision declaring legally sanctioned racial segregation unconstitutional. Whether or not southern white politicians read Friedman, they became the leading proponents of school choice. After a period of insisting that they would never comply with the *Brown* decision, they became outspoken advocates of school choice, expecting that white children would stay in all-white schools and black children would be fearful to seek admission to white schools. School choice was their strategy for evading desegregation.

Schneider recounts the original idea of charter schools, as it was first developed in 1988 by Albert Shanker, president of the American Federation of Teachers, and Ray Budde, a professor at the University of Massachusetts. They hoped to enable greater teacher participation in decision-making and less bureaucracy. Shanker used his national platform to propose charters as schools-within-schools, staffed by union teachers, free to try new methods to educate reluctant and unwilling students, and encouraged to share what they learned with the host public school. By 1993, Shanker realized that his idea had been adapted by businesses that thought they could manage public schools and make a profit. At that point, Shanker renounced charters and declared they were a threat to public schools, like vouchers.

The first state to pass charter legislation was Minnesota in 1991. What began as a bipartisan measure soon became a favorite of conservative politicians, who realized that they could replace "government schools" with private management, and at the same time get rid of teachers' unions. As a result of the financial inducement of President Obama's Race to the Top program, almost every state now authorizes privately managed charter schools. In some states, like Nevada and Ohio, charter schools are among the lowest-performing schools in the state. Few of these states established any process for oversight or accountability, so thousands of charters sprang up, deregulated and unaccountable to public authorities. In Michigan, about 80 percent of charters operate for-profit. They perform on average no better than public schools, and according to a year-long investigation by the *Detroit Free Press,* they make up a publicly subsidized $1 billion per year industry with no accountability.

Schneider documents the encouragement provided by the administrations of George W. Bush and Barack Obama for the growth of the charter industry. And she follows the money trail, showing the millions poured into charter proliferation by the Waltons and other billionaires. Charter advocates say that they support charters because they want to "rescue" poor and minority students from "failing" public schools. Walmart employs an astonishing 1.4 million people in the United States alone, many of whom are paid less than the minimum wage. The Waltons would have a more dramatic impact on the well-being of children by paying their workers a minimum wage of $15 an hour than they do by opening charter schools and enfeebling community public schools.

Why is Wall Street willing to spend millions of dollars to promote charter schools? As Schneider shows, charters can be a very profitable business. Unlike the Edison Project, which first banked on vouchers, then entered into contracts with school districts to run low-performing public schools, the charters get public money, and they start fresh, free to exclude the students they don't want. These are huge advantages.

The profits come in many forms. First, there are federal tax credits for those who invest in charter schools. Under the New Markets Tax Credit established in 2000, investors in charter school construction can receive a 39 percent federal tax credit over seven years. That's a good return. Foreign investors in charter schools can win EB-5 visas for themselves and their families by investing in charter schools. Charter operators have developed a neat trick in which they buy a building, lease it to themselves at high rentals, and get rich from their real estate. Other charter operators, businessmen and lawyers, open charter schools and supply all the needed goods and services to the schools, collecting millions of dollars in profits. Former tennis star Andre Agassi entered into a profitable partnership with an equity investor to build and open charter schools across the country, even though the Las Vegas charter school that bears his name is one of the lowest-performing schools in the state of Nevada.

With so much incentive to make money and so little regulation or oversight, fraud and graft are inevitable. Just this past summer, the founder of the Pennsylvania Cyber Charter School admitted that he had stolen $8 million from the company for his own use. Cyber charters are amazingly lucrative and unpoliced. The largest of them, K12 Inc., was founded by ex-financier Michael Milken and is listed on the New York Stock Exchange. Its academic results are poor, but it is very profitable. Each student gets a computer and an online teacher. The company collects full state tuition, even though it has none of the expenses of a real school – like custodians, transportation, a library, a social worker, groundskeepers, heat, or other utilities.

A for-profit cyber charter in Ohio – the Electronic Classroom of Tomorrow (ECOT) – is known for very poor performance. It has the lowest graduation rate of any high school in the nation (20 percent), and it recently fought in court and lost, trying to prevent the state from auditing its attendance rates, which were grossly inflated. The state is now trying to recoup at least $60 million from the school for students who never logged on to their home computers. The owner of ECOT is one of the state's biggest donors to elected officials who control state government, and until now, has never been held accountable for either attendance or the quality of education it provides.

Schneider writes that the greatest threat posed by school choice is the "systematic defunding of the local-board-run public school in favor of under-regulated charter schools." Even though most charter schools are technically nonprofit, she believes that the profit motive is the main engine behind the charter movement. She offers a simple proposal for those who want to stop "charter school churn" and resist the "parasitic squandering of taxpayer money in the name of charter choice."

Whenever a charter school fails because of a financial scandal, she proposes, the school should lose its charter and be restored to the local school district. If the charter fails to meet its academic promises, or if it is found to have selected a student population that was not typical for its neighborhood, it should get one more chance, then lose its charter and be returned to the local school board if it fails again. One do-over only.

At present, proponents of school choice have the upper hand because they are backed by some of the nation's richest people, whose campaign donations give them an outsize voice in shaping public policy. The issue that the American public must resolve in local and state, as well as national elections is whether voters will preserve and protect the public school system, or allow it to be raided and controlled by the one percent and financial elites.

As these two fine books demonstrate, there is no evidence for the superiority of privatization in education. Privatization divides communities and diminishes commitment to that which we call the common good. When there is a public school system, citizens are obligated to pay taxes to support the education of all children in the community, even if they have no children in the schools themselves. We invest in public education because it is an investment in the future of society.

As the recent state election returns in Massachusetts, Georgia, and Washington State suggest, the tide may be turning against privatization as the public recognizes what is at stake. This shift of public opinion was surely advanced by the national NAACP in October, which called for a moratorium on new charter schools until they are held to the same standards of transparency and accountability as public schools, until they stop expelling the students that public schools are required to educate, until they stop segregating the highest-performing students from others, and until "public funds are not diverted to charter schools at the expense of the public school system."

Whatever its faults, the public school system is a hallmark of democracy, doors open to all. It is an essential part of the common good. It must be improved for all who attend and paid for by all. Privatizing portions of it, as Trump wants, will undermine public support and will provide neither equity nor better education.

# THE WHITE HOUSE PRESS CORPS MUST STAND UP FOR THE FIRST AMENDMENT

HUFFINGTON POST, JANUARY 13, 2017

At his first press conference since last July, Trump dealt with a variety of questions about his plans. Many of the questions were about the dossier that was leaked to the media, alleging that the Russian government has compromising information about Trump's personal and financial affairs. The allegations have not been verified. The document was posted in full by BuzzFeed and reported by CNN and many other media outlets. Trump angrily denounced the dossier as "fake news," which it may or may not be.

When Jim Acosta of CNN tried to ask a question,[123] Trump refused to acknowledge him, and shouted out "You are fake news." When Acosta tried again to ask a question, Trump's communications director Sean Spicer warned him that he would throw him out if he didn't stop asking questions.

Everyone in the White House press corps is accredited. CNN is a reputable mainstream network, not Breitbart or Gawker. The president doesn't get to decide who is allowed to ask questions.

The next time Trump pulls this stunt, the entire press corps should get up and walk out. Together. En masse. A man like Trump can't survive without the media. The media should not let him control them. If we the public are to be informed, every member of the press corps should have the same right to ask questions and expect to get an answer.

We must all protect our Constitutional freedoms and not allow them to be eroded, bit by bit.

# WHY WOULD ANYONE LISTEN TO BETSY DEVOS ON THE SUBJECT OF EDUCATION? IT CAN'T BE RESULTS

## HUFFINGTON POST, JANUARY 18, 2017

*"As a private citizen, DeVos was not known for supporting civil rights causes. She and her family were known for their support for vouchers, anti-gay organizations, creationism, and libertarian activism. She appointed a woman to run the Office for Civil Rights who is known for anti-feminism and opposition to affirmative action. Advocates for students must keep close watch over the activities of the U.S. Office for Civil Rights." – Diane Ravitch's Blog*

During the hearings on Betsy DeVos, Trump's nominee for Secretary of Education, the Republican Senator Richard Burr from North Carolina asked why people get all hung up on process, when they should be talking about "results." DeVos agreed. I was hoping the committee might then discuss the results of DeVos reforms in Michigan and Detroit. Or anywhere else. How awesome is Detroit, which is overrun with charters? On the National Assessment of Educational Progress (NAEP), it is the lowest performing urban district in the nation. How awesome are Milwaukee and Cleveland, which have had vouchers and charters for more than 20 years? They barely top Detroit among the lowest performing urban districts in the nation. Here is what *The New York Times* said about charters in Detroit:[124]

> Michigan leapt at the promise of charter schools 23 years ago, betting big that choice and competition would improve public schools. It got competition, and chaos.
>
> Detroit schools have long been in decline academically and financially. But over the past five years, divisive politics and educational ideology and a scramble for money have combined to produce a public education fiasco that is perhaps unparalleled in the United States.
>
> While the idea was to foster academic competition, the unchecked growth of charters has created a glut of schools competing for some of the nation's poorest students, enticing them to enroll with cash bonuses, laptops, raffle tickets for iPads, and bicycles. Leaders of charter and traditional schools alike say they are being cannibalized, fighting so hard over students and the limited public dollars that follow them that no one thrives.
>
> Detroit now has a bigger share of students in charters than any American city except New Orleans, which turned almost all its schools into charters after Hurricane Katrina. But half the charters perform only as well as, or worse than, Detroit's traditional public schools.
>
> "The point was to raise all schools," said Scott Romney, a lawyer and board member of New Detroit, a civic group formed after the 1967 race riots here. "Instead, we've had a total and complete collapse of education in this city."

This morning I was on the NPR radio show from D.C.[125]

that used to be the Diane Rehm show but is now called "1A," with Rick Hess of the DeVos-funded American Enterprise Institute, and he said that Detroit charters were outperforming Detroit public schools. As Stephen Henderson, the editor of the Detroit Free Press wrote not long ago,[126] the charters in Detroit vary in quality, but many of them are failing and they are no better than the public schools. Henderson deconstructed the CREDO studies that Rick Hess cited, and concluded:

> In a city like Detroit, for instance, where, on average, students perform well below statewide norms, kids in charter schools should more quickly close their gaps than kids in traditional public schools.
>
> Hypothetically.
>
> The problem is they really haven't. Not for 20 years, dating to the beginning of Michigan's charter experiment.
>
> CREDO also found that, for instance, 63% of charters statewide perform no better than traditional public schools in math. And in Detroit, nearly half all charters do no better than traditional public schools in reading.
>
> Overall, about 84% of charter students perform below state averages in math, the number is 80% for reading. That tracks closely with the outcomes for traditional public schools.
>
> The gains for charter students are also clustered, in many instances, in high-performing outliers. But because Michigan does not require charter operators to have proven track records before they open schools or do much to hold them accountable after their schools open, the number of underperforming charter schools far outweighs the high achievers.

> In addition, the CREDO results need to be considered in the context of other data about charter schools.
>
> The Free Press investigation of charter schools, for instance, revealed that even taking poverty into account, charter schools essentially perform the same as traditional public schools, and in some cases, a little worse.

If Detroit, which is still the lowest-performing urban district in the nation, is the DeVos model of "success," then our nation's education system is doomed. The Detroit Free Press reported in May 2016[127] that Michigan's standing on the 2015 National Assessment of Educational Progress had dropped, in some cases dramatically, since 2003 – not long after Michigan committed to "choice" as its strategy for reform. The article cites a 2016 report from The Education Trust-Midwest, warning that the state was on its way to the bottom.[128]

Among the 2015 NAEP results highlighted in the article and the report:

- Michigan ranked 41st in fourth-grade reading, down from 28th in 2003.
- The state ranked 42nd in fourth-grade math, down from 27th in 2003.
- It ranked 31st in eighth-grade reading, down from 27th in 2003.
- It ranked 38th in eighth-grade math, down from 34th in 2003.

Given these dismal results, why would anyone listen to Betsy DeVos on the subject of education? It must be the tens of millions of dollars she has donated to Republicans, including 10 of the 12 who sit on the Senate Health, Education, Labor and Pensions Committee (HELP), which will judge her fitness to serve as Secretary of Education. It can't be results.

# AN OPEN LETTER TO SENATOR LAMAR ALEXANDER ABOUT BETSY DEVOS

### HUFFINGTON POST, JANUARY 22, 2017

*"Now that Betsy is talking numbers, maybe she will pay attention to the research on charters and vouchers and admit that her favorite panacea is not working. But I'm not holding my breath." – Diane Ravitch's Blog*

*From 1991 to 1993, I worked for Secretary of Education Lamar Alexander in the administration of President George H.W. Bush. I was Assistant Secretary in charge of the Office of Education Research and Improvement and also Counselor to the Secretary of Education.*

*Lamar Alexander is now Senator from Tennessee and Chairman of the Senate Health, Education, Labor, and Pensions Committee (HELP), which is evaluating the qualifications of Betsy DeVos to be U.S. Secretary of Education.*

Dear Lamar,

I hope you don't mind my taking the liberty of writing you a public letter.

I was just reading your book of sayings, the *Little Plaid Book.*[129] For those who don't know, this is your book of "311 rules, lessons, and reminders about running for office and making a difference whether it's for president of the United States or president of your senior class."

The main lesson of the book for me is that you should be honest with people. You shouldn't bore them. You shouldn't lecture them or try to impress them. You should get to know them, listen to them, respect their concerns, and try to understand their problems.

Rule 151 is very important at this time in our national life. It says, "When stumped for an answer, ask yourself, 'What's the right thing to do?' Then do it."

Rule 168 says, "Read whatever Diane Ravitch writes about education." It doesn't say that anyone should agree with what I write, it just says you should read it.

So I am writing you this letter in hopes that you will read it and that I can persuade you to do the right thing.

When I worked for you in the early 1990s in the Department of Education, I absorbed important lessons about character and ethics in public life. You were a model of dignity, integrity, and respect for others. You never raised your voice. You smiled and laughed often. You were always well informed. You picked the best person for whatever job was open.

Now you are in the position of selecting a new Secretary of Education. I watched the hearings, and it was evident to all but the most extreme partisans that Ms. DeVos is unqualified, unprepared, and unfit for the responsibility of running this important agency.

When asked direct questions about important federal issues, she was noncommittal or evasive, or displayed her ignorance. She thinks that the Individuals with

Disabilities Act should be left up to the states to decide whether or not to comply, she does not know it is a federal law and is not optional. When asked about higher education, she was stumped. She was unfamiliar with the terminology of education issues.

Her lack of experience leaves her ill-equipped to address the needs of the vast majority of America's schools. I understand that she doesn't like public schools and much prefers religious schools and privately managed charter schools, including those that operate for profit.

Frankly, it is unprecedented for a Secretary of Education to disapprove of public schools. At least eighty-five percent of American school children attend public schools. She has no ideas about how to improve public schools. Her only idea is that students should enroll in non-public schools.

She would be the first Secretary of Education in our history to be hostile to public education. I have written extensively about the history of public education and how important it is to our democracy. It seems strange to return to the early 19th century, when children attended religious schools, charity schools, charter schools, were home-schooled, or had no education at all. This is not "reform." This is backsliding. This is wiping out nearly two centuries of hard-won progress towards public schools that enroll boys and girls, children of all races and cultures, children with disabilities, and children who are learning English. We have been struggling to attain equality of educational opportunity but we are still far from it. School choice promotes segregation and would take us further away from our national goal.

Since Michigan embraced the DeVos family's ideas

about choice, Michigan has steadily declined on the National Assessment of Educational Progress.

In 2003, Michigan ranked 28th among the states in fourth-grade reading. The latest results, in 2015, showed that Michigan had dropped to 41st.

In 2003, Michigan ranked 27th in fourth- grade math. By 2015, it had declined to 42nd among the states.

Michigan has hundreds of charter schools. 80% of them are run by for-profit operators. The Detroit Free Press conducted a one-year review of the charter sector and concluded it was a $1 billion a year industry that operated without accountability or transparency and that did not produce better results than public schools. When the legislature tried to develop accountability standards for the charter industry in June 2016, Ms. DeVos successfully lobbied to block the legislation.

Detroit is awash in charters and few of them perform as well as the public schools. Detroit is the lowest rated urban district in the nation on the NAEP.

As for vouchers, there have been many state referenda over the past 20 years, and the voters have rejected them every time, usually by large margins. When Ms. DeVos and her husband Richard led a movement to change the Michigan state constitution to permit vouchers for religious schools in the year 2000, the referendum was defeated by 69-31%. Even in deep red Utah, the public rejected vouchers overwhelmingly in 2007. Florida was the last state to reject vouchers, but in a 2012 vote deceptively named the Religious Freedom Act it was defeated by 58-42%.

Time and again, the American public has said that

they don't want public money to be spent in religious schools.

We have experience and evidence about vouchers, which have been imposed by legislatures, not by popular vote. Milwaukee, Cleveland, and the District of Columbia offer vouchers, and these districts are among the lowest performing in the nation on national tests. Milwaukee and Cleveland have had vouchers for more than 20 years, and neither district has seen any improvement in its public schools, nor do the voucher schools outperform the public schools. When the taxpayers' precious dollars are divided among two or three sectors, none of them flourishes.

The Every Student Succeeds Act, which you worked so hard to produce in a bipartisan spirit, goes a long way towards devolving control of education to states. I, of course, would have liked to see the elimination of the federal mandate for annual testing, which has proven to be ineffective for 15 years.

But the best way to enable ESSA to work is to appoint a Secretary of Education who comes to the job with knowledge, experience, and a commitment to let districts and states nurture better ideas than those imposed by Washington.

With kind regards and great respect,
Diane Ravitch

# BETSY DEVOS: I WILL REPLACE THE FAILED IDEAS OF BUSH-OBAMA WITH MY OWN FAILED IDEAS

## HUFFINGTON POST, FEBRUARY 23, 2017

*"Charters could never have gotten this far without bipartisan support so it was useful for their advocates to play the "social justice" card. Now that Republicans control so many states and DeVos is Secretary of Education, why not tell the truth? Charters are a way to break up public schools and replace them with competition and choice, while getting rid of unions. They are and always have been a conservative ploy to launch school choice. Obama and Duncan fell for it. So have Corey Booker and Andrew Cuomo. They got fooled into attacking their political base. Will Democrats continue to support charters now that they are clearly part of the Trump-DeVos agenda?" – Diane Ravitch's Blog*

Betsy DeVos gave a speech to the Conservative Political Action Conference (CPAC), explaining that the programs created by George W. Bush and Barack Obama had failed, and she would replace them with her own ideas.[130] She did not point out that her own ideas have failed too. Just look at the mess she has made of Michigan, where the state's rankings on the federal test (NAEP) have plummeted,[131] and where Detroit is a mess[132] thanks to the miasma of school choice.

*The Washington Post* reported on DeVos's CPAC speech:[133]

> DeVos argued Thursday that education is failing too many students, pointing to "flatlined" test scores (presumably on the National Assessment of Educational Progress, also called the Nation's Report Card) and more than 1.3 million youth who drop out of school each year. The Obama administration's $7 billion investment in overhauling the worst schools, called the School Improvement Grant program, didn't work, DeVos said, making reference to a study by the administration that found no increase in test scores or graduation rates at schools that got the money.
>
> "They tested their model, and it failed miserably," she said. She emphasized that she was not indicting teachers.
>
> She has said that she wants to return as much authority over education as possible to states and districts, and intends to identify programs and initiatives to cut at the Education Department. She has also made clear that she intends to use her platform to expand alternatives to public schools, including charter schools, online schools and private schools that students attend with the help of public funds.
>
> "We have a unique window of opportunity to make school choice a reality for millions of families," she said. "Both the president and I believe that providing an equal opportunity for a quality education is an imperative that all students deserve."

Her own model of vouchers has not a single success to its name. Evaluations of voucher programs in Milwaukee, Cleveland, the District of Columbia, Louisiana, and Indiana have found no gains for the students enrolled in voucher schools. Parents are happier, but that's not a good reason to destroy public schools.

The overwhelming majority of charter studies have found that charters perform no better than public schools unless they exclude children with disabilities, English language learners, and children with behavior problems. When the charters kick them out, they go back to the public schools, which must take them.

Cyber charters have been proven to be disastrous failures in every state. In Tennessee, the Tennessee Virtual Academy is the lowest performing school in the state. Ohio boasts the cyber charter with the lowest graduation rate in the nation, called Electronic Classroom of Tomorrow.

DeVos does not have a single innovative idea. It is the same old retreads of the privatization movement.

I recommend that she read *Reign of Error: The Hoax of the Privatization Movement and the Danger to America's Public Schools*, where I patiently demonstrated using data from the U.S. Department of Education that American students as of 2013 had the highest test scores in our history for all groups – white, black, Hispanic, and Asian – as well as the highest graduation rates and the lowest dropout rates in history.

The scores flatlined from 2013 to 2015, and that may have been because of the application of the Common Core standards and the disruptions foisted upon the schools by Obama and Duncan for the past eight years.

DeVos has proven that she is unqualified to be Secretary of Education. She is not dumb, she is just ignorant. She should do some reading and break free of her ideological contempt for public schools.

# ARE DONALD TRUMP AND BETSY DEVOS THE CIVIL RIGHTS LEADERS OF OUR TIME?

HUFFINGTON POST, MARCH 1, 2017

The title of this post may strike you as a strange question, in light of the well-known history of the Trump Organization in discriminating against blacks who sought to rent their properties and the DeVos's longstanding role as the antagonist of government programs of all kinds, especially in education. History in this country shows that government, not the private sector, is the most faithful guarantor of rights and equity.

Yet in his speech last night,[134] Trump picked up on the deceptive line that we have heard from free-market ideologues for the past 15 years:

> Education is the civil rights issue of our time.
>
> I am calling upon Members of both parties to pass an education bill that funds school choice for disadvantaged youth, including millions of African-American and Latino children. These families should be free to choose the public, private, charter, magnet, religious or home school that is right for them.

> Joining us tonight in the gallery is a remarkable woman, Denisha Merriweather. As a young girl, Denisha struggled in school and failed third grade twice. But then she was able to enroll in a private center for learning, with the help of a tax credit scholarship program. Today, she is the first in her family to graduate, not just from high school, but from college. Later this year she will get her master's degree in social work.
>
> We want all children to be able to break the cycle of poverty just like Denisha.

In reality, the true civil rights issue of our time is the fight to save public education as a public responsibility, responsible for all, doors open to all, staffed by well-prepared teachers.

Trump may have given a big boost to the school choice movement – vouchers, charters, cyber charters, and homeschooling – but his embrace should be the kiss of death for those who know that his bona fides as a leader of the civil rights movement are non-existent, and that our public schools are vital to our democracy.

It is not difficult to open the public coffers and have a free-for-all for anyone who wants part of the public treasury. The for-profit, fly-by-night charter schools that populate Michigan's education landscape must have been heartened by Trump's declaration. The basement voucher schools no doubt have dreams of public dollars coming their way. The fraudulent cyber charter operators who rake in millions in profit must be rubbing their hands with glee.

It is hard, by contrast, to build and sustain high-quality public schools in every community.

Clearly this administration has neither the will nor the heart to do what society needs. They do not intend to increase federal funding, they intend to divide it up among all who want a share. That will cripple community public schools, and they know it. The victims will be the great majority of children who are still enrolled in public schools.

*The New York Times* this morning blasted Betsy DeVos's "fake history" of Historically Black Colleges and Universities,[135] recognizing that they began not as "school choice," but as a response to racism and exclusion.

The same editorial board has faithfully parroted the virtues of charters and school choice, and one day may have to deal with its contradictory stance.

Privately owned and managed charters do not improve public schools. They take funding away from public schools, thus disadvantaging them even further. In the name of "choice" for the few, they weaken the schools that serve whoever arrives at the schoolhouse doors.

Let's be clear about "school choice," at least in this country. It was born of racism in the mid-1950s as a way to evade the *Brown v. Board of Education* decision of 1954. Southern governors and senators took up "choice" as their rallying cry. For many years the term itself was stigmatized because of its history.

The fact that it has been revived by entrepreneurs, well-meaning advocates, and closet racists doesn't change its history or its purpose. It will undermine public education. It may "save" a child here or there, while most children will be lost in a free-market system of competition in which the public abandons its responsibility to provide the best possible education for all children.

We cannot let that happen. If choice were the answer, we would all look to Milwaukee as a national model, which has had vouchers, charters, and public schools since 1990. Twenty-six years is time enough for an experiment to demonstrate its worth. Milwaukee today has a public system that disproportionately enrolls the high-needs children that the other schools don't want. It is also one of the lowest performing urban districts in the nation on the federal tests. Not even Trump or DeVos would have the nerve to call it a national model.

Our public schools need our support. Trump and DeVos are wolves in sheep's clothing. Their sheep's clothing is transparent.

No one should be fooled by their phony advocacy for poor kids or education. They advocate for an unregulated free-market in education that will leave most children behind, especially those who are the most disadvantaged by their social and economic circumstances.

They must not be permitted to destroy public education. They must be stopped, by parents, teachers, students, and every one of us who attended public schools. In every community, we must fight for our democracy and stop the raid on our public treasury.

# THE PUBLIC SHOULD PAY ONLY FOR PUBLIC SCHOOLS, NOT RELIGIOUS SCHOOLS

HUFFINGTON POST, APRIL 10, 2017

Robert Natelson, a retired constitutional law professor who is allied with the ultra-conservative Heartland Institute, writes in The Hill[136] that the Supreme Court may well strike down the state prohibitions on funding religious schools – known as "baby Blaine amendments" – because of their origins in anti-Catholic bias. If this happened, it would pave the way for government to divert public funding from public schools to pay for vouchers for religious schools, as Secretary of Education Betsy DeVos advocates.

The Blaine Amendment was proposed by Speaker of the U.S. House of Representatives James G. Blaine in 1875. Blaine was an ambitious politician from Maine who ran for president in 1876, 1880, and 1884. He was interested in a wide range of issues, including trade, monetary policy, and foreign affairs. He is remembered today for the Constitutional amendment he proposed, which passed the House but not the Senate:

> No State shall make any law respecting an establishment of religion, or prohibiting the free exercise thereof; and no money raised by taxation in any State for the support of public schools, or derived from any public fund therefor, nor any public lands devoted

> thereto, shall ever be under the control of any religious sect; nor shall any money so raised or lands so devoted be divided between religious sects or denominations.

Although the Blaine Amendment was not adopted as an amendment to the U.S. Constitution, it was adopted by many states and incorporated into their state constitutions to prohibit spending public money on religious schools.

Natelson is right that the public schools of the 19th century were deeply imbued with Protestant teachings and practices. I wrote about the battle between Protestants and Catholics in my history of the New York City public schools, *The Great School Wars*. The arrival of large numbers of Irish immigrants in the 1840s, mostly Catholic, concurred with the beginnings of public school systems in urban areas.

In New York City, Bishop John Hughes (later Archbishop Hughes) fought the local school authorities over the content of the textbooks, which contained anti-Catholic selections, and the daily Protestant prayers and rituals in the schools. Hughes demanded equal funding for Catholic schools, since the public schools served as Protestant schools. Even if they cleansed the textbooks of Protestant views of history, he said, the schools would still fail to meet the needs of Catholic children for a Catholic education. He did not want nonsectarian schools, he wanted Catholic schools. He proposed that the state fund both Catholic public schools and Protestant public schools. He ultimately lost the battle, but he determined to build an independent Catholic school system that was privately supported to make sure that Catholic children were not exposed to Protestant teachings in the public schools. His example eventually persuaded the American Catholic Church to require all parishes to open their own schools, and to expect all Catholic children to attend them.

The Protestants who then ran the New York City Public School Society tried to placate Bishop Hughes by expurgating textbook content that he found offensive. Their efforts did not satisfy Bishop Hughes because he did not want nonsectarian public schools. He wanted schools that taught the Catholic religion to Catholic children.

In the 1840s and 1850s, the Know-Nothing Party formed to advocate for white Anglo-Protestant nativism and to harass Catholics and immigrants. The popular press was rife with cartoons ridiculing Catholics and articles warning about the Catholic menace. Prejudice against Catholics and Irish immigrants occasionally turned violent, and churches and convents were burned to the ground.

The Blaine Amendment appealed to anti-Catholic sentiment among the dominant Protestant majority. Blaine's mother was Irish-Catholic, and as Natelson points out, there is no evidence that he was prejudiced. Blaine was a member of the moderate faction of the Republican Party and a strong supporter of black suffrage. Ironically, Archbishop Hughes of New York was an opponent of abolitionism.

Natelson maintains that the anti-Catholic origins of the Blaine amendment are reason enough to overturn them.

But it seems to me even more plausible to argue that the public schools today are not "Protestant schools," that they are thoroughly nonsectarian in character, and that they fulfill the original promise of the Blaine Amendment, which is to serve all children on equal terms, regardless of their religion.

Thanks to the Supreme Court ruling *Engel v. Vitale* in 1962 forbidding state-sponsored prayer in the public schools, the public schools no longer impose any religious prayers or practices, as was common in most public schools well into the 20th century.

The motives of James G. Blaine or Catherine Beecher Stowe or Horace Mann or Henry Bernard or any of the other 19th-century founders of public schools are irrelevant today. They matter less than the reality and practices of public schools today that the Blaine Amendments permit and protect.

Because of the states' Blaine Amendments, public schools across the nation welcome children who are of every religion or no religion, whether Catholic, Protestant, Muslim, Jewish, Hindu, Buddhist, atheist, or any other belief.

To rule against the Blaine Amendments would open the door to subsidizing religious schools with public dollars. On many occasions, voucher advocates have asked voters to repeal their state's Blaine amendment to allow vouchers for religious schools, and in every state, voters said no. Betsy DeVos and her husband sponsored a referendum in Michigan in 2000 to roll back that state's ban on vouchers, and voters rejected their proposal overwhelmingly. A proposal to permit vouchers was rejected by voters in Utah in 2007. Jeb Bush promoted a referendum to change the state constitution in Florida in 2012 – he called it the "The Florida Religious Freedom Amendment" – and despite its deceptive name (who would vote no to religious freedom?), voters decisively said no. The voucher programs that now exist were installed by state legislatures circumventing their own state constitution and the will of the voters. The pro-voucher legislators say that the money goes to the family to spend wherever it wants, including religious schools. They go out of their way to try to disguise these voucher programs by calling them something else, like "opportunity scholarships," "tax credits," "education savings accounts," "empowerment savings accounts." But they are still vouchers for religious schools.

The legislators know that the public opposes funding vouchers for religious schools. Thus they try to avoid calling them what they are or asking for a public referendum to change the state constitution. Voters have repeatedly made clear that they do not want to pay their taxes to underwrite religious schools.

The founders were wiser than we are. The First Amendment states clearly that Congress is not allowed to establish any religion. The founders were well aware of the centuries of religious rivalry and factionalism that had brought constant war and bloodshed to Europe, and they did not wish to encourage it in their new nation. The word "education" does not appear in the Constitution. It is a responsibility left to the states. That does not mean that the federal government has no obligation to fund education, in support of the general welfare it does. That does not mean that the federal government does not have the power to protect the civil rights of students, under the Fourteenth Amendment it does.

If the High Court reviews the state Blaine Amendments, I hope the Justices will recognize that the founders knowingly decided to avoid state entanglement with religious establishments. Let the states decide what belongs in their state constitutions, by popular vote. Our public schools are no longer the Protestant public schools that Bishop Hughes fought against. They are an integral part of our democratic society. They are a public good, like the services of police and firefighters, like public beaches, libraries, and parks. Separation of church and state is a valuable principle that protects the church schools from government intervention and mandates. Religious liberty is best protected by keeping it separate from government dollars and government control.

# DON'T LIKE BETSY DEVOS? BLAME THE DEMOCRATS

## THE NEW REPUBLIC, MAY 23, 2017

*"I contend that it is immoral, unjust, and inequitable to advocate for policies that hurt 95% of students so that 5% can go to a private school. It is even more unjust to destabilize an entire school district by introducing a welter of confusing choices, including schools that open and close like day lilies. Why don't the advocates of school choice also advocate for funding to replace the money removed from the public schools?" – Diane Ravitch's Blog*

Of all the corrupt, unqualified, and extremist characters Donald Trump has tapped to lead his administration, none has generated the tsunami of liberal outrage whipped up by Education Secretary Betsy DeVos. And with all due respect to Jeff Sessions, there's good reason for the backlash. The billionaire Amway heiress from Michigan,[137] who long ago made "school choice" her passion project, is the first education secretary in history to be hostile to the very idea of public education.

Prodded by grassroots activists and what's left of teachers' unions, Democrats went all out to defeat DeVos. George Miller, the former congressman from California, slammed her plan to create a $20 billion "school choice" program that would underwrite private and religious schools,[138] calling it "a perfect storm of ignorance, money, and power." Senator Al Franken grilled DeVos at her confirmation hearing, drawing out her jaw-dropping ignorance of federal programs. Senator Michael Bennet called her nomination an "insult to schoolchildren and their families, to teachers and principals and communities fighting to improve their public schools all across the country."[139] And when DeVos was confirmed by a vote of 51 to 50, over unanimous Democratic opposition, Senator Cory Booker went on Facebook, "frustrated and saddened," to sound a sorrowful note: "Somewhere in America, right now, there is a child who is wondering if this country stands up for them."

Listening to their cries of outrage, one might imagine that Democrats were America's undisputed champions of public education. But the resistance to DeVos obscured an inconvenient truth – Democrats have been promoting a conservative "school reform" agenda for the past three decades. Some did it because they fell for the myths of "accountability" and "choice" as magic bullets for better schools. Some did it because "choice" has centrist appeal. Others sold out public schools for campaign contributions from the charter industry and its Wall Street patrons. Whatever the motivations, the upshot is clear: The Democratic Party has lost its way on public education. In a very real sense, Democrats paved the way for DeVos and her plans to privatize the school system.

Thirty years ago, there was a sharp difference between Republicans and Democrats on education. Republicans wanted choice, testing, and accountability. Democrats wanted equitable funding for needy districts, and highly trained teachers. But in 1989, with Democrats reeling from three straight presidential losses, the lines began to blur. That year, when President George H.W. Bush convened an education summit of the nation's governors , it was a little-known Arkansas Democrat named Bill Clinton who drafted a bipartisan set of national goals for the year 2000 ("first in the world" in mathematics, for starters). The ambitious benchmarks would be realized by creating, for the first time, national achievement standards and tests. Clinton ran on the issue, defeated Bush, and passed Goals 2000,[140] [141] which provided grants to states that implemented their own achievement metrics.

The Democrats had dipped a toe in "school reform." Before long, they were completely immersed. After George W. Bush made the "Texas miracle" of improved schools a launching pad for the presidency, many Democrats swallowed his bogus claim that testing students every year had produced amazing results. In 2001, Ted Kennedy, the Senate's liberal lion, teamed with Bush to pass No Child Left Behind.[142] For the first time, the government was mandating not only "accountability" – code for punishing teachers and schools who fall short, but also "choice" – code for handing low-performing public schools over to charter operators.

When Barack Obama took office in 2009, educators hoped he would return the party to its public school roots. By then, even Bill Clinton was calling No Child Left Behind a "train wreck."[143] Instead, Obama and Education Secretary Arne Duncan doubled down on testing, accountability, and choice. Their Race to the Top program was, in essence, No Child Left Behind II: It invited states to compete for $5 billion in funds by holding teachers accountable for test scores, adopting national standards, opening more charter schools, and closing low-scoring public schools.

The Obama years saw an epidemic of new charters, testing, school closings, and teacher firings. In Chicago, Mayor Rahm Emanuel closed 50 public schools in one day. Democratic charter advocates – whose ranks include the outraged Booker and Bennet – have increasingly imported "school choice" into the party's rhetoric. Booker likes to equate "choice" with "freedom" – even though the entire idea of "choice" was created by white Southerners who were scrambling to defend segregated schools after *Brown v. Board of Education.*

It's fitting that Trump and DeVos rely on the same language to tout their vision of reform. They're essentially taking Obama's formula one step further – expanding "choice" to include vouchers,[144] so parents can use public funding to pay for private and religious schools. Democrats are up in arms about the privatization scheme, as they should be – it's a disaster for public schools. But if they're serious about being the party that treats public education as a cornerstone of democracy, they need to do more than grandstand about the consequences they helped bring about. They need to follow the money – their own campaign money, that is.

As Democrats learned years ago, support for mandatory testing and charter schools opens fat wallets on Wall Street. Money guys love deregulation, testing and Big Data, and union-busting. In 2005, Obama served as the featured speaker at the inaugural gathering of Democrats for Education Reform,[145] which bundles contributions to Democrats who back charter schools. Among its favorites have been those sharp DeVos critics George Miller, Michael Bennet, and Cory Booker. Conservative funders like the Walton Foundation also give generously to charter schools and liberal think tanks such as the Center for American Progress.

The money had its intended effect. When Andrew Cuomo decided to run for governor of New York, he learned that the way to raise cash was to go through the hedge funders at Democrats for Education Reform. They backed him lavishly, and Cuomo repaid them by becoming a hero of the charter movement.[146] Connecticut Governor Dan Malloy, often celebrated for his unvarnished liberalism, is another champion of the charter industry – some of its biggest funders live in his state. California Governor Jerry Brown vetoed a bill to ban for-profit charters in the state, and has resisted efforts to make charters more accountable. As mayor of Oakland, he opened two charter schools.[147]

There are plenty of reasons that Democrats should steer clear of the charter industry. Charter corporations have been repeatedly charged with fraud, nepotism, self-dealing, and conflicts of interest. Many charters make money on complex real-estate deals. Worst of all are the "cybercharters", mega-corporations that offer virtual schools, with high attrition, low test scores, and abysmal graduation rates.[148] The biggest cybercharter chain is K12 Inc., started by former junk-bond king Michael Milken and listed on the New York Stock Exchange.

But it's more than a matter of sleeping with the enemy. School choice doesn't work, and "evidence-based" Democrats ought to acknowledge it. Charter schools are a failed experiment. Study after study has shown that they do not get better test scores than public schools unless they screen out English-language learners and students with profound disabilities.[149] It's well-established that school choice increases segregation,[150] rather than giving low-income students better opportunities. And kids using vouchers actually lose ground in private schools.[151]

Support for charters is paving the way for a dual school system – one that is allowed to choose the students it wants, and another that is required to accept all who enroll.

This is what Democrats *should* be yelling about. And if there's ever a moment for them to reclaim their mantle as the party of public education, it's now. The misguided push for "reform" is currently being led not by Obama and Duncan, but by Trump and DeVos, giving Democrats an opening to shift gears on education – though they'll lose some of that hedge-fund money.

But if 2016 taught Democrats anything, it's how unwise it was to allow the demolition of organized labor – including teachers' unions, once a great source of money and grassroots energy. The party needs strong teachers' unions and it needs their enthusiasm.

The agenda isn't complicated. Fight privatization of all kinds. Insist on an evidence-based debate about charter schools and vouchers. Abandon the obsession with testing. Fight for equitable funding, with public money flowing to the neediest schools. Acknowledge the importance of well-educated, professional teachers in every classroom.

Follow the example of Virginia Governor Terry McAuliffe, who vetoed a bill to expand charters in March. Or Montana Governor Steve Bullock, who insists that charters employ certified teachers, allow them to unionize, and fall under the control of local school districts. Democrats should take their cue from Bullock when he declares, "I continue to firmly believe that our public education system is the great equalizer."[152]

There is already an education agenda that is good for children, good for educators, good for the nation, and good for the Democratic Party. It's called good public schools for everyone. All Democrats have to do is to rediscover it.

# THE DEMOLITION OF AMERICAN EDUCATION

## THE NEW YORK REVIEW OF BOOKS - NYR DAILY, JUNE 5, 2017

Donald Trump and Betsy DeVos's proposed budget for the U.S. Department of Education is a boon for privatization and a disaster for public schools and low-income college students. They want to cut federal spending on education by 13.6 percent. Some programs would be eliminated completely, others would face deep reductions. They want to cut $10.6 billion from existing programs, and divert $1.4 billion to charter schools and to vouchers for private and religious schools. This budget reflects Trump and DeVos's deep hostility to public education and their desire to shrink the Department of Education, with the ultimate goal of getting rid of it entirely.

The proposed budget would shrink the assistance programs that now enable 12 million students to attend college. Funding for college work-study programs would be cut in half, thus "saving" $490 million. It would eliminate a student loan forgiveness program, enacted in 2007, that encourages college graduates to enter careers in public service – such as social work, teaching, or working as doctors in rural areas – by relieving them of their college debt at the end of ten years of such employment. Some 550,000 young people have joined this program in the past decade; the first wave are due to have their debts forgiven in 2017, but it is not clear if the administration will follow through on the promise to cancel their debt.

The proposed budget would maintain funding for Pell grants for needy college students, but would eliminate more than $700 million in Perkins loans for disadvantaged students. No attempt would be made to lessen the burden of escalating college costs for students, whether middle-income or poor. Student debt is currently about $1.4 trillion, and many students, whether they graduate or not, spend years, even decades, repaying their loans. These cuts will reduce the number of students who can afford to attend college.

The most devastating cuts are aimed at programs for public schools. Nearly two dozen programs are supposed to be eliminated, on the grounds that they have "achieved their original purpose, duplicate other programs, are narrowly focused, or are unable to demonstrate effectiveness." In many cases, the budget document says that these programs should be funded by someone else – not the U.S. Department of Education, but "federal, state, local and private funds." These programs include after-school and summer programs that currently serve nearly two million students, and which keep children safe and engaged in sports, arts, clubs, and academic studies when they are out of school. They have never been judged by test scores, but the budget claims they do not improve student achievement, and aims to save the government $1 billion by ending support for them. The budget assumes that someone else will pick up the tab, but most states have cut their education budgets since the 2008 recession. No mention is made of how other sources will be able to come up with this funding.

The administration wants to end many programs that are aimed at the poorest students and disadvantaged minorities in particular, while canceling vital enhancements to public school education like arts and foreign-language funding. These include:

- Supplementary educational services for Alaskan Native and Native Hawaiian students ($66 million).
- Arts education ($27 million)

- American history and civics academies ($1.8 million).
- Full-service community schools that provide comprehensive academic, social, and health services to students and their families ($10 million).
- Library-based literacy programs ($27 million)
- "Impact Aid" to districts that lose revenue because of federal facilities like military bases ($66 million)
- International education and foreign language studies ($73 million)
- The Javits program for gifted and talented students ($12 million); preschool development grants to help states build or expand high-quality preschool services ($250 million)
- Special Olympics programs for students with disabilities ($10 million)
- Supporting Effective Instruction State Grants, funds used to train teachers and to reduce class sizes ($2.345 billion).
- In addition, the Trump-DeVos budget would eliminate funding for a potpourri of programs including mental health services, anti-bullying initiatives, and Advanced Placement courses ($400 million).

This is only a sample of the broad sweep of programs that would be eliminated, not just reduced. Some of the programs, like the Special Olympics for handicapped students, are small grants but they have both real and symbolic importance. The cuts to funds for reducing class sizes will have an immediate negative effect.

With billions cut from existing education programs, the only area of increase in the education budget would be grants for school choice. The department's Title I program consists of billions of dollars distributed to states and districts to aid in the education of poor children, by providing smaller classes, extra aides in the classroom, or other assistance. Trump would set aside $1 billion of Title I funding as a reward for states that create open enrollment policies, which allow parents to choose schools that are not their neighborhood schools, and that allow federal, state, and local dollars to follow students to the public school of their choice. In "reform" circles, this is known as the "backpack-full-of-cash" method of financing school. The money goes wherever the student goes.

The other Trump-DeVos initiative is $400 million to "create, develop, implement, replicate, or take to scale entrepreneurial, evidence-based, field-initiated innovations to improve student achievement ... and rigorously evaluate such innovations." This murky statement is aimed at setting aside funds to underwrite vouchers that could be used at private and religious schools, as well as research on the effectiveness of these programs.

Ironically, the Trump administration is modeling some of its approach on the Obama administration's Race to the Top program, which held a contest for states in 2009 and 2010. According to Race to the Top, to be eligible to compete for $4.35 billion in federal funds, states had to agree to increase the number of charter schools in the state, to evaluate teachers by the test scores of their students, to adopt "college and career ready standards," which everyone knew were the freshly-minted Common Core standards that had never been field-tested, and to agree to take dramatic action to restructure or close schools with persistently low test scores. There was no evidence of effectiveness to support any of these policies, but most states changed their laws so they could compete for badly needed funding. A recent evaluation by the Department of Education[153] found that these policies were ineffective, "Overall, across all grades, we found... no significant impacts on math or reading test scores, high school graduation, or college enrollment." But nonetheless the Race was a successful way to lure states into doing "voluntarily" what the federal government wanted them to do, but was prohibited by law from ordering them to do.

Similarly, Trump is offering states a chance to win a slice of the $1 billion Title I pot if they agree to meet his and DeVos's demand for more school choice – more charters, more vouchers, more online schools, more alternatives to public schools. Although they are not offering as much money as Race to the Top, nearly two thirds of the states are now in Republican hands, and most are likely to jump at the chance to introduce school choice and vouchers for religious schools.

Since the enactment of George W. Bush's No Child Left Behind (NCLB), it has become customary for every piece of federal education legislation to insist upon "evidence-based policies," and then to in fact impose policies based on speculation, without any evidence behind them. NCLB made reference to "evidence-based" over one hundred times. NCLB required every public school in the nation to test every child in grades 3-8 every year, and to punish or reward schools based on their test scores, although evidence was lacking for this bold federal intrusion. The "Texas Miracle" was supposed to be the evidence for this strategy – Bush said that if you test everyone every year, scores go up, graduation rates go up, and the achievement gap among the races begins to close. Unfortunately, this was not supported by the actual results. There was no miracle, just – as we say in Texas – "Texas brags," an empty boast.

And now the Trump administration says it wants school choice policies that are "evidence-based ... to improve student achievement." But we have had charter schools and voucher programs since 1990, and there is a growing body of data showing that they do not improve student achievement. Milwaukee opened charter schools and a voucher program for poor children in 1990. It now has three competing sectors – public schools, charter schools, and voucher schools. The latter two sectors get to choose their students and prefer to avoid students with profound disabilities or who are in the process of learning English. The public schools are required to take all comers. Nonetheless, there is little if any difference in test results among the three sectors. And Milwaukee is one of the lowest performing urban districts in the nation on the federal tests called the National Assessment of Educational Progress (NAEP). No rising tide there.

There are voucher programs in several states, such as

Louisiana, Ohio, and Indiana. Recent evaluations have found that voucher students in those states did not perform as well academically as their peers in the public schools. Earlier this year, a federally funded evaluation of the voucher program in the District of Columbia, established by a Republican-led Congress in 2004, found that, on average, students who used the vouchers had worse test scores than their peers who remained in public schools.

DeVos, who has spent decades advocating for school vouchers, responded to the poor results by saying: "When school choice policies are fully implemented, there should not be differences in achievement among the various types of schools." But if the goal is to "improve student achievement," this seems an admission of failure.

DeVos's home state of Michigan embraced the "school choice" ideology, but not vouchers, because in 2000 the public overwhelmingly rejected them in a referendum (funded by DeVos and her husband). Michigan has hundreds of charter schools. Eighty percent of them operate for profit. Charter schools perform worse on state tests than public schools. Over the past fifteen years, as Michigan pursued choice as its reform strategy, the state scores on the NAEP dropped significantly.

Thus, we have a budget for federal education policy that swings a mighty scythe, mostly at programs that serve middle-income and low-income students. Its major innovation is a proven failure. DeVos has no ideas about helping or improving public schools. Her only idea is choice. But we already know how that will turn out.

# PBS RUNS A THREE-HOUR SERIES GLORIFYING THE DEVOS EDUCATION AGENDA

HUFFPOST, JUNE 13, 2017

*"Whenever charter operators are sued, their defense is that they are not public schools. They are privately managed schools that receive public funding. ... Charter schools are run by private entities that receive government contracts. The receipt of public funds does not make an entity public. If it did, then every major defense contractor would be public not private." – Diane Ravitch's Blog*

Public education today faces an existential crisis. Over the past two decades, the movement to transfer public money to private organizations has expanded rapidly. The George W. Bush administration first wrote into federal law the proposal that privately managed charter schools were a remedy for low-scoring public schools, even though no such evidence existed. The Obama administration provided hundreds of millions each year to charter schools, under the control of private boards. Now, the Trump administration, under the leadership of Secretary of Education Betsy DeVos, wants to expand privatization to include vouchers, virtual schools, cyberschools, homeschooling, and every other possible alternative to public education. DeVos has said[154] that public education is a "dead end," and that "government sucks."

DeVos's agenda finds a ready audience in the majority of states now controlled by Republican governors and legislatures. Most states already have some form of voucher program that allow students to use public money to enroll in private and religious schools, even when their own state constitution prohibits it. The Republicans have skirted their own constitutions by asserting that the public money goes to the family, not the private or religious school. The longstanding tradition of separating church and state in K-12 education is crumbling. And Betsy DeVos can testify with a straight face that she will enforce federal law to "schools that receive federal funding," because voucher schools allegedly do not receive the money, just the family that chooses religious schools.

Advocates of the privatization movement like DeVos claim that nonpublic schools will "save poor children from failing public schools," but independent researchers have recently concurred that vouchers actually have had a negative effect on students in the District of Columbia, Indiana, Louisiana, and Ohio.[155] Charters, at best, have a mixed record, and many are known for excluding children with disabilities and English language learners, and for pushing out students who are troublesome.

This is a time when honest, nonpartisan reporting is needed to inform the American public.

But this month the Public Broadcasting System is broadcasting a "documentary" that tells a one-sided story, the story that Betsy DeVos herself would tell, based on the work of free-market advocate Andrew Coulson. Author of "Market Education," Coulson narrates "School, Inc.," a three-hour program, which airs this month nationwide in three weekly broadcasts on PBS.

Uninformed viewers who see this slickly produced program will learn about the glories of unregulated schooling, for-profit schools, and teachers selling their lessons to students on the Internet. They will learn about the "success" of the free market in schooling in Chile, Sweden, and New Orleans. They will hear about the miraculous charter schools across America, and how public school officials selfishly refuse to encourage the transfer of public funds to private institutions. They will see a glowing portrait of South Korea, where students compete to get the highest possible scores on a college entry test that will define the rest of their lives and where families gladly pay for after-school tutoring programs and online lessons to boost test scores. They will hear that the free market is more innovative than public schools.

What they will not see or hear is the other side of the story. They will not hear scholars discuss the high levels of social segregation in Chile, nor will they learn that the students protesting the free-market schools in the streets are not all "Communists," as Coulson suggests. They will not hear from scholars who blame Sweden's choice system for the collapse of its international test scores. They will not see any reference to Finland, which far outperforms any other European nation on international tests, yet has neither vouchers nor charter schools. They may not notice the absence of any students in wheelchairs or any other evidence of students with disabilities in the highly regarded KIPP charter schools. They will not learn that the acclaimed American Indian Model Charter Schools in Oakland do not enroll any American Indians, but have a student body that is 60 percent Asian American in a city where that group is 12.8 percent of the student population. Nor will they see any evidence of greater innovation in voucher schools or charter schools than in properly funded public schools.

Coulson has a nifty way of dismissing the fact that the free market system of schooling was imposed by the dictator Augusto Pinochet. He says that Hitler liked the Hollywood movie "It Happened One Night" (with Claudette Colbert and Clark Gable), so should we stop showing or watching the movie? Is that a fair comparison? Pinochet was directly responsible for the free market system of schooling, including for-profit private schools. Hitler neither produced nor directed "It Happened One Night." Thus does Coulson refer to criticisms, like Sweden's collapsing scores on international tests, and dismisses them as irrelevant.

I watched the documentary twice, preparing to be interviewed by Channel 13, and was repelled by the partisan nature of the presentation. I googled the funders and discovered that the lead funder is the Rose Mary and Jack Anderson Foundation, a very conservative foundation that is a major contributor to the Friedman Foundation for Educational Choice, which advocates for vouchers. The Anderson Foundation is allied with Donors Trust,[156] whose donors make contributions that cannot be traced to them. Mother Jones referred[157] to this foundation as part of "the dark-money ATM of the conservative movement." Other contributors to Donors Trust include the Koch brothers' Americans for Prosperity and the Richard and Helen DeVos Foundation.

The second major funder is the Prometheus Foundation. Its public filings with the IRS show that its largest grant ($2.5 million) went to the Ayn Rand Institute. The third listed funder of "School Inc." is the Steve and Lana Hardy Foundation, which contributes to free-market libertarian think tanks.

In other words, this program is paid propaganda. It does not search for the truth. It does not present opposing points of view. It is an advertisement for the demolition of public education and for an unregulated free market in education. PBS might have aired a program that debates these issues, but "School Inc." does not.

It is puzzling that PBS would accept millions of dollars for this lavish and one-sided production from a group of foundations with a singular devotion to the privatization of public services. The decision to air this series is even stranger when you stop to consider that these kinds of anti-government political foundations are likely to advocate for the elimination of public funding for PBS. After all, in a free market of television, where there are so many choices available, why should the federal government pay for a television channel?

# NICHOLAS KRISTOF DEFENDS FOR-PROFIT TAKEOVER OF SCHOOLS IN AFRICA

## DIANE RAVITCH BLOG POST, JULY 16, 2017

In his column in *The New York Times*,[158] Nicholas Kristof defends the takeover of schooling in Africa by Bridge International Academies.

Kristof says that since the government failed to provide basic education, it is welcome news that BIA is doing it, for a fee. The investors include Bill Gates and Mark Zuckerberg.

He writes that American liberals should get over their squeamishness about privatization and for-profit operation of what are supposed to be public schools.

I think Kristof is wrong because BIA is a short-term fix, not a solution. It cannot possibly educate the hundreds of millions of children whose parents can't afford to pay. By providing this "fix," the governments are relieved of their obligation to establish a universal, free public school system with qualified teachers. If teachers are sleeping in their classrooms, who should take responsibility? Who should supervise them and make sure that every child has a decent education? That is the government's job. Addressing the systemic problems of low-quality public education would accomplish far more than creating a for-profit corporation to offer scripted lessons to some. BIA is not a long-term solution, and surely Kristof knows this. Why is he willing to settle for such a bad deal for the children in impoverished nations? This is a lifeboat strategy – instead of righting the ship, throw life preservers to a few (at a price).

In his column, Kristof chastises progressives and union leaders for their hostility to BIA:

> I've followed Bridge for years, my wife and I wrote about it in our last book, and the concerns are misplaced. Bridge has always lost money, so no one is monetizing children. In fact, it's a start-up that tackles a social problem in ways similar to a nonprofit, but with for-profit status that makes it more sustainable and scalable.
>
> More broadly, the world has failed children in poor countries. There have been global campaigns to get more children in school, but that isn't enough. The crucial metric isn't children attending school, but children learning in school.

Although Kristof presents BIA as a grand venture in philanthropy, it was billed by its founders as a start-up that had the potential to grow into a billion-dollar company. Did he read Peg Tyre's article[159] in *The New York Times Magazine* about BIA? Tyre wrote:

> Bridge operates 405 schools in Kenya, educating children from preschool through eighth grade, for a fee of between \$54 and \$126 per year, depending on the location of the school. It was founded in 2007 by May and her husband, Jay Kimmelman, along with a friend, Phil Frei. From early on, the founders' plans for the world's poor were audacious. "An aggressive start-up company that could figure out how to profitably deliver education at a high quality for less than \$5 a month could radically disrupt the status quo in education for these 700 million children and ultimately create what could be a billion-dollar new

global education company," Kimmelman said in 2014. Just as titans in Silicon Valley were remaking communication and commerce, Bridge founders promised to revolutionize primary-school education. "It's the Tesla of education companies," says Whitney Tilson, a Bridge investor and hedge-fund manager in New York who helped found Teach for America and is a vocal supporter of charter schools.

The Bridge concept – low-cost private schools for the world's poorest children – has galvanized many of the Western investors and Silicon Valley moguls who learn about the project. Bill Gates, the Omidyar Network, the Chan Zuckerberg Initiative and the World Bank have all invested in the company; Pearson, the multinational textbook-and-assessment company, has done so through a venture-capital fund. Tilson talked about the company to Bill Ackman, the hedge-fund manager of Pershing Square, which ultimately invested $5.8 million through its foundation. By early 2015, Bridge had secured more than $100 million, according to *The Wall Street Journal.*

The fact that Bridge was a for-profit company gave pause to some NGOs that work in developing countries. But others reasoned that in the last decade, for-profit companies backed by what are called social-impact investors – people and institutions that make money by doing good – had successfully brought about important innovations, like solar-power initiatives and low-cost health clinics, in poor countries. Bridge's model relied on similar investors but was even more ambitious in its dreams of scale. "There is a great demand for this," May said in an M.I.T. video from 2016. Some of the company's backers, she said, were "not social-impact investors," continuing that "t was straight commercial capital who saw, 'Wow, there

> are a couple billion people who don't have anyone selling them what they want.' " For a 2010 case study on the company, Kimmelman told the Harvard Business School that return on investment could be 20 percent annually.

So, some investors were making philanthropic investments (what's a few millions to Gates or Zuckerberg?), but the founders imagined a company returning 20 percent annually. BIA currently has schools operating in Kenya, Nigeria, and Uganda and is opening in India. It planned to go public this year. As Tyre wrote:

> By 2016, they planned to enroll more than 750,000 students, at which point they would be breaking even. By 2022, they estimated that they would educate 4.1 million students and generate $470 million in revenue.

Tyre shows that many families can't afford BIA's fees. If the parents don't pay, the students are sent home.

Kristoff says, "So what, as long as the children are learning?" He cites a study commissioned and released by BIA called "The Bridge Effect," which showed the success of its model, and Kristoff cites it as evidence of success. Tyre took it to two independent experts, who found it inconclusive because 50% of the BIA students dropped out during the course of the study:

> I asked two experts in statistics – Nat Malkus, from the American Enterprise Institute, and Bryan Graham, from the University of California, Berkeley – to help me evaluate the findings. "This is good evidence of positive effects," says Malkus. Both pointed out that the study's results are complicated by Bridge's high dropout rate: While a third of public-school students dropped out, nearly half of Bridge students left during the study and were unable to take the final assessment. "The high attrition rate should give one pause," Malkus says, "when considering the full effect of

> the program." Graham, co-editor of The Review of Economics and Statistics, says that "organizations are under a lot of pressure to do these studies and 'prove' their program works. Reasonable and informed people could look at the information in that report and come to widely different conclusions about the effect of Bridge on academic achievement as they measure it. It's information, just not especially actionable information."
>
> Another area of achievement that Bridge trumpets is the success of its students on the eighth-grade K.C.P.E. test. In 2015, according to Bridge, 63 percent of Bridge students who had been there for at least two years passed, compared with 49 percent of Kenyan students nationwide. But it's unclear whether Bridge's approach will be sustainable as the company grows. Former Bridge employees told me that in preparation for the 2015 exam, those on track to get a lower score were asked to repeat a year. The rest were taken to a residential cram school and prepped for the test by teachers who flew in from the United States.

Tyre reports that BIA has had trouble hiring and retaining teachers. Turnover was high. Then BIA signed them to two-year contracts and warned that they would be docked the cost of training if they left before two years. That reduced churn. Teachers read their lessons from a script on a tablet called a Nook. The teachers are "managed" by text messages or robocalls.

> Some Bridge staff members described what they saw as a stark contrast between their hopes for Bridge and a grittier reality. One school administrator, an academy manager, described how the pressure to ensure that parents made their payments on time was disheartening. "I didn't realize how hard it would be to talk to parents," he said. "They're ill, they're out of work, they had a fire. No one is in the house who's

> making any money. How can they pay when they have no money for food?" And working at Bridge, teachers said, can disrupt a career: Instructors are required to sign an employment agreement that includes a non-compete clause that prevents them from working at other nearby schools for a year after they leave.
>
> In the public and informal Kenyan schools I visited school administrators welcomed my impromptu drop-ins warmly, showed me their classrooms and introduced me to their teachers, who spoke frankly about their challenges. Bridge teachers and managers say that sort of openness is not allowed. At some Bridge schools I visited unescorted, staff members said that they would need to contact superiors if I didn't leave.

The most peculiar part of Kristof's article is his defense of the situation of for-profit schools in the U.S., most of which are notoriously corrupt and thrive by using public funds for lavish marketing. Kristof writes:

> But my travels have left me deeply skeptical that government schools in many countries can be easily cured of corruption, patronage and wretched governance, and in the meantime we fail a generation of children.
>
> In the United States, criticisms of for-profit schools are well grounded, for successive studies have found that vouchers for American for-profit schools hurt children at least initially (although the evidence also shows that in the U.S., well-run charters can help pupils).

I don't think Nick reads much about education, only what he sees in his own newspaper, although he clearly missed Peg Tyre's article.

If he thinks governments are corrupt, he should take a look

at the for-profit charter sector in the U.S. Furthermore his reference to voucher schools is wrong. The latest research shows that students who enroll in voucher schools (whether for-profit or not) lose ground academically, but if they persist for four years, they catch up to their peers in public schools. How is that helping children? If the same money were spent reducing class sizes in their public schools, all students would benefit.

# BAD NEWS FOR BRIDGE INTERNATIONAL ACADEMIES

## DIANE RAVITCH BLOG POST, SEPTEMBER 10, 2017

The Liberian government received a report on the various for-profit corporations providing schooling. The bottom line – scores went up, but the cost of services varied dramatically. The most expensive of all the providers was Bridge International Academies, the for-profit corporation that is funded by Bill Gates, Mark Zuckerberg, and other luminaries of the tech sector. Their costs were so much higher than that of any other service that it is doubtful that they are sustainable.

The so-called Partnership schools received double the funding of the public schools, $100 instead of only $50. And the Ministry of Education made sure that the Partnership schools were well-supplied with teachers, including the best-trained.

Four of the networks managed to produce results for less than $100 per pupil. Bridge, however, cost more than $1,000 per pupil, a figure dramatically higher than any other network, and their results were not markedly better.

Will Nicholas Kristof reconsider his fulsome praise for Bridge International Academies? The skeptics were right to be concerned about sustainability and scalability. Why did the billionaires think it was a good idea to try to turn a profit off the backs of the poorest people in the world? These Silicon Valley geniuses may be good at selling product, but they are not very good at creating or providing an education system.

Download the brief here.[160] Download the report here.[161]

# UGANDA CRACKS DOWN ON FOR-PROFIT PRIVATE SCHOOLS RUN BY WESTERNERS

## DIANE RAVITCH BLOG POST, MAY 20, 2018

In the past few years, a group of Western investors have introduced low-cost for-profit private schools into African nations. Their company is called Bridge International Academies. It is a "tech startup" developed by entrepreneurs who hoped to do well by doing good. Veteran journalist Peg Tyre wrote a balanced yet implicitly scathing article about BIA in *The New York Times Magazine.*[162] Some of the investors are Mark Zuckerberg, Pearson, the World Bank, Bill Gates, and Pierre Omidyar. The schools seek to replace the public schools, which are free but usually underfunded and poorly equipped. Bridge teachers teach from tablets loaded with scripted curriculum – apparently written in Boston by charter school teachers who understand how to write scripted curricula. It claims to get better results than the public schools, but at a higher price. Even though these schools are "low cost," most families in poor nations cannot afford to pay. It is operating schools in Kenya, Uganda, and Nigeria, and a few in India.

Are they philanthropic saviors of African children or neocolonialists?

The government of Uganda is aggressively pushing back

against the Bridge schools. Janet K. Museveni is First Lady and Minister of Education and Sports. In her December 17, 2017 article in Uganda's leading daily newspaper *New Vision*,[163] she explains that the 63 Bridge schools operating in Uganda are unlicensed and do not meet the standards required to operate. Museveni writes:

> The media has been awash with news about the intransigent manner in which Management of the Bridge International Academies (BIA) which were recently renamed Bridge Schools are acting when faced with closure by the Ministry of Education and Sports for lack of licenses to operate in Uganda.
>
> It must be puzzling to the public particularly when all they see, as a result of the aggressive media campaign by Bridge operators, are pictures of children that look fairly "organised" as they march on streets and demonstrate at Parliament to protect the interests of the proprietors – at the risk of simply being used as pawns in a game they hardly comprehend.

The Bridge tactic of organizing pupils to march on behalf of the school corporation will sound familiar to Americans.

Museveni goes on to describe the requirements of the law and the power of the Ugandan government to set standards. She describes the efforts made by the Government to regulate and inspect Bridge schools. These were the findings of the investigation:

> Key findings of the multi-disciplinary team that were brought to the attention of the Bridge team during this meeting are summarised hereunder:
>
> **Issue #1: – Curriculum**
>
> Early childhood Development (ECD):
>
> Children are kept for long hours at school without any designated resting places; did not use the approved

ECD Learning Framework and the Caregivers' Guide; administered written examinations which are against Government Policy.

Lower Primary:

The preparation, language of instruction and pedagogy were not in line with the approved curriculum.

Upper Primary

Curriculum Content, Schemes of Work, Lesson Plans, Textbooks, Schools and Class timetables did not conform to the approved Ugandan curriculum which they purport to implement. Many teachers were not free to adjust what they received on the tablets to teach from a central source and appeared to live in fear; claiming to be underpaid and lacking a forum for airing their grievances. Most of the Head Teachers, referred to as "Academy Managers" were not professionally trained and could not provide instructional leadership.

**Issue #2: – Teacher Qualification/Competence**

There were no clear documents on teachers' qualifications in the Managers' ('Head Teachers') Office; most teachers had no contracts; and about a half had no authentic Teacher Registration numbers.

Notwithstanding the well-known benefits of introducing technology into the delivery process, teachers should have the freedom to adapt their classroom schemes of work, lesson plans, assessment and remedial activities to the practicalities of the specific teaching-learning context rather than be enslaved to the restrictions of centrally prepared and delivered lessons.

**Issue #3: – Bridge Schools Infrastructure**

All the facilities were temporary with School structures made of roofing sheet material (both walls and roof) and wire mesh, which are unsuitable for students during very hot weather conditions. The structures have no windows and battened wooden doors were used without proper framing. Soundproofing between Classrooms is inadequate. There is no protection against lightening on any of the structures. Sanitation facilities are shared amongst students (boys and girls) and teachers. The facilities were not fit to be a school.

Based on the findings/observations outlined above, specific and general recommendations were made on curriculum, teachers and facilities to enable them meet the basic requirements and minimum standards.

She and the Government of Uganda are serious about regulating Bridge schools:

I should, however, add that the impunity being exhibited by Bridge Management, and its likes, will not be tolerated and that Government will spare no effort to use all legal means to enforce the requirements of the Law to protect our children and our future, as a country.

# BIG MONEY RULES

## THE NEW YORK REVIEW OF BOOKS, JULY 12, 2017

*"Americans for Prosperity opposes all government programs. Its primary purpose is to protect the Koch billions from taxation to pay for any programs that benefit others. If it was up to the Koch Brothers, they would eliminate Social Security, Medicare, and every other social program. They are rabid libertarians who oppose taxation and government. Their interest is protecting the Koch billions, not anyone else." – Diane Ravitch's Blog*

I grew up in the 1950s, an era when many believed that our society would inevitably progress toward ever greater economic equality. Desperate poverty would recede, it was assumed, as new federal programs addressed the needs of those at the very bottom of the ladder and as economic growth created new jobs. The average CEO at the time earned only 20 times as much as the average worker, and during the Eisenhower administration the marginal tax rate for the highest earners was 91 percent. Today, the goal of equality appears to be receding. The top marginal tax rate is only 39 percent, far below what it was during the Eisenhower years, and most Republicans would like to lower it even more. Employers now make 271 times as much as the average worker, and half the children in American schools are officially classified by the federal government as low-income and eligible for free or reduced-price lunch. Union membership peaked in the mid-1950s and has declined ever since. The largest unions today are in the public sector and only about 7 percent of private sector workers belong to a union.

Despite these alarming developments, however, politicians who support the deregulation of business and champion pro-employer legislation – from state legislators to members of Congress – have a firm electoral foothold in most states. During the 2016 presidential campaign, candidate Trump promised to support basic government services like Medicare and pledged to bring back jobs that had been outsourced to other nations. However, once he was president, Trump endorsed health care bills that would have left millions of low- and lower-middle-income Americans without health insurance, and his insistence on reducing corporate tax rates suggests his determination to act in the interest of wealthy elites.

Two recent books – Nancy MacLean's *Democracy in Chains: The Deep History of the Radical Right's Stealth Plan for America* and Gordon Lafer's *The One Percent Solution: How Corporations Are Remaking America One State at a Time* – seek to explain several puzzling aspects of American politics today. Why do people of modest means who depend on government-funded health care and Social Security or other supplements to their income continue to vote for candidates who promise to privatize or get rid of those very programs? Why do people who are poor vote for politicians who promise to cut corporate taxes?

Both books follow in the path of Jane Mayer's *Dark Money: The Hidden History of the Billionaires Behind the Rise of the Radical Right* (2016), which documented an astonishing effort by the Koch brothers, the DeVos family, and other billionaires to purchase politicians in support of such goals as the elimination of welfare programs and the privatization of health care and education. Lafer's describes how in recent years those goals have been achieved in state after state. MacLean's book, which set off a heated dispute among historians and economists when it appeared in June, aims to describe their historical, theoretical, and academic underpinnings.

At the center of Democracy in Chains is the work of the Nobel Prize winning economist James M. Buchanan, who died in 2013. Buchanan is associated with the doctrine of economic libertarianism. He is widely credited as one of the founding fathers of the "public choice" model of economics, which argues that bureaucrats and public officials serve their own interests as much as or more than the public interest, and he was the leading figure in the Virginia School of economic thought. He trained many economists who came to share his libertarian views, and his acolytes have protested MacLean's view that he had "a formative role" in the evolution of an anti-democratic "strand of the radical right."

MacLean discovered Buchanan by chance. About a decade ago, she began researching a book about Virginia's decision to issue state vouchers that would allow white students to attend all-white schools, avoiding compliance with the *Brown v. Board of Education* decision of 1954. While studying the writings of the voucher advocate Milton Friedman, she came across Buchanan's name. She started reading his work and visited a disorganized archive of his writings and papers at the Fairfax, Virginia, campus of George Mason University, where she found materials scattered in boxes and file cabinets. In uncatalogued stacks of papers she came across personal correspondence between Buchanan and the billionaire Republican donor Charles Koch.

What she pieced together, she writes, was a plan "to train a new generation of thinkers to push back against *Brown v. Board of Education* and the changes in constitutional thought and federal policy that had enabled it." This was indeed a bold project. Most mainstream economists in the postwar era had long accepted Keynesian doctrines that affirmed the power of the federal government to regulate the economy and protect the rights of workers to organize in unions. Buchanan's rejection of governmental actions that he thought infringed on individual liberty and his defense of states' rights gave intellectual ammunition to those who opposed both Keynesian economics and federal interventions in the states to enforce desegregation.

In 1956 Buchanan founded a research-and-design center at the University of Virginia to combat what he called "the powerful grip that collectivist ideology already had on the minds of intellectuals" and the "increasing role of government in economic and social life." Three years later, as the state of Virginia sought a way to avoid racial integration in schools, Buchanan and a colleague proposed using tax-funded vouchers to avoid compliance with the Brown decision. This would destroy public education and preserve racial segregation, since white children could use publicly funded vouchers to attend all-white schools.

During his years at UVA, Buchanan collaborated with such "old-fashioned libertarians" as Frank Knight of the University of Chicago, F.A. Hayek, Ludwig von Mises, and other partisans of the Austrian School who railed against socialism and championed the virtues of individual self-reliance and economic liberty. In 1969, after a brief and unhappy stint at UCLA, he took his center – now called the Center for Study of Public Choice – with him to Virginia Tech. Thirteen years later he brought it to George Mason University (GMU), where it remains today.

GMU had been founded in 1957 in a shopping mall in suburban Washington as a two-year college. Buchanan was its prize catch. When he was hired in 1982, he came with a team of colleagues and graduate assistants and attracted what the school's senior vice-president later called "literally millions of dollars" in funding from corporate-friendly political interests, such as Charles Koch and the Scaife Family Charitable Trusts. The economics department and the law school of GMU were devoted to advancing his ideas.

By the mid-1980s, MacLean argues, the center had become a channel through which scholars were funneled into "the far-flung and purportedly separate, yet intricately connected, institutions funded by the Koch brothers and their now large network of fellow wealthy donors," notably the Cato Institute, whose founding seminar Buchanan attended, and the Heritage Foundation, which gave him a welcoming reception when he arrived at GMU. Stephen Moore, the research director for Ronald Reagan's Commission on Privatization who later served on *The Wall Street Journal's* editorial board, was one of GMU's early master's degree recipients. Three of Buchanan's first doctoral students at the school went on to work in the Reagan administration, which made the reduction of federal authority one of its primary goals.

In MacLean's account, Buchanan was responding to the threats that democratic institutions posed to the preservation of wealth in America. Early American democracy had limited this threat by confining the franchise to white male property owners. But as voting rights were extended, the nation's elites had to reckon with the growing power of formerly disenfranchised voters, who could be expected to support ever more expensive government programs to benefit themselves and ever more extensive ways to redistribute wealth. MacLean asserts that Buchanan supplied his benefactors with arguments to persuade the American public to go along with policies that protect wealth and eschew federal programs reliant on progressive taxation.

If everyone is motivated by self-interest, he argued, government can't be trusted to do what it promises. Indeed, it cannot be trusted at all. Bureaucrats can be expected to protect their turf, not the public interest. Every politician, Buchanan wrote, "can be viewed as proposing and attempting to enact a combination of expenditure programs and financing schemes that will secure him the support of a majority of the electorate." For Buchanan, this was reason enough to endorse economic liberty, freedom from taxes, and privatization of public services, such as schools, Social Security, and Medicare. In MacLean's view, those proposals promised a return to the kind of political economy that prevailed in America at the opening of the twentieth century, when the mass disenfranchisement of voters and the legal treatment of labor unions as illegitimate enabled large corporations and wealthy individuals to dominate Congress and most state governments alike, and to feel secure that the nation's courts would not interfere with their reign.

Charles Koch well understood the power of academic experts, and he directed millions of dollars toward developing what are now called "thought leaders" to defend his self-interested political and economic vision. Buchanan was one of those academics. Koch bypassed Milton Friedman and his "Chicago boys," MacLean writes, because "they sought 'to make government work more efficiently when the true libertarian should be tearing it out at the root.'" Instead, in the early 1970s, he funded the Libertarian Party and the Cato Institute, designed to advocate for what MacLean summarizes as:

> ... the end of public education, Social Security, Medicare, the U.S. Postal Service, minimum wage laws, prohibitions against child labor, foreign aid, the Environmental Protection Agency, prosecution for drug use or voluntary prostitution – and, in time, the end of taxes and government regulations of any kind.

Koch also funded the libertarian Reason Foundation, which advocated for privatizing all government functions. Another Koch-backed organization, the Liberty Fund, hired Buchanan to run summer conferences for young social scientists.

Buchanan's challenge was to develop a strategy that would enlist the public's support for the ideas he shared with Charles Koch. This challenge was especially daunting in the case of Social Security. Overwhelming majorities of Americans supported Social Security because it ensured that they would not be impoverished in their old age. In an influential 1983 paper, Buchanan marveled that there was "no widespread support for basic structural reform" of Social Security "among any membership group" in the American political constituency – "among the old or the young, the black, the brown, or the white, the female or the male, the rich or the poor, the Frost Belt or the Sun Belt." Pinochet's Chile – which Buchanan visited for a week in May 1980 to give what MacLean calls "in-person guidance" to the regime's minister of finance, Sergio de Castro – had privatized its social security system, and libertarians hoped to do the same in the United States. We now know that the privatization of social security in Chile was a disaster for many, but the libertarians were unshakable in their enthusiasm for market solutions and ignored the risks.

Buchanan laid out the strategy needed to divide the political coalition that supported Social Security. The first step was to insist that Social Security was not viable, that it was a "Ponzi scheme." If "people can be led to think that they personally have no legitimate claim against the system on retirement," he wrote in a paper for the Cato Institute, it will "make abandonment of the system look more attractive." Then those currently receiving benefits must be reassured that nothing will change for them. "Their benefits," as MacLean puts it, "would not be cut." Taxpayers, in turn, would have to be promised, as Buchanan says, "that the burden of bailing out would not be allowed to fall disproportionately on the particular generation that would pay taxes immediately after the institutional reform takes place." Cultivating these expectations would not only make taxpayers more ready to abandon the system, it would also build resentment among those who expect never to get payments comparable to those receiving the initial bailout.

After they announce the insolvency of Social Security, Buchanan argued, the system's critics should "propose increases in the retirement age and increases in payroll taxes," which would, MacLean writes, "irritate recipients at all income levels, but particularly those who are just on the wrong side of the cutoff and now would have to pay more and work longer." Calls for protecting Social Security with progressive taxation formulas would emphasize the redistributive character of the program and isolate progressives. "To the extent that participants come to perceive the system as a complex transfer scheme between current income classes instead of strictly between generations," Buchanan predicted, "the 'insurance contract' image will become tarnished" and its public support will be compromised.

Critics of MacLean claim she overstates her case because Buchanan was merely presenting both sides of the issue. But it is indisputable that Cato and other Koch-funded policy centers favor privatization of government programs like Social Security and public education. The genius of their strategy was in describing their efforts to change government programs as "reforms," when in fact they were intended from the outset to result in their destruction. This rebranding depended on think tanks amply funded by Charles Koch, his like-minded brother David, and other ideologically friendly sponsors. Charles Koch funded the James Buchanan Center at GMU with a gift of $10 million. The libertarian philosophy funded by Koch and developed by Buchanan has close affinities with the Tea Party and Freedom Caucus of the Republican Party, which oppose federal spending on almost anything other than the military and has placed its members at the highest levels of the Trump administration, including Vice President Mike Pence and Mick Mulvaney, the director of the Office of Management and Budget.

MacLean's argument that Buchanan knowingly engineered a strategy for the wealthy to preserve their hold on American democracy has prompted intense resistance. She has been repeatedly attacked on libertarian blogs, historical websites, and even in *The Washington Post*. The attacks are sometimes personal. Steve Horwitz, a libertarian economist who called MacLean's book "a travesty of historical scholarship," earned his degrees at GMU, where Buchanan was one of his professors. Most of her prominent critics – Michael Munger, David Bernstein, Steven Hayward, David Boaz – are libertarians, some receive funding from the Koch brothers. They accuse her of unjustly berating a legitimate area of economic inquiry and overstating the evidence against Buchanan in support of her position. Other critics have come from the political center. The political scientists Henry Farrell and Steven Teles, for instance, have argued that MacLean overstates the extent to which Buchanan and his supporters were "implementing a single master plan with fiendish efficiency." MacLean has replied to her critics that her book demonstrates that Buchanan was part of a much larger movement.

MacLean's reputation will no doubt survive. She has written a carefully documented book about issues that matter to the future of our democracy and established the close and sympathetic connections between Buchanan and his far-right financial patrons. However fierce they might be, her critics have been unable to refute the central message of her important book –

that the ongoing abandonment of progressive taxation and the social benefits it gives most people is undergirded by a libertarian economic movement funded by wealthy corporate benefactors. The dismantling of basic government functions by the Trump administration, such as Betsy DeVos's efforts to privatize public education, shows the continuing influence of Buchanan's libertarian ideas.

Gordon Lafer's *The One Percent Solution* is a worthy companion to *Democracy in Chains*. Lafer does not write about Buchanan and the Virginia School, but he meticulously demonstrates how the Koch brothers and the Supreme Court's *Citizens United* decision of 2010 have influenced elections and public policy in the states. He opens his book with a revealing anecdote about Bill Haslam, the Republican governor of Tennessee. In 2015 Haslam wanted to expand his state's Medicaid program to include some 200,000 low income residents who had no health insurance under the Affordable Care Act. He had just been re-elected with 70 percent of the vote. Republicans, who controlled both branches of the state legislature, approved of Haslam's plan. The public liked the idea. But then the Koch brothers' advocacy group Americans for Prosperity sent field organizers into the state to fight the expansion, ran television ads against it, and denounced it as "a vote for Obamacare." The Medicaid expansion proposal was defeated by the legislature.

Lafer reviews bills passed in the fifty state legislatures since the *Citizens United* decision removed limits on corporate spending in political campaigns. He identifies corporate influences on state-level decision making and finds that those same policies provided a template for corporate lobbying in Congress. His most striking discovery is the "sheer similarity of the legislation – nearly identical bills introduced in cookie-cutter fashion in states across the country." What Lafer documents is a coherent strategic agenda on the part of such business lobbies as the National Association of Manufacturers and the National Federation of Independent Business to reshape the nation's economy, society, and politics – state by state.

The many goals of this agenda can be summed up in a few words – lower taxes, privatization of public services, and deregulation of business. The lobbies Lafer studies oppose public employee unions, which keep public sector wages high and provide a source of funding for the Democratic Party. The tobacco industry opposes anti-smoking legislation. The fossil fuel industry wants to eliminate state laws that restrict fracking, coal mining, and carbon dioxide emissions. The soft-drink industry opposes taxes on sugary beverages. The private prison industry advocates policies that increase the population of for-profit prisons, such as the detention of undocumented immigrants and the restriction of parole eligibility. Industry lobbyists oppose paid sick leave, workplace safety regulations, and minimum wage laws. They support "right to work" laws that undermine unions. They oppose teachers' unions and support the privatization of education through charter schools and vouchers.

These are not sporadic efforts to affect state policy. There is an organization that coordinates the efforts of industry lobbyists and turns their interests into legislation. It is a secretive group formed in 1973 called the American Legislative Exchange Council (ALEC). It is sponsored by scores of major corporations, which each pay a fee of $25,000 (or more) to be members. Lafer lists the group's current and past corporate members, including Alcoa, Amazon, Amoco, Amway, AT&T, Boeing, BP, Chevron, Coca-Cola, Corrections Corporation of America, CVS, Dell, Dupont, Exxon Mobil, Facebook, General Electric, General Motors, Google, Home Depot, IBM, Koch Industries, McDonald's, Merck, Microsoft, Sony, the U.S. Chamber of Commerce, Verizon, Visa, and Walmart. In addition to these corporations, two thousand state legislators are members of ALEC – collectively one quarter of all state legislators in the nation. They include state senate presidents and house speakers.

ALEC writes policy reports and drafts legislation designed to carry out its members' goals.* It claims, Lafer writes, "to introduce eight hundred to one thousand bills each year in the fifty state legislatures, with 20 percent becoming law." The "exchange" that ALEC promotes is between corporate donors and state legislators. The corporations pay ALEC's expenses and contribute to legislators' campaigns. In return, legislators carry the corporate agenda into their statehouses. In the first decade of this century, ALEC's leading corporate backers contributed more than $370 million to state elections, and over one hundred laws each year based on ALEC's model bills were enacted.

The keynote speaker at ALEC's lavish annual conference in Denver earlier this year was Betsy DeVos, who used the occasion to belittle public schools and unions and to tout the virtues of school choice. She quoted Margaret Thatcher that "there is no such thing" as "society," only individual men and women and families. This position supports a vision of America in which the country's citizens express themselves individually as consumers rather than collectively as, for example, voting majorities or empowered unions. When they fall victim to fires, hurricanes, or earthquakes – or, for that matter, when the economy collapses – these individual men and women and families can expect to be on their own.

Lafer contends that ALEC and its compatriots are engineering what he calls "a revolution of falling expectations." They have cynically played on the resentments of many citizens, purposefully deepening antagonism toward government programs that benefit unspecified "others." Many people are losing their economic security while others are getting government handouts. Why should others get pensions? Why should others get health insurance? Why should others have job protections? Why should unions protect their members? "We are the only generation in American history to be left worse off than the last one," reads a post from the Kochs' advocacy group Generation Opportunity urging young people in Michigan to vote down a ballot proposal to raise the state's sales tax. "We are paying more for college tuition, for a Social Security system and a Medicare system we won't get to use, $18 trillion in national debt and now an Obamacare system – all that steals from our generation's paychecks."

It is ironic that this fraudulently populist message, encouraging resentment of government programs, was funded by billionaires who were, Lafer writes, "willing to spend previously unthinkable sums on politics." The *Citizens United* decision allowed a tiny percentage of the population, the richest, to direct vast amounts of money into political campaigns to promote privatization, discredit unions, and divert attention from the dramatic growth of income inequality. "For the first time ever," Lafer writes, "in 2012 more than half of all income in America went to the richest 10 percent of the population."

Lafer writes that this concentration of wealth has produced a new generation of mega-donors: "More than 60 percent of all personal campaign contributions in 2012 came from less than 0.5 percent of the population." In 2010, Republicans swept state legislatures and governorships, they used their resulting advantage to gerrymander seats and attack the voting rights of minorities. Even state and local school board elections became the target of big donors, like the anti-union Walton family, the richest family in America, who poured millions into state and local contests to promote charter schools, more than 90 percent of which are non-union.

ALEC and likeminded organizations are particularly interested in discrediting labor unions. Lafer gives much attention to understanding why this is. Corporations want to eliminate unions to cut costs. Republicans resist them because they provide money and volunteers for Democrats. Getting rid of them also reduces employee health care costs and pensions. But, Lafer argues, the greatest threat posed by unions is that their very existence raises the expectations of those who are not in unions. When they function well, unions have the power to raise wages, reduce working hours, and demand better working conditions. Stifling this power and making every worker an at-will employee lowers the expectations of the non-unionized workforce.

Quite simply Lafer argues, labor unions are the only political bodies that can impede the efforts of ALEC's members to:

- Roll back minimum-wage, prevailing-wage, and

living-wage laws.
- Eliminate entitlements to overtime or sick leave.
- Scale back regulation of occupational safety.
- Make it harder for employees to sue over race or sex discrimination or even to recover back wages they are legally owed.
- Replace adult employees with teenagers and guest workers.

In education, technology corporations are using their influence to replace teachers with computers as a cost-saving device, a move opposed by parents and teachers' unions. Corporations, libertarians, and right-wing politicians pursue these goals even in states where unions are weak or nonexistent. The rise of the "gig economy," in which every employee is a self-employed contractor with no collective bargaining rights, advances this trend, empowering big employers who put a monopolistic downward pressure on labor costs.

Reading these two books together is not a happy experience. They give reason to fear for the future. But they also remind us why it is important to join with others and take action. An informed public is a powerful public. The best counterweight to the influence of big money on politics is the ballot. When you see the strategy that libertarians, billionaire donors, and corporations have devised, you understand why low voter turnout is their ally and why high voter turnout is the only way to save our democracy.

* *Since 2011 the Center for Media and Democracy has maintained a website, ALECexposed.org, that tracks the organization's activities. It features lists of corporations involved with ALEC, politicians associated with it, and the full texts of hundreds of "model" bills and resolutions ALEC has sponsored.*

# YES, IT IS TRUE! I DON'T LIKE SCHOOL CHOICE! I ADMIRE TEACHERS' UNIONS!

HUFFPOST, OCTOBER 11, 2017

*"The Kochs and their political action group Americans for Prosperity are relentless in trying to replace public schools with charters and vouchers and eliminate unions. The goal of the Koch brothers is to install their free-market ideology in high schools across the country." – Diane Ravitch's Blog*

One of the most annoying aspects of the privatization movement is that they pretend to be progressives. They are not. They are reactionaries, and they have the history to prove it.

They stole the word "Reform," so they could pretend that they want to make schools better, instead of admitting they want to replace public schools with religious schools, private schools, for-profit schools, online schools, anything but public schools. Hint: Destruction is not reform.

Take Jeanne Allen, the CEO of the misnamed Center for Education Reform. Jeanne worked for the far-right Heritage Foundation before she launched CER many years ago. She wants School Choice. She is indistinguishable from Betsy DeVos. She loves charter schools, vouchers, anything but public schools. She pretends that School Choice is a progressive cause. No, it is not.

She recently wrote an article[164] criticizing some of us who support public schools – like nearly 90 percent of all families. She criticized Matt Damon, who narrated[165] a new pro-public school film called "Backpack Full of Cash," because the film criticizes privatization. The film was made by professional filmmakers.

I urge everyone to arrange a screening in your community – public television showed a four-part series called "School" by the same team in 2000, but won't touch "Backpack" because it's too controversial.

Allen criticizes me too, because I flipped from being a supporter of charters to being an outspoken critic. She blames my conversion on my friendship with a union leader.

She had me stumped there.

Did she mean Al Shanker? He was president of the American Federation of Teachers when I first met him in 1974. He read my first book, a history of the New York City public schools, and he called out of the blue to say he loved it.

He wrote a weekly column in *The New York Times*, and he asked, "Do you want me to praise it or blast it?" We became good friends, had dinner, exchanged ideas. In the late 1980s, I visited newly freed Soviet satellite nations as part of an AFT group promoting democracy and civic education. Arch-conservative Checker Finn was part of the same group sponsored by the AFT. We visited Hungary, Czechoslovakia, Poland and Romania to talk to newly unionized teachers. Al Shanker was a great intellectual and one of my heroes. I was proud to call him my friend.

Did Allen mean Sandy Feldman? I knew her for many years too. I had many great dinners with her and her husband Arthur Barnes.

Maybe she meant Randi Weingarten? I have known Randi since 1998. I consider her a close friend, although I admit we sometimes have fights over issues. We differ over the Common Core – she likes it, I don't. We differ over charters. She likes some (the ones that join the union), I see them as the gateway to privatization. Despite our differences, we agree on the importance of public education, a strong teaching profession, well-funded schools, and the right of workers to join unions to bargain collectively.

I am also friendly with Lily Eskelsen Garcia, presidency of the NEA. We shared an evening of pizza and wine and laughs in my apartment not so long ago.

I have never belonged to a union, but I believe in them as democratic institutions. Jeanne Allen and her libertarian friends hate teachers' unions, and they think they can smear people by accusing them of being friends of unions. The reactionary right has done a good job of destroying unions, and they hurt our democracy by their anti-unionism.

Here is why.

Unions give working people a collective voice. A single worker has no voice. They can be fired arbitrarily. Unions protect a teacher's right to due process if their boss wants to fire them. They are entitled to a hearing and to know the charges against them. Unions fight to improve wages and working conditions. Unions protect public schools against budget cuts that harm education.

Above all, unions create a path into the middle class. As unions shrink, so does the middle class. As unions shrink, income inequality grows. Unions are especially important for people of color, who need a strong organization to fight for their job rights.

Jeanne Allen, Betsy DeVos, Donald Trump, the Koch brothers, and their billionaire buddies – some of whom are on the board of Allen's Center for Education Reform – would like to roll back the New Deal. Not I. I want us to have a vibrant society, strong unions, well-funded public schools, a respected teaching profession, and a genuine narrowing of the income inequality that blights our society.

We need to strengthen the New Deal, not get rid of it. Public schools are part of the promise of America. We cannot let libertarians destroy our public institutions by privatizing them. The good news is that the public supports public schools, not privatization. There have been 19 state referenda on vouchers, and vouchers lost overwhelmingly every time. Last fall, Massachusetts held a referendum on whether to expand the number of charters, and the proposal was voted down in almost every school district in the state – only the rich districts, which did not want charters for themselves, voted in favor.

I confess, I favor public schools. I oppose charters and vouchers. I support teachers unions. I am proud of my friendship with union leaders.

# DETROIT NEEDS A NEW MODEL OF EDUCATION

## DIANE RAVITCH BLOG POST,DECEMBER 13, 2017

*"The odd thing about our culture is that it is so attached to the present moment that anything that happened or was written about a month ago tends to disappear in the ether." – Diane Ravitch's Blog*

Education in Detroit and in Michigan is in crisis. Detroit is consistently ranked as the lowest performing urban district in the nation. Michigan's student performance has sunk nearly to the bottom of national tests in the past decade.

Education is a crucial investment in children and in the future of our society, but something is terribly wrong in this city and state.

Detroit has been a petri dish for free-market reformers for the past generation. Since 1993, the state has operated on the theory that competition among public schools and privately managed charter schools will lead to rising achievement in both sectors. After nearly 25 years of trying school choice, it is time to admit that the theory was wrong.

Gov. Rick Snyder and the Legislature tried another experiment on Detroit – The Education Achievement Authority. The lowest scoring schools were gathered into a single district where they were immersed in technology and were subjects of another trial of privatization. That failed too.

What works?

First, children should start school healthy and ready

to learn. Just days ago, the Kresge and Kellogg foundations announced a 10-year, $50 million program to improve and coordinate programs for early childhood education and health for the children of Detroit. That's a wonderful step forward.

Second, honesty requires a frank acknowledgment that Michigan's unique experiment in free-market ideology has failed. Nearly 80 percent of the charter schools in the state operate for-profit, and these for-profit schools perform worse than nonprofit schools, according to a report last June by the Center for Research on Educational Outcomes at Stanford. Why continue to fund failure? Why waste taxpayers' dollars?

Third, the competition between charter schools and public schools has drained the public schools of the resources they need to thrive and improve. Yet most charters are no better than the public schools.

Since 1993, the state of Michigan has been engaged in a massive experiment that has thoroughly tested whether school choice is the answer to poor academic outcomes. Two generations of children have passed through the schools of Michigan since the school choice experiment began.

The experiment has failed.

In 2003, Michigan was ranked in the middle of the pack on national tests. By 2015, Michigan had fallen to the bottom. A 2016 report by The Education Trust-Midwest[166] concluded that the declines had been across the board, among all racial groups and income groups:

> It's a devastating fall. Indeed, new national assessment data suggest Michigan is witnessing systemic decline across the K-12 spectrum. White, black, brown, higher-income, low-income – it doesn't matter who they are or where they live, Michigan students' achievement levels in early reading and middle school math are not keeping up with the rest of the U.S., much less our international competitors.

The only way to improve education in Detroit and Michigan

is to admit error and change course.

Michiganders should acknowledge that competition has not produced better schools. Detroit needs a strong and unified public school system that has the support of the business and civic community. There should be a good public school in every neighborhood.

Every school should be staffed with credentialed and well-qualified teachers. Class sizes should be no larger than 20 in elementary schools, no larger than 24 in middle and high schools. Every school should offer a full curriculum, including the arts, civics, history, and foreign languages. Every school should have a library and media center staffed by a qualified librarian. Every school should have fully equipped laboratories for science. Every school should have a nurse and a social worker. Every school should be in tip-top physical condition.

Students should have a program that includes physical education and sports teams, dance, chorus, robotics, dramatics, videography, and other opportunities for intellectual and social development.

That is what the best suburban communities want for their children. That's what will work for the children of Detroit and the rest of Michigan.

# SETTLING FOR SCORES WHY ARE SCHOOLS STILL JUDGED BY THE RESULTS OF STANDARDIZED TESTS?

## THE NEW REPUBLIC, DECEMBER 27, 2017

*"My view: The federal government should not dictate any testing. The decision to test or not should be left to every state. Contrary to the belief promoted by ex-Secretary Duncan, NAEP testing gives us all the information we need based on sampling about performance in math and reading, by race, language, gender, poverty status, disability status, and also achievement gaps. Annual tests of every child are a waste of instructional time and money. They provide no useful information." – Diane Ravitch's Blog*

In 1979, the psychologist Donald Campbell proposed an axiom. He wrote:[167]

> The more any quantitative social indicator is used for social decision-making, the more subject it will be to corruption pressures and the more apt it will be to distort and corrupt the social processes it is intended to monitor.... Achievement tests may well be valuable indicators of general school achievement under conditions of normal teaching aimed at general competence. But when test scores become the goal

> of the teaching process, they both lose their value as indicators of educational status and distort the educational process in undesirable ways.

Put simply, when the measure becomes the goal, and when people are punished or rewarded for meeting or not meeting the goal, the measure is corrupted. As Richard Rothstein has shown in his superb monograph, *Holding Accountability to Account*,[168] tying high stakes to measurable goals affects behavior in negative ways in every field, not just education. Judge heart surgeons by the mortality rate of their patients, and they will turn away risky patients. The classic (and probably apocryphal) illustrations of Campbell's law come from the Soviet Union. When workers were told that they must produce as many nails as possible, they produced vast quantities of tiny and useless nails. When told they would be evaluated by the weight of the nails, they produced enormous and useless nails. The lesson of Campbell's law – do not attach high stakes to evaluations, or both the measure and the outcome will become fraudulent.

For the last 16 years, American education has been trapped, stifled, strangled by standardized testing. Or, to be more precise, by federal and state legislators' obsession with standardized testing. The pressure to raise test scores has produced predictable corruption – test scores were inflated by test preparation focused on what was likely to be on the test. Some administrators gamed the system by excluding low-scoring students from the tested population, some teachers and administrators cheated, some schools dropped other subjects so that more time could be devoted to the tested subjects.

In his new book, Daniel Koretz, an eminent testing expert at Harvard University, has skillfully dissected the multiple negative consequences of the education reforms of the 2000s, most of them unintended. His title, *The Testing Charade: Pretending to Make Schools Better*, sums up his conclusion that the reform movement failed badly because of its devotion to high-stakes testing as the infallible measure of educational quality. Koretz says the results of the testing inflated scores and were not valid.

But reformers did not withdraw their support for testing even when the harm it inflicted on children and public schools became evident. Some were ignorant of the evidence of failure, others believed tests provided valuable information, despite the corruption of the data by high stakes. Since federal law required states to label schools with low scores as failing, and since those schools were often turned into charter schools, a whole industry benefited from this system – even though the same measures labeled many charters as failing, too. The Every Student Succeeds Act (ESSA), passed in 2015, still requires that every child be tested every year – a practice unknown in any high-performing nation.

Legislators' and policymakers' obsession with testing has been locked into place since January 8, 2002, when President George W. Bush signed into law his signature domestic legislation, the No Child Left Behind Act.[169] Before NCLB, every state had its own tests and its own accountability measures, but none was as harsh, punitive, and unrealistic as NCLB. None required every school to reach 100 percent proficiency or face mass firings or closure or both.

When Bush campaigned for the presidency, he portrayed himself as a "compassionate conservative" who knew how to overcome "the soft bigotry of low expectations." He said he knew how to raise test scores, raise graduation rates, and close the achievement gaps between children of different races and classes. Test every child every year from grades three to eight, publish the scores for every subgroup by race, gender, disability status, and so on, then reward the schools that raised scores, embarrass those that didn't, and voilà! Problem solved. Test scores and graduation rates go up, achievement gaps close. It was all common sense – get the incentives and sanctions right, and results were sure to follow.

Bush's surrogates claimed there had been a "Texas miracle," that annual testing had dramatically raised scores and graduation rates in the state while he was governor.[170] In fact, there was no miracle. Texas was not a model for the nation in 2000, nor is it now. But Congress bought it, and NCLB required every public school in the nation to test every child, every year, in reading and mathematics from grades three to eight. Schools were required to reach 100 percent proficiency on standardized tests by the year 2014,[171] only twelve years later, or face dire sanctions, including closure or privatization. Not only did the Bush administration vastly expand the federal government's role in education, venturing where no other administration of either party had dared to go, it set a goal that was literally impossible for schools, districts, and states to meet. Democrats as well as Republicans supported this massive federal intrusion into pedagogical and local matters. Senator Ted Kennedy and Democratic Congressman George Miller of California, both noted liberals, proudly supported Bush's folly.

When Obama took office in 2009, the failure of NCLB was already apparent,[172] but the president and his secretary of education, Arne Duncan, were true believers in George W. Bush's vision, and they doubled down on standardized test scores as the definition of success. Under their Race to the Top program, thousands of educators were fired, and countless public schools were closed or handed over to private charter operators. The devout belief in standardized tests as the measure of learning and the equally devout belief in turning public schools over to charter entrepreneurs came to be known as the "reform movement." It was, in reality, a giant federal wrecking ball that did immeasurable damage to students, teachers, and public education.

Koretz excoriates the reform movement for its indifference to the harm it caused. He criticizes its iconic leaders – Joel Klein, Michelle Rhee, and Arne Duncan – for their fanatical devotion to standardized tests without regard to how the scores were obtained. Duncan demanded that all teachers must raise the test scores of their students, that they must be rated by their ability to raise scores, and that those who couldn't consistently raise scores year on year should be fired. No excuses. Teachers of the gifted, whose students were already at the top, would be rated ineffective if they didn't raise those scores even higher – say from 3.97 out of 4 to 3.98. Teachers of art and physical education and other subjects that were not tested were assigned a rating based on the scores of students they didn't teach, in subjects they didn't teach. Duncan applauded when Los Angeles and New York City publicly released the rankings of teachers, even though the rankings were rife with errors. Rigoberto Ruelas, a teacher in a tough Los Angeles neighborhood, committed suicide after his average ranking was made public. No one apologized.

The reformers' obsession with test scores, Koretz writes, prepares students to take tests, but it does not prepare them to apply what they have learned to real life situations. Typically, students are prepped to take a specific test. Switch to another test in the same subject for which the students have not prepped, and their scores are likely to plummet. Placing so much importance on test scores, Koretz writes, was certain to produce score inflation, not better education. Teachers were told to give "interim assessments" frequently during the year to prepare for the real test, but doing so took time away from non-tested subjects like history, the arts, civics, even physical education and recess. Reformers point to higher scores as "proof" that their reforms worked. This is circular reasoning.

Will the Common Core standards fix this mess? Koretz says no. The standards mistakenly assume that one curriculum is right for everyone. The whole reform package was mandated without regard for evidence. Reformers suffer, Koretz writes, from an "arrogant assumption that we know so much that we don't have to bother evaluating our ideas before imposing them on teachers and students." This assumption is especially startling when you realize how few of the reformers ever taught or taught for more than two years as members of Teach for America.

Koretz is not anti-testing. He is not even anti–standardized testing. He opposes the misuse of tests and would prefer to see them used as diagnostic tools, disconnected from rewards and punishments. Koretz proposes that standardized tests should be coupled with teacher tests and other measures of student performance, and that teachers get extra help to improve classroom instruction. He recognizes that nearly two decades of test-driven accountability, attached to harsh sanctions, has deeply embedded the power of standardized testing in the psyche of teachers and principals, and that it will take years to make policymakers and educators aware of the pernicious effects of high-stakes testing.

But there are, Koretz finds, two reasons to feel hopeful about the future. One is that 2015's ESSA is somewhat less punitive than NCLB. The other is the opt-out movement. In New York, for example, one-fifth of parents refused to allow their children to take the federally mandated state tests. The students sit for the tests in the spring, sometimes for as long as 18 hours – longer than the bar exams for lawyers – over two weeks, which is unreasonable, especially for children so young. The test results are not reported until summer or fall, when the students have different teachers. Neither the students nor the teachers are allowed to discuss the test questions to find out what they got wrong and how they can do better. The students are given a numerical ranking: They learn how they compare to others of their age. But because of test secrecy,[173] the tests have no diagnostic value. None.

Worse, they teach young children to look for the right answer instead of looking for the right question. Some test questions may have two right answers or no right answer. The thoughtful child may choose an answer that is plausible but judged "wrong." As a teaching tool, the tests are deeply flawed because they quash imagination, creativity, and divergent thinking. These are mental habits we should encourage, not punish.

Since test scores are highly correlated with parental income and education, children from affluent homes learn they did well. Children from poor homes learn they did poorly. The British author Michael Young wrote in the introduction to the revised edition of his classic book *The Rise of the Meritocracy* about the pernicious social effects of standardized tests. The children from elite homes are convinced by their test scores that they deserve their high status because their scores demonstrate their superiority. And children of the poor learn early on that they rank poorly because their test scores confirm their lowly status.

Despite the clear failure of test-based accountability, which

Koretz amply documents, policymakers cling stubbornly to this corrosive doctrine. When Betsy DeVos says she will leave decisions about testing to the states, what she means is that the status quo of federally mandated annual testing in grades three to eight will remain undisturbed. Supporters of privatization appreciate the testing regime because every year it produces failing schools, the bottom 5 percent that can be closed and handed over to entrepreneurs and charter chains. Testing taps into Americans' love of competition, incentives, and scores. It makes perfect sense to rank baseball players and teams by their wins and losses, but it doesn't transfer to children or schools. Children may be talented in the arts or sports or other areas, and it won't show on the tests. Education is a developmental process, a deliberate cultivation of knowledge and skills, a recognition of each child's unique talents, not a race.

# TODAY IS THE ANNIVERSARY OF THE WORST FEDERAL EDUCATION LAW EVER PASSED

HUFFPOST, JANUARY 8, 2018

*"Race to the Top offered $4.35 billion to 11 states and DC, but will cost the nation tens of billions that might have been spent to build health clinics or support pre-K or the arts." – Diane Ravitch's Blog*

On January 8, 2002, President George W. Bush signed No Child Left Behind into law.

NCLB, as it was known, is the worst federal education legislation ever passed by Congress. It was punitive, harsh, stupid, ignorant about pedagogy and motivation, and ultimately a dismal failure. Those who still admire NCLB either helped write it, or were paid to like it, or were profiting from it.

It was Bush's signature issue. He said it would end "the soft bigotry of low expectations." It didn't.

When he campaigned for the presidency, he and his surrogates claimed there had been a "Texas miracle." There wasn't.

All that was needed, they said, was to test every child in grades 3-8 every year in reading and math. Make the results for schools public. Reward schools that raised scores. Punish schools for lower scores. Then watch as test scores soar, graduation rates rise, and achievement gaps closed. It didn't happen in Texas nor in the nation.

The theory was simple, simplistic, and stupid. Test, then punish or reward.

Congress bought the claim of the Texas miracle and passed NCLB, co-sponsored by leading Republicans and Democrats, including Ted Kennedy of Massachusetts and Congressman George Miller of California.

Congress mandated that every student in every school must be proficient on standardized tests of reading or math or the school was a failure, facing closure or privatization by 2014. NCLB was a ticking time bomb, set to destroy American public education by setting an impossible goal, one that almost every school in every state would ultimately fail.

It was the largest expansion of the federal role in history. It was the largest intrusion of the federal government into state and local education decision-making ever.

Bush's original proposal was a 28-page document. I was invited to the White House ceremony where it was unveiled. At the time, I was a member in good standing of the conservative policy elite. By the time the bill passed, the new law exceeded 1,000 pages. A Republican Congressman from Colorado told me that he thought he was the only member who read the whole bill. He voted against it.

NCLB took the place of the Elementary and Secondary Education Act of 1965, a component of President Lyndon B. Johnson's "Great Society" Program. The primary purpose of ESEA was to send federal funds to the poorest districts. During the Clinton administration, ESEA was renamed the Goals 2000 Act, and incorporated the lofty education goals endorsed by the first Bush administration.

To learn more about this history and why NCLB failed, read my book *The Death and Life of the Great American School System: How Testing and Choice Are Undermining Education.* To learn more about the negative effects of NCLB, read Daniel Koretz's book, *The Testing Charade: Pretending to Make Schools*

*Better*. To learn more about the unintended negative effects of accountability, google Richard Rothstein's monograph *Holding Accountability to Account*.[174]

This is what we got from NCLB – score inflation, cheating, narrowing the curriculum, obsession with test scores, more time devoted to testing, less time for the arts, physical education, history, civics, play, and anything else that was not tested. Among other consequences – demoralization of teachers, a national teacher shortage, more money for testing companies, and less money for teachers and class size reduction.

We also got a load of "reforms" that had no evidence to support them, such as closing schools, firing teachers and principals because of low scores, handing schools with low scores over to charter operators or the state.

NCLB, in turn, led to its ugly spawn, Race to the Top, which was even meaner and more punitive than NCLB. Race to the Top turned up the heat on test scores, making them the measure of teacher quality despite decades of social science that refuted that policy. More teachers and principals were fired, more public schools were closed, and enrollments in professional education programs plummeted across the country.

NCLB was the Death Star of American education. Race to the Top was the Executioner, scouring the land with a giant scythe in search of teachers, principals, and schools to kill if student scores didn't go up.

When the law was passed, I went to an event at the Willard Hotel in D.C. where key senators discussed it. One of them was Senator Lamar Alexander, former governor of Tennessee and former U.S. Secretary of Education, for whom I worked as Assistant Secretary of Education in charge of the Office of Education Research and Improvement. At the end of the panel, when it was time for questions, I asked Senator Alexander whether Congress really believed that every student in the nation would be proficient by 2014. He said that Congress knew they would not be, but "it's good to have goals."

# WHAT THE TEACHERS ARE ASKING FOR

## HUFFPOST,APRIL 26, 2018

*"The economy is changing in ways that none of us fully understands but in ways that increase income inequality, enriching the top 1-10% and almost no one else. We need fresh thinking about who we are and what we are becoming." – Diane Ravitch's Blog*

The teacher walkouts began in West Virginia, where public school employees were woefully underpaid and faced spiraling health care costs. They stayed out for nine days and won a 5 percent salary increase.[175] Oklahoma teachers soon followed suit, seeking a raise and increased education funding for their schools and students. They too won concessions.[176] Then came Kentucky teachers,[177] angry because the state planned to restructure their pensions for the worse. Starting Thursday, public school teachers in Arizona will walk out.[178] On Friday several districts in Colorado will be closed.[179]

What is happening? Almost all these states are red states, controlled by Republicans. Almost all are right-to-work states, with weak unions. Yet in these states, teachers have said enough is enough. Typically, it has not been their unions that spurred the walkouts. Time and again, the uprisings were from the grass roots, beginning with a page on social media calling other teachers to get together and protest working conditions.

As educators often say, teachers' working conditions are students' learning conditions. It is not merely low pay that is sending the teachers into the streets. It is also large class sizes, obsolete textbooks, crumbling buildings and the fact that many teachers (already underpaid) are shelling out $1,000 or more each year to pay for classroom supplies that their schools no longer provide.[180]

In short, teachers are calling on their legislatures to fund their schools and their students adequately.

For years, the red states have been working from a common playbook, low taxes for corporations and budget cuts for schools, universities and other public services.

The result? Many teachers have to work two or three jobs (sometimes even more) to feed their families, pay their mortgages and make their car payments. Some move in with their parents. Some leave the state and look for work where they can make a living wage. Teacher shortages are growing,[181] especially in hard-to-staff positions teaching mathematics and science and educating students with disabilities.

What started the rebellion? It might have been sheer exasperation from their efforts to obtain fair wages for the important work they do for other people's children.

Perhaps it was encouraged by the example of the fearless students at Marjory Stoneman Douglas High School in Parkland, Florida, who launched a national movement for gun control after a massacre at their school on Valentine's Day. The West Virginia walkout began on February 22nd.

Most certainly the teachers agreed that they could not continue to live on promises, praise and low wages.

To understand the teacher uprisings, look at the data compiled by researchers at the Education Law Center and professor Bruce Baker of Rutgers University in the report "Is School Funding Fair?"[182] The answer is no. Public school funding is not fair. Nor is it adequate in most states.

New York spent the most per pupil in 2015. Idaho spent the least, only about one-third of what was spent in New York. Other states at the bottom of the spending ranks, in ascending order, are Arizona, North Carolina, Utah, Oklahoma, Mississippi,

Tennessee, Nevada and Florida. With the exception of Nevada, their legislatures are solidly red. Although Utah was one of the lowest-spending states, it was tops in the nation for spreading its meager funding fairly among poor and wealthy schools. Watch these states for future teacher walkouts.

The ability to attract and retain good teachers is crucial to the success of state school systems. When it comes to salaries, according to the report, teachers on average earn about 82 percent of their similarly educated counterparts who enter other fields. The best states in terms of wage competitiveness in 2015 were Wyoming, Alaska and Iowa. The least competitive were Colorado, New Hampshire, Virginia, Utah, Washington, Georgia, Arizona, Missouri and Texas. In those states, teachers earned 69 to 75 percent of what their comparably qualified counterparts in other fields made.

The somber conclusion of this report is that most states have underinvested in education. Most do not provide enough funding for disadvantaged children to achieve even average outcomes.

Americans want good public schools, good roads, well-prepared emergency response departments and other public services.

But we are not willing to pay for it.

Another important study, published in November, 2017 by the Center for Budget and Policy Priorities,[183] found that many states were spending less on K-12 education than they were a decade ago, when the depression of 2008 struck. After that bruising economic crisis, public spending on schools never recovered.

The CBPP wrote:

> Public investment in K-12 schools – crucial for communities to thrive and the U.S. economy to offer broad opportunity – has declined dramatically in a number of states over the last decade. Worse, some of the deepest-cutting states have also cut income tax rates, weakening their main revenue source for supporting schools.

As of 2015, there were 29 states whose spending on education had not increased since 2008, even as student enrollments went up and inflation increased costs. Several of those states cut income taxes – Arizona, Idaho, Kansas, Michigan, Mississippi, North Carolina and Oklahoma – while they refused to increase spending on their schools from 2008 levels. Thus the funding source for schools shrank.

America cannot retain its position as a global leader unless it educates its children well. Investing in our children is investing in our future. The states' refusal to pay teachers appropriately, as professionals, is an admission by their leaders that they don't care about tomorrow and they don't care about the children of their constituents.

The push for charter schools and vouchers is simply a way of changing the subject. Privatization benefits the 1 percent, who don't want to pay more taxes, but it does not address the funding inequities that rob our students and teachers.

Until now, we have been a world leader in science, medicine, technology, music, entertainment, the arts, sports and higher education. We can thank our teachers for that. Without the groundwork they provide, none of these achievements are possible.

If we kill our future, it hurts everyone. Without well-supported, professional teachers, we are nowhere.

# CHARTER SCHOOLS DAMAGE PUBLIC EDUCATION

## THE WASHINGTON POST, JUNE 22, 2018

*"Almost every day, I get an email from some sponsor telling me how entrepreneurs will reinvent education and make money at the same time. I wish they would stick to soap and toothpaste and leave our children alone." – Diane Ravitch's Blog*

In 1988, teachers union leader Albert Shanker had an idea.[184] What if teachers were allowed to create a school within a school, where they could develop innovative ways to teach dropouts and unmotivated students? The teachers would get the permission of their colleagues and the local school board to open their school, which would be an R&D lab for the regular public school. These experimental schools, he said, would be called "charter schools."

Five years later, in 1993, Shanker publicly renounced his proposal. The idea had been adopted by businesses seeking profits, he said, and would be used, like vouchers, to privatize public schools and destroy teachers unions. He wrote that "vouchers, charter schools, for-profit management schemes are all quick fixes that won't fix anything."[185]

Shanker died in 1997, too soon to see his dire prediction come true. Today, there are more than 7,000 charter schools with about 3 million students[186] – total enrollment in public schools is 50 million.[187] About 90 percent of charter schools are non-union.[188] Charters are more segregated than public schools, prompting the Civil Rights Project at UCLA in 2010 to call charter schools "a major political success" but "a civil rights failure."[189] They compete with public schools instead of collaborating. Charter proponents claim that the schools are progressive, but schools that are segregated and non-union do not deserve that mantle.

The charter universe includes corporate chains that operate hundreds of schools in different states. The largest is KIPP, with 209 schools. The-second-largest has 167 schools and is affiliated with Turkish preacher Fethullah Gulen. About one of every six charters operates for profit,[190] in Michigan, 80 percent are run by for-profit corporations.[191] Nationally, nearly 40 percent of charter schools are run by for-profit businesses known as Educational Management Organizations.[192]

The largest online charter chain, K12 Inc.,[193] was founded with the help of former junk-bond king Michael Milken and is listed on the New York Stock Exchange. The biggest single virtual charter was the Ohio-based Electronic Classroom of Tomorrow, which collected $1 billion from Ohio taxpayers from 2000 until its bankruptcy earlier this year.[194] The charter's 20 percent graduation rate was the lowest in the nation.[195]

Charter schools pave the way for vouchers. More than half of states now have some form of public subsidy for religious and private schools. Voucher schools are not bound by civil rights laws and may exclude students based on religion, disabilities and LGBT status.

Charters are publicly funded but privately managed. They call themselves public schools, but a federal court ruling in 2010 declared[196] they are "not state actors." The National Labor Relations Board ruled in 2016 that charters are private corporations, not public schools.[197] As private corporations, they are not subject to the same laws as public schools.

The anti-union Walton Family Foundation is the biggest private financier of charters. The foundation in 2016 unveiled a plan to spend $200 million annually over five years for charter schools,[198] and the organization claims credit for opening one of every four charters in the nation. The Waltons and Education

Secretary Betsy DeVos, using both public and private funds, are pouring hundreds of millions annually into what amounts to a joint effort to privatize public education. The federal government spends $400 million annually on charter schools[199] and a congressional budget proposal seeks to increase that amount for fiscal 2019.

On average, charters do not get better academic results than public schools, according to the National Education Policy Center,[200] except for those that have high attrition rates and that control their demographics to favor high-scoring groups.

The lowest-scoring urban district in the nation is Detroit, where more than half the children are enrolled in charters.[201] The highest-ranked charters in the nation are the BASIS charters in Arizona, where 83 percent of students are either Asian or white,[202] double the proportion of these students in the state.

Charter schools drain resources and the students they want from public schools. When students leave for charters, the public schools must fire teachers, reduce offerings and increase class sizes. Some districts, such as Oakland's, teeter on the edge of financial ruin because public funds have been diverted to charters.

In 2016, the NAACP called for a moratorium on new charter schools until charters are held to the same accountability standards as public schools, until "public funds are not diverted to charter schools at the expense of the public school system" and until charter schools "cease expelling students that public schools have a duty to educate."[203]

American education seems to be evolving into a dual school system, one operated under democratic control and overseen by a board that was either elected by the people or appointed by an elected official, the other under private control.

One is required to find a place for every student who shows up, no matter that student's academic skills, language or disability.

The privately managed charter sector can limit its enrollment, exclude students it doesn't want, and accept no new students after a certain grade level. Charters can even close school for the day to take students to a political rally for the school management's financial benefit.

That is not fair competition, and it is not healthy for democracy.

# REFERENCES


1. NAACP Legal Defense Fund. (June 26, 2010). *Framework for Providing All Students an Opportunity to Learn through Reauthorization of ESEA.* http://naacpldf.org/update/civil-rights-groups-release-framework-priorities-esea-reauthorization

2. Darling-Hammond, L.; Amrein-Beardsley, A.; Haertel, Edward H. & Rothstein, J. (September 14, 2011). *Getting Teacher Evaluation Right: A Background Paper for Policy Makers.* American Educational Research Association & National Academy of Education. http://www.aera.net/Portals/38/docs/News_Media/AERABriefings/Hill%20Brief%20-%20Teacher%20Eval%202011/GettingTeacherEvaluationRightBackgroundPaper(1).pdf

3. Burris, C.C. & Strauss, Valerie. (February 19, 2012). 'You are so smart…why did you become a teacher?' *The Washington Post.* http://www.washingtonpost.com/blogs/answer-sheet/post/you-are-so-smartwhy-did-you-become-a-teacher/2012/02/19/gIQA-2vBNNR_blog.html

4. Anderson, Jerry. (February 19, 2012). States Try to Fix Quirks in Teacher Evaluations. *The New York Times.* http://www.nytimes.com/2012/02/20/education/states-address-problems-with-teacher-evaluations.html

5. Hess, Rick. (February 10, 2012). A Shameless Display on Waivers. *Education Week.* http://blogs.edweek.org/edweek/rick_hess_straight_up/2012/02/a_shameless_display_on_waivers.html

6. Loveless, T. (February 16, 2012). The 2012 Brown Center Report on American Education. *Brookings.* https://www.brookings.edu/research/the-2012-brown-center-report-on-american-education

7. Loveless, T. (February 2012). *The 2012 Brown Center Report on American Education: How Well Are American Students Learning?*

The Brown Center on Education Policy at Brookings. https://www.brookings.edu/wp-content/uploads/2016/06/0216_brown_education_loveless.pdf

8. Ravitch, D. (February 12, 2012). No Student Left Untested. *The New York Review of Books – NYR Daily.* http://www.nybooks.com/blogs/nyrblog/2012/feb/21/no-student-left-untested/

9. Amos, Jason. (March 19, 2012). *The MetLife Survey Of The American Teacher: Teachers, Parents, And The Economy: Teacher Job Satisfaction at Lowest Level in Two Decades, Survey Finds.* Alliance for Excellent Education. Vol.12 No. 6. https://all4ed.org/articles/the-metlife-survey-of-the-american-teacher-teachers-parents-and-the-economy-teacher-job-satisfaction-at-lowest-level-in-two-decades-survey-finds/

10. *The MetLife Survey of the American Teacher: Teachers, Parents, and the Economy.* (March 2012). https://files.eric.ed.gov/fulltext/ED530021.pdf

11. Ravitch, D. (March 8, 2012). No Student Left Untested. *The New York Review of Books – NYR Daily.* http://www.nybooks.com/articles/archives/2012/mar/08/schools-we-can-envy

12. Ravitch, D. (March 22, 2012). How, and How Not, to Improve the Schools. *The New York Review of Books – NYR Daily.* http://www.nybooks.com/articles/archives/2012/mar/22/how-and-how-not-improve-schools

13. Kopp, Wendy. (March 13, 2012, Updated May 13, 2012). In Defense of Optimism in Education. *Huff Post.* http://www.huffingtonpost.com/wendy-kopp/in-defense-of-optimism-in_b_1338763.html

14. Obama, B. (January 25, 2011). *Remarks by the President in State of Union Address.* The White House: President Barack Obama. https://obamawhitehouse.archives.gov/the-press-office/2011/01/25/remarks-president-state-union-address

15. Klein, J. I., Rice, C., Levy, J., et al. (March 2012). *U.S. Education Reform and National Security.* Council on Foreign Relations, Independent Task Force Report No. 68. http://www.cfr.org/united-states/us-education-reform-national-security/p27618

16. Loveless, T. (February 16, 2012). The 2012 Brown Center Report on American Education. *Brookings.* https://www.brookings.edu/research/the-2012-brown-center-report-on-american-education

17. Ravitch, D. (March 7, 2012). Flunking Arne Duncan. *The New York Review of Books – NYR Daily* http://www.nybooks.com/blogs/nyrblog/2012/mar/07/flunking-arne-duncan/

18. Rado, D. (December 23, 2012). Illinois schools win share of federal money. *Chicago Tribune.* http://articles.chicagotribune.com/2011-12-23/news/ct-met-race-to-the-top-1223-20111223_1_grant-money-illinois-schools-overhaul-education

19. Editorial. (September 11, 2012). Chicago Teachers' Folly. *The New York Times – Opinion.*http://www.nytimes.com/2012/09/12/opinion/chicago-teachers-folly.html

20. Ravitch, D. (March 7, 2012). Flunking Arne Duncan. *The New York Review of Books – NYR Daily.* http://www.nybooks.com/blogs/nyr-blog/2012/mar/07/flunking-arne-duncan/

21. Ravitch, D. (September 12, 2012). Two Visions for Chicago's Schools. *The New York Review of Books – NYR Daily.* http://www.nybooks.com/blogs/nyrblog/2012/sep/12/two-visions-chicagos-schools/

22. Ravitch, D. (April 11, 2011). The Education of Lord Bloomberg. *The New York Review of Books – NYR Daily.* http://www.nybooks.com/blogs/nyrblog/2011/apr/11/mayor-bloomberg-lord-schools/

23. Darling-Hammond, L.; Amrein-Beardsley, A.; Haertel, Edward H. & Rothstein, J. (September 14, 2011). *Getting Teacher Evaluation Right: A Brief for Policymakers.* American Educational Research Association & National Academy of Education. https://edpolicy.stanford.edu/sites/default/files/publications/getting-teacher-evaluation-right-challenge-policy-makers.pdf

24. Shulevitz, J. (August 15, 2013). Don't You Dare Say "Disruptive": It's the most pernicious cliché of Our Time. *The New Republic.* https://newrepublic.com/article/114125/disruption-silicon-valleys-worst-buzzword

25. Blow, Charles M. (August 21, 2103). The Common Core and the Common Good. *The New York Times – Opinion.* http://www.nytimes.com/2013/08/22/opinion/blow-the-common-core-and-the-common-good.html

26. School District Operators. (September 15, 2009). *School Closure Guide: Closing Schools as a Means for Addressing Budgetary Challenges.* The Broad Foundation. https://failingschools.files.wordpress.com/2011/01/school-closure-guide1.pdf

27. Carnoy, M. & Rothstein, R. (January 28, 2013). *What Do International Tests Really Show About U.S. Student Performance?* Economic Policy Institute. http://www.epi.org/files/2013/EPI-What-do-international-tests-really-show-about-US-student-performance.pdf

28. Stewart, W. (July 26, 2013). Is PISA Fundamentally Flawed? *Times Educational Supplement.* https://www.tes.com/news/pisa-fundamentally-flawed

29. Somerby, R. (December 20, 2012). Fooled About Schools: Black kids beat Finland! *The Daily Howler.* http://dailyhowler.blogspot.com/2012/12/fooled-about-schools-black-kids-beat.html

30. Klein, J. I., Rice, C., Levy, J., et al. (March 2012). *U.S. Education Reform and National Security.* Council on Foreign Relations, Independent Task Force Report No. 68. http://www.cfr.org/united-states/us-education-reform-national-security/p27618

31. Kosar, K. (April 14, 2011). Historic Use of the Term "Failing School". *Federal Education Policy History.* http://federaleducationpolicy.wordpress.com/2011/04/14/historic-use-of-the-term-failing-school/

32. Prohaska, T. (August 29, 2013). Cuomo Seeks Death Penalty to Deal with Failing Schools. *The Buffalo News.* http://www.buffalonews.com/city-region/buffalo-public-schools/coumo-urges-death-penalty-for-failing-schools-20130829

33. Goldman, H. & Abelson, M. (September 4, 2013). Wealthy New Yorkers Call De Blasio's Tax Plan Offensive. *Bloomberg.* https://www.bloomberg.com/news/articles/2013-09-04/wealthy-new-yorkers-call-de-blasio-s-tax-plan-offensive

34. Rich, M. (September 10, 2013). Loud Voice Fighting Tide of New Trend in Education. *The New York Times.* http://www.nytimes.com/2013/09/11/education/loud-voice-fighting-tide-of-new-trend-in-education.html

35. Somerby, R. (September 11, 2013). Adult Abuse: Two different worlds! *The Daily Howler.* http://dailyhowler.blogspot.com/2013/09/adult-abuse-two-different-worlds.html

36. Red Queen in LA. (September 30, 2013). Today's Homework: Dr. Diane Ravitch. Do you know the name "Diane Ravitch"? Do you know who she is? http://redqueeninla.k12newsnetwork.com/2013/09/30/todays-homework-dr-diane-ravitch/

37. Enfield, H. et al. *Women: Know Your Limits!* Harry Enfield and Chums - BBC One Comedy, Series 2 Episode 1. http://www.youtube.com/watch?v=LS37SNYjg8w

38. Schneider, M. (August 27, 2013). A Brief Audit of Bill Gates' Common Core Spending. *Deutsch29 Blog.* http://deutsch29.wordpress.com/2013/08/27/a-brief-audit-of-bill-gates-common-core-spending/

39. Schneider, M. (September 3, 2013). Gates Money and Common Core– Part II. *Deutsch29 Blog.* http://deutsch29.wordpress.com/2013/09/03/gates-money-and-common-core-part-ii/

40. Schneider, M. (September 11, 2013). Gates Money and Common

Core– Part III. *Deutsch29 Blog.* http://deutsch29.wordpress.com/2013/09/11/gates-money-and-common-core-part-iii/

41. Schneider, M. (September 17, 2013). Gates Money and Common Core– Part IV. *Deutsch29 Blog.* http://deutsch29.wordpress.com/2013/09/17/gates-money-and-common-core-part-iv/

42. Schneider, M. (September 25, 2013). Gates Money and Common Core– Part V. *Deutsch29 Blog.* http://deutsch29.wordpress.com/2013/09/25/gates-money-and-common-core-part-v/

43. Schneider, M. (October 5, 2013). Gates Money and Common Core– Part VI. *Deutsch29 Blog.* http://deutsch29.wordpress.com/2013/10/05/gates-money-and-common-core-part-vi/

44. Thompson, J. (October 14, 2013). Should Diane Ravitch Be More Careful to Not Hurt Reformers' Feelings? *Schools Matter Blog.* http://www.schoolsmatter.info/2013/10/should-diane-ravitch-be-more-careful-to.html

45. Providence Student Union Campaign. (January 2013-June 2014). *More Than a Test Score.* http://vimeo.com/76769828

46. Layton, L. (October 16, 2013). Study: Poor children are now the majority in American public schools in South, West. *The Washington Post.* http://www.washingtonpost.com/local/education/study-poor-children-are-now-the-majority-in-american-public-schools-in-south-west/2013/10/16/34eb4984-35bb-11e3-8a0e-4e2cf80831fc_story.html

47. Rich, M. (October 23, 2013). Better News in New Study That Assesses U.S. Students. *The New York Times.* http://www.nytimes.com/2013/10/24/education/better-news-in-new-study-that-assesses-us-students.html

48. Layton, L. (October 23, 2013). Study: Eighth-graders in more than half of U.S. states better than average in math and science. *The Washington Post.* http://www.washingtonpost.com/local/education/2013/10/23/fa4374d0-3c1f-11e3-a94f-b58017bfee6c_story.html

49. Rubinstein, G. (November 7, 2013). On the latest D.C. NAEP Miracle. *Teach For Us.* http://garyrubinstein.teachforus.org/2013/11/07/on-the-latest-d-c-naep-miracle/

50. The Commission on Excellence in Education. (April, 1983). *A Nation At Risk: The Imperative For Educational Reform.* U.S. Department of Education, Washington D.C. http://www2.ed.gov/pubs/NatAtRisk/risk.html

51. Strauss, V. (December 3, 2013). Key PISA test results for U.S. students. *The Washington Post.* http://www.washingtonpost.com/blogs/

answer-sheet/wp/2013/12/03/key-pisa-test-results-for-u-s-students/

52. Loveless, T. (February 16, 2012). The 2012 Brown Center Report on American Education. *Brookings.* https://www.brookings.edu/research/the-2012-brown-center-report-on-american-education

53. Hiltzik, M. (March 9, 2014). Cultural production of ignorance provides rich field for study. *Los Angeles Times.* http://articles.latimes.com/2014/mar/09/business/la-fi-hiltzik-20140307

54. NYC Department of Education InfoHub. (2018). *Test Results.* http://schools.nyc.gov/Accountability/data/TestResults/ELAandMathTestResults

55. New York Communities Organizing Fund, Inc. (January 19, 2013). *Charter Schools in Public School Buildings: Best Practices for Co-Location.* ISSUELAB, A Service of Foundation Center. http://www.issuelab.org/resource/charter_schools_in_public_school_buildings_best_practices_for_co-location

56. Baker, B. D. (February, 2014). *Review Of: "Should Charter Schools Pay Rent?"* National Education Policy Center (NEPC). http://nepc.colorado.edu/files/ttr-charter-rent_0.pdf

57. Decker, G. (January 17, 2014). Success Academy donors give big to Cuomo campaign. *Chalkbeat.* http://ny.chalkbeat.org/2014/01/17/success-academy-donors-flood-cuomos-coffers-filings-show/

58. American National Standards Institute (ANSI). *Overview of the U.S. Standardization System.* http://www.ansi.org/about_ansi/introduction/introduction.aspx

59. American National Standards Institute (ANSI). *United States Standards Strategy.* http://www.ansi.org/standards_activities/nss/usss.aspx

60. The New York Times Poll. (August 16, 2013). New Yorkers' Views on Their Mayor and His Programs. *The New York Times.* http://www.nytimes.com/interactive/2013/08/18/nyregion/new-yorkers-views-on-bloomberg-poll.html

61. Ravitch, D. (March 10, 2014). The Smear Campaign Against Mayor Bill de Blasio. *Diane Ravitch's Blog.* http://dianeravitch.net/2014/03/10/the-smear-campaign-against-mayor-bill-de-blasio/

62. Hernández, J. C. (March 23, 2014). Gentler Words About Charter Schools From de Blasio. *The New York Times.* http://www.nytimes.com/2014/03/24/nyregion/de-blasio-strikes-conciliatory-tone-on-charter-schools.html

63. Ravitch, D. (March 12, 2014). Fact-Checking Eva's Claims on National

Television. *Diane Ravitch's Blog.* http://dianeravitch.net/2014/03/12/fact-checking-evas-claims-on-national-television/

64. Powell, M. (March 12, 2014). Gilded Crusade for Charters Rolls Onward. *The New York Times.* http://www.nytimes.com/2014/03/13/nyregion/gilded-crusade-for-charters-rolls-onward.html

65. Karlin, R. (March 14, 2014). Judge bars comptroller audit of charter schools. *Times Union.*https://www.timesunion.com/local/article/Judge-bars-comptroller-audit-of-charter-schools-5319373.php

66. Matthews, K. (March 26, 2014). Report: NY schools are most racially segregated. *Democrat & Chronical.* https://www.democratand-chronicle.com/story/news/2014/03/26/report-ny-schools-racially-segregated/6930731/

67. Savio, M. (December 2, 1964). Sit-in Address on the Steps of Sproul Hall, The University of California at Berkeley. https://www.ameri-canrhetoric.com/speeches/mariosaviosproulhallsitin.htm

68. Inaugural Camp Philos, (May 2014). Lake Placid, New York https://campphilos.org/camp-philos-2014/

69. American Statistical Association (ASA). (April 8, 2014). *ASA Statement on Using Value-Added Models for Educational Assessment.* www.amstat.org/asa/files/pdfs/POL-ASAVAM-Statement.pdf

70. Darling-Hammond, L.; Amrein-Beardsley, A.; Haertel, Edward H. & Rothstein, J. (September 14, 2011). *Getting Teacher Evaluation Right: A Brief for Policymakers.* American Educational Research Association & National Academy of Education.https://edpolicy.stanford.edu/sites/default/files/publications/getting-teacher-evaluation-right-challenge-policy-makers.pdf

71. Martin, J. (April 19, 2014). Republicans See Political Wedge in Common Core. *The New York Times.* http://www.nytimes.com/2014/04/20/us/politics/republicans-see-political-wedge-in-common-core.html

72. Schneider, M. (April 18, 2014). David Brooks, Common Core Circus Performer. *Deutsch29 blog.* http://deutsch29.wordpress.com/2014/04/18/david-brooks-common-core-circus-performer/

73. Balkhy, I. (April 16, 2014, updated December 19, 2014). Economist Thomas Piketty Explains Why Income Inequality Is Just Getting Started. *HuffPost.* https://www.huffingtonpost.com/2014/04/16/thomas-piketty-inequality_n_5159937.html

74. Mishel, L. (September 15, 2011). *Huge disparity in share of total wealth gain since 1983.* Economic Policy Institute. http://www.epi.org/publication/large-disparity-share-total-wealth-gain/

75. Bivens, J.; Gould E.; Mishel L. & Shierholz H. (September, 2012). *The State of Working America, 12th Edition.* Economic Policy Institute. http://stateofworkingamerica.org/12th-edition-press-release/ http://stateofworkingamerica.org/fact-sheets/inequality-facts/

76. Leonhardt, D. & Quealy, K. (April 22, 2014). The American Middle Class Is No Longer the World's Richest. *The New York Times.* http://www.nytimes.com/2014/04/23/upshot/the-american-middle-class-is-no-longer-the-worlds-richest.html

77. Economic Policy Institute. (June 18, 2012). *The State of Working America.* http://stateofworkingamerica.org/chart/swa-income-figure-2q-average-effective-federal/

78. Gilens, M. & Page, B.I. (September 18, 2014). Testing Theories of American Politics: Elites, Interest Groups, and Average Citizens. *Perspectives on Politics.* Vol 12, Issue 3, pp. 564-581. https://www.cambridge.org/core/services/aop-cambridge-core/content/view/62327F513959D0A304D4893B382B992B/S1537592714001595a.pdf/testing_theories_of_american_politics_elites_interest_groups_and_average_citizens.pdf; https://doi.org/10.1017/S1537592714001595

79. Liptak, A. (April 2, 2014). Supreme Court Strikes Down Overall Political Donation Cap. *The New York Times.* http://www.nytimes.com/2014/04/03/us/politics/supreme-court-ruling-on-campaign-contributions.html

80. Bureau of Labor Statistics, U.S. Department of Labor. (December 2015). *Projections of occupational employment, 2014–24.* http://www.bls.gov/ooh/most-new-jobs.htm

81. Fowler, M. (January 18, 2012). From Eisenhower to Obama: What the Wealthiest Americans Pay in Taxes. *ABC News/Yahoo News.* http://news.yahoo.com/eisenhower-obama-wealthiest-americans-pay-taxes-193734550--abc-news.html; https://abcnews.go.com/beta-story-container/Politics/eisenhower-obama-wealthy-americans-mitt-romney-pay-taxes/story?id=15387862

82. Bradford, H. (November 15, 2011). Warren Buffett: 'My Class Has Won' And 'It's Been A Rout'. *HuffPost.* http://www.huffingtonpost.com/2011/11/15/warren-buffett-tax-code-l_n_1095833.html

83. Buffett, W.E. (August 14, 2011). Stop Coddling the Super-Rich. *The New York Times.* http://www.nytimes.com/2011/08/15/opinion/stop-coddling-the-super-rich.html

84. Tone, H. (May 13, 2014). The 8 Most Ridiculous Attacks On Public Education In Glenn Beck's New Book. *Media Matters For America.* http://mediamatters.org/blog/2014/05/13/the-8-most-ridiculous-attacks-on-public-educati/199284

85. Keyes, S. (May 19, 2014). Florida Lawmaker: Common Core Will Turn 'Every One Of Your Children' Gay. *ThinkProgress.* http://thinkprogress.org/lgbt/2014/05/19/3439163/state-rep-common-core-gay/

86. Bakeman, J. (May 30, 2014). Business groups fighting back in support of Common Core. *Politico.* http://www.capitalnewyork.com/article/albany/2014/05/8546262/business-groups-fighting-back-support-common-core

87. Layton, L. (June 7, 2014). How Bill Gates pulled off the swift Common Core revolution. *The Washington Post.* http://www.washingtonpost.com/politics/how-bill-gates-pulled-off-the-swift-common-core-revolution/2014/06/07/a830e32e-ec34-11e3-9f5c-9075d5508f0a_story.html

88. Schneider, M. (August 29, 2013, updated October 29, 2013). A Brief Audit of Bill Gates' Common Core Spending. *HuffPost.* http://www.huffingtonpost.com/mercedes-schneider/a-brief-audit-of-bill-gat_b_3837421.html

89. Ravitch, D. (February 26, 2013). Why I Cannot Support the Common Core Standards. *Diane Ravitch's Blog.* https://dianeravitch.net/2013/02/26/why-i-cannot-support-the-common-core-standards/

90. Ravitch, D. (January 18, 2014). My Speech about Common Core to MLA. *Diane Ravitch's Blog.* https://dianeravitch.net/2014/01/18/my-speech-about-common-core-to-mla/

91. Loveless, T. (April 13, 2012). Does the Common Core Matter? *Education Week.* http://mobile.edweek.org/c.jsp?DISPATCHED=true&cid=25983841&item=http%3A%2F%2Fwww.edweek.org%2Few%2Farticles%2F2012%2F04%2F18%2F28loveless_ep.h31.html

92. Treu, Judge Rolf M. (June 10, 2014). Vergara vs. State of California (Defendants) & California Teachers Association (Intervenors), Case No. BC48642, Tentative Decision. *Superior Court of the State of California, County of Los Angeles.* http://studentsmatter.org/wp-content/uploads/2014/06/Tenative-Decision.pdf

93. Ravitch, D. (June 11, 2014). The Expert Witnesses for the Plaintiffs in the Vergara Trial. *Diane Ravitch's Blog.* https://dianeravitch.net/2014/06/11/the-expert-witnesses-for-the-plaintiffs-in-the-vergara-trial/

94. Sink, J. (June 6, 2014). Obama: US must 'strengthen unions'. *The Hill.* https://thehill.com/homenews/administration/209648-obama-us-must-strengthen-unions

95. Wright, D. (June 26, 2014). Robert Gibbs To Lead National Campaign Against Teachers Unions. *Shadowproof.* http://news.firedo-

glake.com/2014/06/26/robert-gibbs-to-lead-national-campaign-against-teachers-unions/

96. Strauss, V. (June 27, 2014). A disturbing look at Common Core tests in New York. *The Washington Post.* http://www.washingtonpost.com/blogs/answer-sheet/wp/2014/06/27/a-disturbing-look-at-common-core-tests-in-new-york/

97. Simon, S. & Emma, C. (July 2, 2014). New twist in Common Core wars. *Politico.* http://www.politico.com/story/2014/07/common-core-test-anxiety-108527.html

98. Layton, L. (June 7, 2014). How Bill Gates pulled off the swift Common Core revolution. *The Washington Post.* http://www.washingtonpost.com/politics/how-bill-gates-pulled-off-the-swift-common-core-revolution/2014/06/07/a830e32e-ec34-11e3-9f5c-9075d5508f0a_story.html

99. Bryant, J. (July 17, 2014). Waking Up To Our Broken Education Policies. *Education Opportunity Network.* http://educationopportunitynetwork.org/waking-up-to-our-broken-education-policies/

100. Travis, S. (August 29, 2014). Palm Beach County School Board considers opting out of high-stakes testing. *South Florida Sun Sentinel.* http://www.sun-sentinel.com/news/education/fl-palm-opt-out-testing-20140827,0,4524415.story

101. Bergner, D. (September 3, 2014). The Battle for New York Schools: Eva Moskowitz vs. Mayor Bill de Blasio. *The New York Times Magazine.* http://www.nytimes.com/2014/09/07/magazine/the-battle-for-new-york-schools-eva-moskowitz-vs-mayor-bill-de-blasio.html

102. Gonzalez, J. (June 18, 2014). Gonzalez: Students of much-touted Success Academy charter school score too low on entrance exam for top city high schools. *New York Daily News.* http://www.nydailynews.com/new-york/education/gonzalez-success-charter-students-fail-top-city-schools-article-1.1833960

103. Zelon, H. (August 20, 2014). Why Charter Schools Have High Teacher Turnover. *City Limits.* http://www.citylimits.org/news/articles/5156/why-charter-schools-have-high-teacher-turnover

104. Success Academy Employee Reviews. (Updated January 11, 2019). *Glassdoor.* http://www.glassdoor.com/Reviews/Success-Academy-Charter-Schools-Reviews-E381408.htm

105. Ravitch, D. & Blaustein, A. (March 12, 2014, updated May 12, 2014). Mayor de Blasio and Education: Fact-Checking Eva Moskowitz's Claims. *HuffPost.* http://www.huffingtonpost.com/diane-ravitch/mayor-de-blasio-eva-moskowitz_b_4948262.html

106. Fisher, M. (April 15, 2013). Map: How 35 countries compare on child poverty (the U.S. is ranked 34th). *The Washington Post.* http://www.washingtonpost.com/blogs/worldviews/wp/2013/04/15/map-how-35-countries-compare-on-child-poverty-the-u-s-is-ranked-34th/

107. Lien Foundation, (2012). *Starting Well: Benchmarking early education across the world.* Economist Intelligence Unit, The Economist. http://www.lienfoundation.org/sites/default/files/sw_report_2.pdf

108. Born Too Soon Global Map. (2010). *March of Dimes.* http://www.marchofdimes.org/mission/global-preterm.aspx

109. Zumbrun, J. (October 7, 2014). SAT Scores and Income Inequality: How Wealthier Kids Rank Higher. *The Wall Street Journal.* http://blogs.wsj.com/economics/2014/10/07/sat-scores-and-income-inequality-how-wealthier-kids-rank-higher/

110. Wade, L. (December 8, 2013). Sociological Images: U.S. Rare in Spending More Money on the Education of Rich Children. *The Society Pages.* http://thesocietypages.org/socimages/2013/12/08/u-s-rare-in-spending-more-money-on-the-education-of-rich-children/

111. American Statistical Association (ASA). (April 8, 2014). *ASA Statement on Using Value-Added Models for Educational Assessment.* www.amstat.org/asa/files/pdfs/POL-ASAVAM-Statement.pdf

112. Layton, L. (July 8, 2015). Even as Congress moves to strip his power, Arne Duncan holds his ground. *The Washington Post.* http://www.washingtonpost.com/local/education/as-congress-moves-to-strip-his-power-duncan-is-staying-until-the-final-buzzer/2015/07/08/cb0c9d28-15d4-11e5-9ddc-e3353542100c_story.html

113. Strauss, V. (April 3, 2016). Diane Ravitch: Why all parents should opt their kids out of high-stakes standardized tests. *The Washington Post.* https://www.washingtonpost.com/news/answer-sheet/wp/2016/04/03/diane-ravitch-why-all-parents-should-opt-their-kids-out-of-high-stakes-standardized-tests/

114. Covert, B. (May 14, 2014). School Closings Are Shutting The Doors On Black And Hispanic Students. *ThinkProgress.* http://thinkprogress.org/education/2014/05/14/3437826/school-closings-race/

115. National Assessment of Educational Progress (NAEP). (2015). *The Nation's Report Card: 2015 Mathematics and Reading Assessments.* National Center for Education Statistics (NCES), U.S. Department of Education and the Institute of Education Sciences (IES). http://www.nationsreportcard.gov/reading_math_2015/#mathematics/scores?grade=4

116. Rich. M. (October 28, 2015). Nationwide Test Shows Dip in Students' Math Abilities. *The New York Times.* http://www.nytimes.

com/2015/10/28/us/nationwide-test-shows-dip-in-students-math-abilities.html

117. Layton, L. (June 7, 2014). How Bill Gates pulled off the swift Common Core revolution. *The Washington Post*. https://www.washingtonpost.com/politics/how-bill-gates-pulled-off-the-swift-common-core-revolution/2014/06/07/a830e32e-ec34-11e3-9f5c-9075d5508f0a_story.html

118. Brown, E. (April 5, 2016). Alaska cancels all K-12 standardized tests for the year, citing technical problems. *The Washington Post*. https://www.washingtonpost.com/news/education/wp/2016/04/05/alaska-cancels-all-k-12-standardized-tests-for-the-year-citing-technical-problems

119. Schaeffer, R. (September 6, 2015, updated December 21, 2018). Computerized Testing Problems – Chronology. *FairTest – The National Center for Fair and Open Testing*. http://fairtest.org/computerized-testing-problems-chronology

120. Finn, C. E. Jr. (August 2, 2016). An Open Letter to Mark Zuckerberg and Priscilla Chan. *Education Next*. http://educationnext.org/open-letter-to-mark-zuckerberg-and-priscilla-chan-philanthropy/

121. Tucker, M. (August 18, 2016). (Another) Open Letter to Mark Zuckerberg and Priscilla Chan. *Education Week*. http://blogs.edweek.org/edweek/top_performers/2016/08/another_open_letter_to_mark_zuckerberg_and_priscilla_chan.html

122. Ivory, D., Protess, B. & Bennett, K. (June 25, 2016). When You Dial 911 and Wall Street Answers. *The New York Times*. https://www.nytimes.com/2016/06/26/business/dealbook/when-you-dial-911-and-wall-street-answers.html

123. Lavender, P. (January 11, 2017). Donald Trump Refuses To Take A Question From CNN Reporter, Calls Network 'Fake News'. *HuffPost*. http://www.huffingtonpost.com/entry/donald-trump-cnn_us_58765783e4b05b7a465ccc0b

124. Zernike, K. (June 28, 2016). A Sea of Charter Schools in Detroit Leaves Students Adrift. *The New York Times*. https://www.nytimes.com/2016/06/29/us/for-detroits-children-more-school-choice-but-not-better-schools.html

125. Hess, F. & Ravitch, D. (January 18, 2017). Betsy DeVos: School Advocate or Adversary? *1A – American University Radio*. http://the1a.org/shows/2017-01-18/betsy-devos-school-advocate-or-adversary

126. Henderson, S. (December 10, 2016). Betsy DeVos' trouble with data. *Detroit Free Press*. http://www.freep.com/story/opinion/columnists/stephen-henderson/2016/12/10/betsy-devos-trouble-

data/95207844/

127. Higgins, L. (May 18, 2016). Michigan students sliding fast toward the bottom. *Detroit Free Press.* http://www.freep.com/story/news/education/2016/05/18/michigan-students-sliding-toward-bottom/84535876/

128. Arellano, A., Bedi, S. & Gallagher, T. (2016). *Michigan's Talent Crisis: The Economic Case for Rebuilding Michigan's Broken Public Education System.* The Education Trust-Midwest. https://midwest.edtrust.org/wp-content/uploads/sites/2/2013/10/MIAchieves2016_5-15-16WEB.pdf

129. Alexander, L. (May 1998). *Lamar Alexander's Little Plaid Book: 311 rules, lessons, and reminders about running for office and making a difference whether it's for president of the United States or president of your senior class.* Nashville, TN: Rutledge Hill Press.

130. Strauss, V. (February 23, 2017). 'The system is failing too many kids' – text of Education Secretary DeVos's speech at CPAC. *The Washington Post.* https://www.washingtonpost.com/news/answer-sheet/wp/2017/02/23/the-system-is-failing-too-many-kids-text-of-education-secretary-devoss-speech-at-cpac/

131. Lewis, S. D. (February 20, 2017). Michigan test score gains worst in nation. *The Detroit News.* http://www.detroitnews.com/story/news/local/michigan/2017/02/20/michigan-test-score-gains-worst-nation/98144368/

132. Levy, K. (February 20, 2017). The Last Cut? We the People of Detroit Documentary on School Closings. *Vimeo.* https://vimeo.com/204933347

133. Brown, E. (February 23, 2017). DeVos defiant at CPAC: 'My job isn't to win a popularity contest'. *The Washington Post.* https://www.washingtonpost.com/news/education/wp/2017/02/23/devos-defiant-at-cpac-my-job-isnt-to-win-a-popularity-contest

134. Trump's Speech to Congress: Video and Transcript. (February 28, 2017). *The New York Times.* (Beginning at time 39:25). https://www.nytimes.com/2017/02/28/us/politics/trump-congress-video-transcript.html

135. The Editorial Board. (March 1, 2017). Ms. DeVos's Fake History About School Choice. *The New York Times.* https://www.nytimes.com/2017/03/01/opinion/ms-devoss-fake-history-about-school-choice.html

136. Natelson, R. (April 8, 2017). How the travel ban ruling could change public education. *The Hill.* http://thehill.com/blogs/pundits-blog/the-judiciary/327957-how-the-travel-ban-ruling-could-

change-public-education

137. Stanton, Z. (January 15, 2017). How Betsy DeVos Used God and Amway to Take Over Michigan Politics. *Politico.* http://www.politico.com/magazine/story/2017/01/betsy-dick-devos-family-amway-michigan-politics-religion-214631

138. Freedberg, L. (February 10. 2017). DeVos confirmation triggered outpouring of support for public education system. *EdSource.* https://edsource.org/2017/devos-confirmation-triggered-outpouring-of-support-for-system-of-public-education/576911

139. Editorial. (February 7, 2017). Michael Bennet calls Betsy DeVos' nomination "an insult" in speaking marathon on Senate floor. *The Denver Post.* http://www.denverpost.com/2017/02/07/michael-bennet-betsy-devos-nomination/

140. Austin, T. L. Goals 2000 – The Clinton Administration Education Program. *University of Notre Dame.* https://www3.nd.edu/~rbarger/www7/goals200.html

141. Holland, R. (July 21, 1999). GOALS 2000: The Hour Has Arrived To Re-Evaluate The Federal Role In Education Reform. https://www.lexingtoninstitute.org/wp-content/uploads/2013/11/goals-2000.pdf

142. 107th Congress. *H.R.1 – No Child Left Behind Act of 2001.* https://www.congress.gov/bill/107th-congress/house-bill/1

143. Cleveland 19 News. (February 1, 2008). Former President Clinton Says 'No Child Left Behind' A Train Wreck, Faults Bush, Kennedy. *Cleveland 19 News.* http://www.cleveland19.com/story/7809000/former-president-clinton-says-no-child-left-behind-a-train-wreck-faults-bush-kennedy/

144. Goldstein, D. (November 23, 2016). How Trump Could Gut Public Education. *Slate.* http://www.slate.com/articles/life/education/2016/11/how_trump_and_education_secretary_betsy_devos_could_gut_public_education.html

145. Graves, L. (March 31, 2016). How DFER Leaders Channel Out-of-State Dark Money. *Center for Media and Democracy - PR Watch.* http://www.prwatch.org/news/2016/03/13065/how-dfer-leaders-channel-out-state-dark-money-colorado-and-beyond

146. Hernández, J. C. & Craig, S. (April 3, 2014). Cuomo Played Pivotal Role in Charter School Push. *The New York Times.* https://www.nytimes.com/2014/04/03/nyregion/cuomo-put-his-weight-behind-charter-school-protections.html

147. Gammon, R. (April 28, 2010). Jerry Brown Raised $12 Million for His Two Oakland Schools. *East Bay Express.* http://www.eastbay-

express.com/oakland/jerry-brown-raised-12-million-for-his-two-oakland-schools/Content

148. Saul, S. (December 12, 2011). Profits and Questions at Online Charter Schools. *The New York Times.* http://www.nytimes.com/2011/12/13/education/online-schools-score-better-on-wall-street-than-in-classrooms.html

149. Chapman, B. (August 20, 2011). Charters score better than district schools, but have fewer special-needs students. *New York Daily News.* http://www.nydailynews.com/new-york/education/charters-score-better-district-schools-special-needs-students-article-1.949043

150. Chingos, M. M. May 15, 2013. Does Expanding School Choice Increase Segregation? *Brookings.* https://www.brookings.edu/research/does-expanding-school-choice-increase-segregation/

151. Carey, K. (February 23, 2017). Dismal Voucher Results Surprise Researchers as DeVos Era Begins. *The New York Times.* https://www.nytimes.com/2017/02/23/upshot/dismal-results-from-vouchers-surprise-researchers-as-devos-era-begins.html

152. Schontzler, G. (September 11, 2016). Bullock, Gianforte differ on education. *Bozeman Daily Chronicle.* http://www.bozemandailychronicle.com/news/education/bullock-gianforte-differ-on-education/article_8888a3ee-20bd-5a0e-9716-419488f2ef1b.html

153. Dragoset, L., Thomas, J., Herrmann, M., Deke, J., James-Burdumy, S., Graczewski, C., Boyle, A., Upton, R., Tanenbaum, C., & Giffin, J. (2017). *School Improvement Grants: Implementation and Effectiveness (NCEE 2017- 4013).* Washington, DC: National Center for Education Evaluation and Regional Assistance, Institute of Education Sciences, U.S. Department of Education. https://ies.ed.gov/ncee/pubs/20174013/pdf/20174013.pdf

154. Zernike, K. & Alcindor, Y. (January 17, 2017). Betsy DeVos's Education Hearing Erupts Into Partisan Debate. *The New York Times.* https://www.nytimes.com/2017/01/17/us/politics/betsy-devos-education-senate-hearing.html

155. Carey, K. (February 23, 2017). Dismal Voucher Results Surprise Researchers as DeVos Era Begins. *The New York Times.* https://www.nytimes.com/2017/02/23/upshot/dismal-results-from-vouchers-surprise-researchers-as-devos-era-begins.html

156. Source Watch. (December 2, 2014). Rose-Marie and Jack R. Anderson Foundation. *The Center for Media and Democracy.* http://www.sourcewatch.org/index.php/Rose-Marie_and_Jack_R._Anderson_Foundation

157. Kroll, A. (February 5, 2013). Exposed: The Dark-Money ATM of

the Conservative Movement. *Mother Jones.* http://www.motherjones.com/politics/2013/02/donors-trust-donor-capital-fund-dark-money-koch-bradley-devos/

158. Kristof, N. (July 15, 2017). A Solution When a Nation's Schools Fail. *The New York Times.* https://www.nytimes.com/2017/07/15/opinion/sunday/bridge-schools-liberia.html

159. Tyre, P. (June 27, 2017). Can a Tech Start-Up Successfully Educate Children in the Developing World? *The New York Times Magazine.* https://www.nytimes.com/2017/06/27/magazine/can-a-tech-start-up-successfully-educate-children-in-the-developing-world.html

160. Romero, M., Sandefur, J. & Sandholtz, W.A. (September 6, 2017). *Can a Public-Private Partnership Improve Liberia's Schools? : Preliminary Results From Year One Of A Three-Year Randomized Evaluation.* Center for Global Development. https://greatschoolwars.files.wordpress.com/2017/09/psl-midline-brief_2017-09-06_watermarked.pdf

161. Romero, M., Sandefur, J. & Sandholtz, W.A. (September 6, 2017). *Can outsourcing improve Liberia's schools? Preliminary results from year one of a three-year randomized evaluation of Partnership Schools for Liberia.* Center for Global Development Working Paper 462. https://greatschoolwars.files.wordpress.com/2017/09/psl_report.pdf

162. Tyre, P. (June 27, 2017). Can a Tech Start-Up Successfully Educate Children in the Developing World? *The New York Times Magazine.* https://www.nytimes.com/2017/06/27/magazine/can-a-tech-start-up-successfully-educate-children-in-the-developing-world.html

163. Museveni, J. K. (February 15, 2018). Enforcement of the Standard Operating Procedure (SOP) for private schools and school charges in Uganda. *New Vision.* https://www.newvision.co.ug/new_vision/news/1471272/enforcement-standard-operating-procedure-sop-private-schools-school-charges-uganda

164. Allen, J. (October 9, 2017). C'mon, Matt Damon. You're Better Than This. *HuffPost.* https://www.huffingtonpost.com/entry/cmon-matt-damon-youre-better-than-this_us_59dc3ad9e4b060f005fbd684

165. Stone Lantern Films & Turnstone Productions. (January 2016). *Backpack Full Of Cash.* https://vimeo.com/189823117; https://www.backpackfullofcash.com/

166. Arellano, A., Bedi, S. & Gallagher, T. (2016). *Michigan's Talent Crisis: The Economic Case for Rebuilding Michigan's Broken Public Education System.* The Education Trust-Midwest. https://midwest.edtrust.org/wp-content/uploads/sites/2/2013/10/MIAchieves2016_5-15-16WEB.pdf

167. Campbell, D.T. (1979). Assessing the impact of planned social

change. *Evaluation and Program Planning.* Volume 2, Issue 1, Pages 67–90. https://doi.org/10.1016/0149-7189(79)90048-X; http://citeseerx.ist.psu.edu/viewdoc/download?doi=10.1.1.170.6988&rep=rep1&type=pdf

168. Rothstein, R. February. (2008). *Holding Accountability to Account: How Scholarship and Experience in Other Fields Inform Exploration of Performance Incentives in Education.* Economic Policy Institute. http://www.epi.org/publication/wp_accountability/

169. Klein, A. (April 10, 2015). No Child Left Behind: An Overview. *Education Week.* https://www.edweek.org/ew/section/multimedia/no-child-left-behind-overview-definition-summary.html

170. Stanford, J. (February 18, 2013, updated September 13, 2013). Bush's 'Texas Miracle' debunked, Lone Star State sparks anti-testing revolution. *MSNBC.* http://www.msnbc.com/msnbc/bushs-texas-miracle-debunked-lone-star-st

171. Kamenetz, A. (October 11, 2014). It's 2014. All Children Are Supposed To Be Proficient. What Happened? *nprEd.* http://www.npr.org/sections/ed/2014/10/11/354931351/it-s-2014-all-children-are-supposed-to-be-proficient-under-federal-law

172. Neill, M., Gisbond L. & Schaeffer, R. (May, 2004). *Failing Our Children: How 'No Child Left Behind' Undermines Quality And Equity In Education.* FairTest: The National Center For Fair And Open Testing. https://nepc.colorado.edu/sites/default/files/EPRU-0405-62-OWI%5B1%5D_0.pdf

173. Strauss, V. (March 25, 2016). 'Why is the material in a standardized test treated as more confidential than .... Hillary Clinton's emails?' *The Washington Post.* https://www.washingtonpost.com/news/answer-sheet/wp/2016/03/25/why-is-the-material-in-a-standardized-test-treated-as-more-confidential-than-former-secretary-of-state-hillary-clintons-emails/

174. Rothstein, R. (February, 2008). *Holding Accountability to Account: How Scholarship and Experience in Other Fields Inform Exploration of Performance Incentives in Education.* Economic Policy Institute. http://www.epi.org/publication/wp_accountability/

175. Jamieson, D. (March 7, 2018). The West Virginia Teacher Strike Was Rare, Militant And Victorious. *HuffPost.* https://www.huffingtonpost.com/entry/what-makes-the-west-virginia-teacher-strike-so-powerful_us_5a9db476e4b0a0ba4ad6f723

176. Jamieson, D. (April 12, 2018). Oklahoma Teachers Union Calls For End To Walkout. *HuffPost.* https://www.huffingtonpost.com/entry/oklahoma-teachers-union-calls-for-end-to-walkout_us_5ad01667e4b077c89ce6f67b

177. Waldron, T. (March 30, 2018). Kentucky Teachers Shut Down Schools After Public Pension Overhaul. *HuffPost.* https://www.huffingtonpost.com/entry/kentucky-school-shutdown-pension_us_5abe4233e4b0f112dc9baeee

178. Cano, R. (April 24, 2018). #RedForEd walkout school closures will impact 840,000 Arizona students. *Azcentral.* https://www.azcentral.com/story/news/local/arizona-education/2018/04/24/redfored-walkout-school-closures-impact-820000-arizona-students/546294002/

179. Whaley, M. (April 24, 2018). Denver Public Schools, the state's largest school district, cancels classes on Friday due to teacher walkout. *The Denver Post.* https://www.denverpost.com/2018/04/24/denver-public-schools-classes-canceled-teacher-strike/

180. Figueroa, A. (December 19, 2017). How Much Do Teachers Spend On Classroom Supplies? *nprEd.* https://www.npr.org/sections/ed/2017/12/19/569989782/how-much-do-teachers-spend-on-classroom-supplies

181. Strauss, V. (August 28, 2017). Teacher shortages affecting every state as 2017-18 school year begins. *The Washington Post.* https://www.washingtonpost.com/news/answer-sheet/wp/2017/08/28/teacher-shortages-affecting-every-state-as-2017-18-school-year-begins

182. Education Law Center. (2015). *Fairness Indicators.* Rutgers Graduate School of Education. http://www.schoolfundingfairness.org/is-school-funding-fair/interactive-data

183. Leachman, M., Masterson, K. & Figueroa, E. (November 29, 2017). *A Punishing Decade for School Funding.* Center on Budget and Policy Priorities. https://www.cbpp.org/research/state-budget-and-tax/a-punishing-decade-for-school-funding

184. Shanker, A. (March 31, 1988). National Press Club Speech. https://reuther.wayne.edu/files/64.43.pdf

185. Kahlenberg, R. D. *Tough Liberal: Albert Shanker and the Battles Over Schools, Unions, Race, and Democracy.* New York: Columbia University Press. (August, 2007). https://cup.columbia.edu/book/tough-liberal/9780231134972

186. David, R. & Hesla, K. (March 2018). *Estimated Public Charter School Enrollment, 2017-2018.* National Alliance for Public Charter Schools. https://www.publiccharters.org/sites/default/files/documents/2018-03/FINAL%20Estimated%20Public%20Charter%20School%20Enrollment%2C%202017-18.pdf

187. *Fast Facts.* (2018). Institute of Educational Sciences: National Center for Education Statistics, U.S. Department of Education. https://nces.

ed.gov/fastfacts/display.asp?id=372

188. Ravitch, D. (August 9, 2016). Worldwide, Public Education Is Up for Sale. *U.S. News & World Report.* https://www.usnews.com/news/best-countries/articles/2016-08-09/worldwide-public-education-is-up-for-sale

189. Frankenberg, E., Siegel-Hawley, G., Wang, J. (January, 2010). *Choice without Equity: Charter School Segregation and the Need for Civil Rights Standards.* Los Angeles, CA: The Civil Rights Project/Proyecto Derechos Civiles at UCLA; www.civilrightsproject.ucla.edu. https://www.civilrightsproject.ucla.edu/research/k-12-education/integration-and-diversity/choice-without-equity-2009-report/frankenberg-choices-without-equity-2010.pdf; https://escholarship.org/uc/item/4r07q8kg

190. Rotherham, A.J. (May 17, 2017). Don't Ban For-Profit Charters: A ban might clean up bad actors, but it would throw out the working options, too. *U.S. News & World Report.* https://www.usnews.com/opinion/knowledge-bank/articles/2017-05-17/states-shouldnt-rush-to-ban-for-profit-charter-schools

191. Binelli, M. (September 5, 2017). Michigan Gambled on Charter Schools. Its Children Lost. *The New York Times Magazine.* https://www.nytimes.com/2017/09/05/magazine/michigan-gambled-on-charter-schools-its-children-lost.html

192. Baker, B. & Miron, G. (December 10, 2015). *The Business of Charter Schooling: Understanding the Policies that Charter Operators Use for Financial Benefit.* National Education Policy Center. https://nepc.colorado.edu/publication/charter-revenue; http://nepc.colorado.edu/files/rb_baker-miron_charter_revenue_0.pdf

193. Layton, L. & Brown, E. (November 26, 2011). Virtual schools are multiplying, but some question their educational value. *The Washington Post.* https://www.washingtonpost.com/local/education/virtual-schools-are-multiplying-but-some-question-their-educational-value/2011/11/22/gIQANUzkzN_story.html

194. Bischoff, L.A. (May 29, 2018). Dems want to pin ECOT blame on GOP in fall election: What's really going on. *Dayton Daily News.* https://www.mydaytondailynews.com/news/dems-want-pin-ecot-blame-gop-fall-election-what-really-going/W0ex4WZK4pE1JglflaBG7K/

195. Rich, M. (May 18, 2016). Online School Enriches Affiliated Companies if Not Its Students. *The New York Times.* https://www.nytimes.com/2016/05/19/us/online-charter-schools-electronic-classroom-of-tomorrow.html

196. Stephen S. Trott, S.S., McKeown, M.M. & Ikuta, S.S. Circuit Judges.

(January 4, 2010). *Caviness v. Horizon Community Learning, D.C. Case No. CV-07-00635-FJM*. U.S. Court of Appeals for the Ninth Circuit, Opinion No. 08-15245. http://www.nabse.org/legislative/9thCircuitCavinessvHorizon_1-2010.pdf

197. Brown, E. (August 30, 2016). National Labor Relations Board decides charter schools are private corporations, not public schools. *The Washington Post*. https://www.washingtonpost.com/news/education/wp/2016/08/30/national-labor-relations-board-decides-charter-schools-are-private-corporations-not-public-schools

198. Sullivan, M. (January 8, 2016). Walton Family Foundation Aims To Bolster Charter Schools With $1 Billion In Grants. *Forbes*. https://www.forbes.com/sites/maureensullivan/2016/01/08/walton-family-foundation-aims-to-bolster-charter-schools-with-1-billion-in-grants/#59d609852d0d

199. Balingit, M, & Douglas-Gabriel, D. March 24, 2018. Congress rejects much of Betsy DeVos's agenda in spending bill. *The Washington Post*. https://www.washingtonpost.com/news/education/wp/2018/03/21/congress-rejects-much-of-betsy-devoss-agenda-in-spending-bill

200. Miron, G, Mathis, W.J. & Welner, K.G. (February 23, 2015). *NEPC Review: Separating Fact & Fiction: What You Need to Know About Charter Schools*. National Education Policy Center (NEPC). https://nepc.colorado.edu/thinktank/review-separating-fact-and-fiction; https://nepc.colorado.edu/sites/default/files/ttr-charterclaims-mmw-1.pdf

201. Higgins, L. (July 26, 2017). NAACP releases report on charter schools, cites Detroit and Michigan. *Detroit Free Press*. https://www.freep.com/story/news/2017/07/26/naacp-charter-school-report-detroit/512724001

202. Strauss, V. (March 30, 2017). What the public isn't told about high-performing charter schools in Arizona. *The Washington Post*. https://www.washingtonpost.com/news/answer-sheet/wp/2017/03/30/what-the-public-doesnt-know-about-high-performing-charter-schools-in-arizona/?utm_term=.95808207adbd

203. NAACP. (October 15, 2016). *Statement Regarding The NAACP's Resolution On A Moratorium On Charter Schools*. National Association for the Advancement of Colored People (NAACP). http://www.naacp.org/latest/statement-regarding-naacps-resolution-moratorium-charter-schools/

# ABOUT DIANE RAVITCH

Diane Ravitch is a Research Professor of Education at New York University and a historian of education. She is the Founder and President of the Network for Public Education (NPE).

Before entering government service, she was Adjunct Professor of History and Education at Teachers College, Columbia University. From 1991 to 1993, she was Assistant Secretary of Education and Counselor responsible for the Office of Educational Research and Improvement in the U.S. Department of Education, and she led the federal effort to promote the creation of voluntary state and national academic standards. From 1997 to 2004, she was a member of the National Assessment Governing Board, which oversees the National Assessment of Educational Progress (NAEP), the federal testing program. From 1995 until 2005, she held the Brown Chair in Education Studies at the Brookings Institution and edited Brookings Papers on Education Policy.

She is the author of 11 books, her two most recent being *Reign of Error: The Hoax of the Privatization Movement and the Danger to America's Public Schools* (2014) and *The Death and Life of the Great American School System: How Testing and Choice Are Undermining Education* (2010). Her books have been translated into many languages, including Chinese, Arabic, Spanish, Swedish, and Japanese. In addition, she has edited fourteen books, and has written more than 500 articles and reviews for scholarly and popular publications. She has lectured worldwide on democracy and civic education, and her lectures have been translated by the USIA into many languages, including Polish, Spanish, Lithuanian, Latvian, Russian, Belarussian, and Ukrainian.

She is an honorary life trustee of the New York Public Library and a former Guggenheim Fellow. She was a member of the Koret Task Force at the Hoover Institution from 1999 to 2009, and a member of the board of the Thomas B. Fordham Foundation from 1996 to 2009. In 1989, she advised Teachers Solidarity and the Ministry of Education in Poland, and was awarded a medal for this work in 1991 by the Polish Government.

She was elected to membership in the National Academy of Education (1979), the Society of American Historians (1984), the American Academy of Arts and Sciences (1985), and as the Eleanor Roosevelt Fellow of the American Academy of Political and Social Sciences (2002). She was selected as a Phi Beta Kappa Visiting Scholar in 1984-85, the first person chosen from the field of education studies. She was awarded the Henry Allen Moe prize in the humanities by the American Philosophical Society in 1986. In 1988, she was designated an "honorary citizen of the state of California" by the State Legislature in recognition of her contributions to the state's history curriculum and its human rights curriculum. In 1989, she received the Wellesley College Alumnae Achievement Award. She was honored as a Literary Lion by the New York Public Library in 1992. The Library of Congress invited her to deliver lectures in 1993 in honor of the 250th birthday of Thomas Jefferson. She received the Leadership Award of the Klingenstein Institute at Teachers College in 1994 and the Horace Kidger Award of the New England History Teachers Association in 1998.

In 2004, she received the Leadership Award of the New York City Council of Supervisors and Administrators. In 2005, she received the John Dewey award from the United Federation of Teachers of New York City, the Gaudium Award of the

Breukelein Institute, and the Uncommon Book Award from the Hoover Institution. In 2006, the Kenneth J. Bialkin/Citigroup Public Service Award was conferred on her.

In 2010, the National Education Association selected her as its "Friend of Education", and she was awarded the Charles W. Eliot Award by the New England Association of Schools and Colleges. In 2011, she was honored with the Outstanding Friend of Education Award from the Horace Mann League, the American Education Award from the American Association of School Administrators, the National Association of Secondary School Principals' Distinguished Service Award, and the Distinguished Alumni Award from Teachers College at Columbia University. Also in 2011, she received the Daniel Patrick Moynihan Prize of the American Academy of Political and Social Science.

She was awarded an honorary degree, Doctor of Humane Letters, by the following institutions: Williams College, Reed College, Amherst College, the State University of New York, Ramapo College, St. Joseph's College of New York, Siena College, Middlebury College Language Schools, and Union College.

A native of Houston, she is a graduate of the Houston public schools. She received a B.A. from Wellesley College in 1960 and a Ph.D. in history from Columbia University's Graduate School of Arts and Sciences in 1975.